G000079558

Cognitive Therapy in Practice

A Guide to the Assessment and Treatment
of
Common Psychological Problems

Dr. Chris L Hamilton

Published 2008 by arima publishing

www.arimapublishing.com

ISBN 978-1-84549-253-3

Printed and bound in the United Kingdom

Abramis is an imprint of arima publishing

www.abramis.co.uk

arima publishing

ASK House, Northgate Avenue

Bury St Edmunds, Suffolk IP32 6BB

t: (+44) 01284 700321

Acknowledgements

As the chapters in the following book illustrate, our emotional and psychological development begins to evolve from our earliest experiences. Each experience both good and bad serves to "shape" our personalities and our emotional resolve. Throughout my own life, my personality and resolve has been "shaped" like many others from failure and success and from sadness and happiness. The success however, would not have been possible without the support of those close to me; my family, the teachers who have shown belief in me and those people who have suffered that I have had the privilege of working with. I remain indebted to each and am grateful for their input. It is thanks to all those individuals that I have come to believe that real "success" in life can only be achieved in the "thought for the week" that I read as a young child in my mining village in South Wales and this is that, *"True Education is Learning How to Live"*. Hopefully some of the ideas discussed throughout the book will go a little way to helping the life long process of learning how to live.

Dr Chris L Hamilton

Foreword

Dr P. Burnett - GP

It is intriguing that we enter the 21st century able to identify microscopic cancers with radioisotopes, able to engineer strands of DNA to "genetically modify" species and soon we hope to avert predicted illness. The laboratories have never been so startlingly high-tech and expectant. But here at the "coal-face" of primary care we continue to struggle in the darkness with an unholy alliance. Depression and anxiety as this book so clearly acknowledges very readily move together and are inextricably linked in a manner that continues to bring misery and emotional torture to many. Like the last of the "phantoms", the "humours" mercurial and intangible. We have tried but have never adequately achieved success in measuring them and the closest we can hope for is a reasonable "assessment" of these emotional predators. They remain elusive and to a great extent unpredictable and often volatile and catastrophic in their subtlety – bringing increasing depression and malaise and destroying lives at an ever increasing rate. They are over-diagnosed on one level yet under-diagnosed on another, over-treated whilst under-treated. Ever increasingly they remain masters of symptom disguise. In medical school one learns that TB and diabetes are "the great mimickers" to be remembered when struggling with a diagnosis. In primary care – many years later – it becomes clear that depression in particular deserves a place on that list. In truth it should be at the head of that list. Depression remains as destructive and disruptive as most of the commonly feared illnesses and rarely as straightforward for doctor, patient or carer to identify. Indeed, I have read numerous medicals that often include a cartoon or "joke" whereby the patient presents to his GP feeling extremely unwell and starts ranting and raving with words such as, *"Please Doc! Tell me I've got some form of cancer, tell me I've got incurable heart disease – just don't tell me it's all in my head"*. If this scenario wasn't so true then maybe it would be laughable. However, the facts couldn't be more further from the truth with many patients stating that if they could have a limb removed and their depression and/or anxiety would disappear as if by magic then they would have that procedure done immediately.

This book unravels much of this mystery and more importantly gives direction for those charged with intervention in the potential "minefield" of adult mental health. I have worked alongside Dr Chris Hamilton in full-time general practice for over 10 years and he arrived when the 7-minute consultation was still the bedrock of healthcare. Depression remained well camouflaged – multiple secondary referrals, haphazard investigations and polypharmacy and futility the inevitable consequences. That Dr Chris Hamilton was able to offer and deliver an alternative and successful approach in the face of our traditional scepticism and resigned inertia is down to his energy, knowledge and clinical ability to push against the boundaries of the old and archaic establishments and structures in order to push through and clarify procedures that bring sense and order to an area of healthcare that has for so long floundered. The clinical results continue to stand the test of time and his approach, which in fairness is a combination of good science, creativity and a great deal of interpersonal skill and energy remains at the cutting edge of primary care mental health. The techniques outlined in this book are now an essential part of our armoury and our own clinical practice has become an easier place to live as we continue to see positive results from patients, some who have been dragged back from the abyss of depression and some who now know how to manage and cope with a "simple" panic attack. It is hard to imagine how primary care mental health problems were conceived and treated only 10 years ago, this book will open the eyes for many health care professionals, carers and those interested in understanding depression and anxiety. We remain indebted to Dr Chris Hamilton's continued energy in a field that has seen many a good and caring practitioner suffer in the potentially demoralising world of depression and anxiety. This book not only has the potential to empower individuals interested in mental health and well being, it also has the potential to give interested parties a renewed direction with regard to both the assessment and treatment of common psychological problems. To this extent, this is the type of book that needs to be available to every general practice and to those individuals who remain committed to working with those suffering with depression and anxiety including those who are keen to take up the challenge of working in this demanding and rewarding field of health care.

Contents

Introduction

When we use the general term "stress" most people will have an idea of what we are referring to. Indeed, most individuals will say that they have suffered with stress at some stage in their life. For most of us experiencing such difficulties this is perhaps a relatively "normal" part of everyday life and problems such as these may be related to specific situations such as dealing with conflict at work or difficulties within the family. These difficulties are of course part of everyday life and whilst they inevitably cause us a degree of stress or anxiety we eventually return to some "normal" state of being and pick up and start again.

For many however, stress and anxiety can take on a far greater meaning and can begin to significantly affect the day to day functioning of people often resulting in painful psychological problems such as depression and anxiety. Over the past 20 years it has been recognised that as many as one in four GP consultations are for people who are suffering with some form of psychological or emotional difficulty such as anxiety or depression (Dept. of Health 2001). Remarkably, out of these patients, 90% of the "treatment" will be provided solely within the primary care setting and this places a huge demand on those trying to treat these difficulties. Presenting problems are numerous and include moderate to severe episodes of depression, anxiety related problems such as panic attacks and obsessive-compulsive difficulties and various problems with sleeping, eating and general well-being. This list is by no means exhaustive and will be all too familiar to practicing GP's and other health care professionals in the primary care setting and beyond. Unfortunately, despite the continuing increase in common mental health problems, the quality of care provided for these patients can be extremely variable and often fragmented. There are numerous reasons for this but in general it is a consequence of time and workload constraints within the primary care setting and of course limited mental health resources and training. Despite a number of Mental Health Trusts and other interested organisations being committed to developing more effective primary care mental health treatments it is accepted practice that mental health services often target their resources on those patients suffering with severe and enduring mental health problems such as schizophrenia and bi-polar affective disorder. Therefore, the great majority of those suffering with a "mild to moderate" mental health problem, and I think we should be careful when we term the problem, "mild to moderate", will often receive little in the way of a formal psychological assessment and an appropriate treatment plan that includes a clinical rationale for the treatment itself.

What the above statistics and general information on mental health suggest is that there is a desperate need to provide more effective and efficient ways of working with these large volumes of patients who continue to suffer with a vast array of mental health difficulties. This becomes more apparent when we realise that problems such as these, if not treated appropriately at the earliest onset may lead to a further deterioration for the person in question with all the misery and complexity that may arise. This need is further highlighted by recent estimates made by the World Health Organization (WHO) who suggest that by the year 2020, depression will be one of the main contributors to overall morbidity in the western world. Therefore, the need to assess and treat this patient population more effectively remains paramount. Indeed, judging by the figures of one in four patients who potentially have these problems and this is a consistent finding, one can suggest that within a relatively small practice of 4000 patients there may well be as many as 1000 who are having to cope with some form of psychological or emotional problem. Naturally, not all of those will present for psychological help and the "hidden" burden to society at large and those family and friends connected to the sufferer is probably unknown. Indeed, psychological symptoms are likely to manifest themselves in a variety of different ways that often include physical problems such as headaches, irritable bowel, impotence and chronic fatigue. Rather than seek help for example, it may be more likely that individuals start to drink or smoke more in order to try to "cope" with their problems or involve themselves in other maladaptive coping strategies. Others may eat more or start to avoid situations as their confidence gradually drains away. Whatever the individual response to depression or anxiety there remains a need to address both the cause of these difficulties and the maladaptive or dysfunctional management that often serves to maintain the problematic condition.

In the main, mental health difficulties fall under two "umbrellas". First of all there are individuals who are suffering with ***depressive problems***, possibly as a result of factors such as marital breakdown, job loss or bereavement and secondly there are those who are suffering with ***anxiety related problems*** that include panic attacks, phobias and various levels of post-traumatic stress. There are a number of other mental health difficulties such as eating difficulties and sleeping problems that may overlap but occasionally do not sit comfortably underneath the above depression and anxiety "umbrellas". Whilst we have separated out depression and anxiety within the following chapters there is naturally a degree of overlap between the symptoms and therefore, the formal differences between the two will be addressed within the book itself when we look at defining mental health problems. Irrespective of definition, there remains little doubt that depression and anxiety continue to be major problems in the western world and as such the impact of these problems cannot be underestimated or treated in an ad hoc fashion. To reinforce this further we only have to look at conservative estimates that suggest that every year one woman in every fifteen and one man in every 30 will be affected by depression whilst most of the 4000 suicides committed each year in England are solely attributed to depression (Dept. of Health 2001).

The knock-on effect of depression is devastating both for the sufferers and for those close to the individual. The associated morbidity often results in additional problems being carried on within the family and within the workplace, often resulting in divorce and/or separation and a loss of time from work and occasionally a loss of ones job. Understandably, these factors further compound the problem and often lead to a deeper depression and a negative vicious cycle is set in motion. The classic symptoms that accompany depression include disturbed sleep and appetite, a low or sad mood and a general loss of interest or pleasure in most if not all activities. There is often very little motivation and a degree of pessimism and hopelessness consumes the individual with regard to the future.

In general the anxiety related symptoms differ from the depressive difficulties in one major area and that is with regard to the often intense and heightened physiological arousal that accompanies anxiety in all of its guises. Whether it is a panic attack or a phobia the patient will often experience an increase in adrenalin that sets off a physiological chain reaction that includes rapid breathing, hyperventilation, sweating, dry mouth and nausea. The patient feels panicky, out of control and faint and the overall experience can be extremely distressing for the individual concerned. Anxiety can "freeze" the individual in a state of immense fear, even though there is no "real" or actual harm that will occur. Only those that have experienced such fear will adequately understand this statement and due to the acute distress caused by anxiety, they are likely to be unconvinced by the fact that no actual or "real" harm is going to come to them.

Despite the morbid and quite distressing picture of depression and anxiety, research over the past 20 years has produced a considerable body of evidence that suggests that there are numerous psychological techniques and strategies that can be applied to psychological problems associated with depression and anxiety that can significantly alleviate much of the emotional and psychological suffering that has been described above. Psychological suffering that has perhaps been experienced by far too many people for far too long.

What we are referring to above are treatments that have come to be known as the cognitive psychotherapies. Cognitive psychotherapy has a number of differing forms depending on specific orientations and it is often referred to as cognitive-behaviour therapy (CBT), cognitive-analytical therapy (CAT) or just cognitive therapy. The semantic and orientation difficulties will become clearer throughout the book and for our present purposes it is useful just to focus on understanding some of the basic principles behind the general approach and the strategies involved in its application.

The treatment is well summed up in the title of a review of psychological therapies that appeared in the British Medical Journal (1997). The article that revealed that cognitive therapy was by far the most effective psychological treatment for treating a vast array of psychological problems including depression, panic attacks and general anxiety difficulties was simply entitled *"Talk that works"*. The simplicity is in the title and whilst to the casual or naïve observer cognitive therapy may appear rather simplistic, there is a great danger and misconception to assume this. Conversely, once the basic tenets and components of the treatment process have been established the principles and practice of cognitive therapy should be relatively simple to apply by many health care providers either as a first line approach or as an adjunct to their existing method of treatment. Either way, an understanding of cognitive therapy can only benefit all potential clinicians who have an interest in the psychological well-being of individuals.

Whilst not intending to be a panacea for all things mental health, cognitive therapy has provided clinicians, therapists and counsellors with a pragmatic and empirically based psychological treatment that has been shown to be extremely beneficial for treating a wide range of psychological and emotional problems.

The historical foundations of cognitive therapy can be traced back to the 1960s and probably beyond that to some extent. Cognitive therapy for example, was initially developed as a treatment for depression by American psychiatrist Aaron Beck. Beck initially argued that negative or morbid thinking is not simply a symptom of psychological distress but one of the primary maintaining factors. The original aim of therapy therefore was to eliminate any negative or "irrational" thinking by teaching people to understand those underlying factors that contributed to their depression in a more constructive fashion. People would then be in a better position to begin to challenge their own beliefs and underlying assumptions in a more adaptive way. Put simply, it was partly a rewording of Descartes' *"I think therefore I am"*. This suggests therefore, that if I start thinking anxious thoughts and *"what ifs"*, then the chances are that I am going to become more anxious. In essence, once our mood has dropped it tends to take on a mind and will of its own and therefore we start to believe in what we are thinking. This doesn't just have to be the mood changing it may also be a consequence of a lack of self-belief or confidence that begins to put doubt in our minds. One of the "techniques" I use in the clinical setting for example is to ask clients/patients if they can remember the slogan of the "Nike" sports firm. Some often remember others haven't got a clue what I am referring to. In essence, I point out that the slogan of the Nike sports firm is *"just do it"*. This is actually a cognitive strategy as what the sports firm is actually pointing out is that when you start thinking about something, especially when there's a significant amount of adrenalin running through your body then you start to put doubt in your mind and this is the last thing you need to be doing. What often follows from this point on is a combination of emotional thinking that in turn can have a dramatic impact on our behaviour. As we shall see in the following chapters' one of the most classical examples of emotional thinking occurs when we are under real and/or imagined pressure, which in turn leads us to become increasingly anxious. In this situation we often think in terms of *"I can't"* or *"I'm afraid"*. This in turn tends to lead to avoidance behaviour and the next time the situation arises we are even less likely to be able to deal with it. This brief and simplistic explanation will be elaborated on in great detail further in the book but hopefully it will serve as a brief example of how our thoughts, emotions and behaviour remain inextricably linked.

Since its initial inception the original CBT approach has been elaborated on and tailored over time in order to treat many different psychological problems. For many informed practitioners it is now seen as the first line approach to treating a vast range of psychological and emotional problems such as those described earlier. The approach is such that there remains tremendous scope for all health professionals including GPs, practice nurses, therapists, counsellors and informed carers from all orientations to improve their skill when working with depression and anxiety. The skills we are referring to specifically include, assessment skills both qualitative and quantitative, and a range of treatment skills and general knowledge of cognitive psychotherapy. If these components can be acquired (and they can be) then there is little doubt that they will significantly improve the clinical effectiveness of those working with psychological and emotional problems. Just as important is the fact that an increased knowledge can also help improve recognition of mental health problems that may often be masked or entrenched in a multitude of physical problems or maladaptive behaviours.

One of the main emphases of this book therefore, is to try to contribute to the existing skills of therapists and other clinicians so that they are able to fully understand the rationale of cognitive therapy in practice and subsequently be able to select from a menu of cognitive strategies that are specifically tailored to work with a range of psychological and emotional problems that present in primary care, private practice and beyond. By achieving this aim, the book would have been able to provide practitioners with a comprehensive understanding of the clinical nature and very essence of the cognitive approach and hopefully readers will be in a far more informed position to provide therapy and advice that is relevant, applicable and effective in order to get the client/patient functioning again. Indeed, by offering people new insights and techniques for working on their difficulties the client/patient is likely to have a far more optimistic outlook than if they were just provided with anti-depressants and/or provided with some reflective or "supportive" counselling per se.

As one will discover throughout the book, a significant part of cognitive therapy involves providing information in order to "educate" the client or patient with regard to their problem. To some extent this aspect has its philosophical premise in the term, *"knowledge is power"*. Indeed, I am still a little surprised and bemused how few people (including health care staff) are aware for example, of how many times we should be breathing in and out in a minute and the deleterious physiological consequences of over or rapid breathing. Just an explanation of this can provide significant insight and psychological relief in itself.

The appropriate term for this therapeutic approach is of course: *psycho-educative* and cognitive based therapies have a large *psycho-educative* component. The additional benefit of this is that patients retain this information and as such they become in effect, their own therapists in the future. This subsequently has the added benefit of acting as a psychological buffer and helps prevent against future relapse.

The following chapters will give an introduction and rationale with regard to cognitive therapy in practice before going on to outline the main psychological problems that appear to be contributing to depression and anxiety in the western world. Each clinical problem will be described in detail and physical and psychological signs and symptoms that are unique to each problem will be outlined followed by a number of "real" case examples from clinical practice. The book will review the common depressive and anxiety related problems such as loss, bereavement, phobias and post-traumatic stress. Attention will also be given to the influence of personality factors involved in the onset of depression and anxiety and there will be an attempt to evaluate the contribution of cognitive therapy in trying to work with these complex problems. The book will also look at what to do when therapy *per se* is seen not to work and hopefully this will provide the clinician with a more informed way of working with "heart sink" clients and patients who appear unable to move forward. Throughout the book there will be anecdotes and quotes that will hopefully help to illustrate certain points. Hopefully these components will combine to encourage and inspire the reader to be creative in their own practice.

Throughout the book there will be references to The American Psychiatric Association's *Diagnostic and Statistical Manual (DSM-IV)*. The Diagnostic and Statistical Manual was originally compiled in 1952 to assist the national census of what was then termed *mental disability*. Since then it has been continuously revised and transformed. The fourth edition was published in 1994 and is now internationally recognised as the prime definition of how to recognise depression and, importantly how and when to treat it. Elements from the DSM-IV are included in the book to further inform the reader how mental health problems are formally classified. Whilst this may be seen as a little reductionist for many therapists and treating clinicians it nonetheless should provide some good insight into how certain problems are classified. This should not however affect the richness of the therapeutic process and I would encourage all clinicians to be as creative as they are compassionate as I believe the more informed they are then potentially the better able they are to conduct therapy.

Outlined above are some of the aims of the book in general. To be more specific however, the book itself is largely concerned with helping readers assess and treat people suffering with psychological and emotional problems. To this extent a significant amount of time has been given to the assessment process itself and this will be twofold consisting of both a qualitative assessment and a quantitative assessment – don't be put off by the words as the assessment process, when understood is relatively straightforward – it's just a case of knowing what questions to ask and what salient information to gather. To ease the assessment process from a quantitative perspective a number of very useful anxiety and depression instruments have been outlined and they should provide the reader with some useful insights into how and why we need to quantify the assessment process. Naturally, following on from the assessment will be the treatment or therapeutic options and these will naturally be governed by, (i) the presenting problem itself, (ii) information from the assessment and (iii) the personal resources of the client/patient. Finally, and possibly most importantly, the book has been written for those who are generally working with clients and patients suffering with mild to moderate difficulties and hence this needs to be borne in mind when reading through the texts and case examples. The material is applicable for severe and complex psychological difficulties, however the book has been specifically written to cater for those working at the mild-moderate end of the spectrum and this should be acknowledged. When referring to people who suffer with depression and anxiety the terms client and patient will be used interchangeably as the chosen description largely depends on the philosophical or clinical approach taken.

Problems call forth our courage and our wisdom; indeed, they create our courage and our wisdom. It is only because of problems that we grow mentally and spiritually. It is through the pain of confronting and resolving problems that we learn

M. Scott-Peck – Psychiatrist and writer

Part 1: Cognitive Behaviour Therapy

1. What is Cognitive Behaviour Therapy?
2. Short-term / Long term therapy – Comparative dominant values
3. The Cognitive Bias

1 – What is Cognitive Behaviour Therapy?

Whilst cognitive behaviour therapy and the cognitive approach in general can be seen as a relatively recent development in the field of psychological therapies its beginnings can actually be traced back to many of the earlier treatment approaches. Indeed, writers have long pointed out that whilst Cognitive therapy largely evolved out of the writings of Aaron Beck's, *"The Self Concept in Depression"* with D. Stein in 1960 there is clear evidence of its existence well before this with many of the psychodynamic theories having inherent cognitive components. For example, Freud, in *"Mourning and Melancholia"*, published in 1917, suggests that melancholia (depression) can occur in response to an imaginary or perceived loss, and that self-critical aspects of the ego are responsible in part for depression. Indeed, I will suggest that on occasion the only difference between the cognitive and the more psychodynamic or psychoanalytical therapy is the *language* used to describe and explain the problem and its evolution. What I am suggesting here is that there may well be semantic differences in the description of these therapeutic orientations that serve to "widen" the actual gap between differing therapeutic approaches. More often than not therefore, each discipline may be using a different terminology and language to describe what in essence may be similar principles and components. However, whilst there are similarities between the more psychoanalytical and psychodynamic approaches in comparison to the cognitive orientation this is not the place to get overly pedantic as there are of course theoretical and philosophical differences that cannot be compared or contrasted, although *"Freud's Cognitive Psychology"* written by Matthew Hugh Erdelyi is a brave attempt at bridging this gap. Indeed, at the very least this type of book does a reasonable job of bridging the clinical divides between therapists that so often serve to maintain a prevailing clinical approach rather than to embrace new developments. This is something that will remain a partial theme throughout the book.

One of the fundamental differences between the more psychodynamic therapies and the cognitive therapies lies in the motivational assumptions made by the therapists themselves, and the techniques used to effect change. Psychodynamic theories for example presume that the maladaptive cognitions arise from specific internal needs (such as the need for affection, acceptance, sexual gratification, etc.), or from unresolved developmental conflicts from childhood. The cognitive therapists however, presume that the maladaptive cognitions may arise from faulty social learning, or from a lack of experiences that would allow adaptive learning to occur, or from dysfunctional family experiences, or traumatic events, etc. In other words, therapists using a more cognitive therapeutic approach recognize that psychological problems may develop from a variety of life experiences, depending on the individual. As a consequence of these experiences the individual starts to "shape" their view of themselves and the world around them and whether they see the world through *rose tinted glasses* or through *dark grey lenses* will largely depend on their genetic makeup and their social, psychological and interpersonal experiences.

A full understanding of the underlying basis and theoretical rationale of the cognitive approach is naturally less simplistic, but it should still be well within the grasp of the average clinician. What is apparent is that these life experiences can have a **significant** impact on an individuals' development whether this experience involves the loss of a parent as a child, the failing of the 11 + when at a crucial stage of development or the experiencing of a traumatic event. These types of issues will be elaborated on further in the book and serve to illustrate just a few of the innumerable difficulties that can shape a person's mind and their overall perception of themselves and the world around them.

Cognitive therapy has significantly changed the face of psychological therapy over the past 20 years. Its growth in popularity is due largely to the vast growing empirical literature that has consistently illustrated the effectiveness of this approach for treating a wide range of emotional and psychological problems. As a result of this scientific rigour and empirical success cognitive therapy has become the treatment of choice for many individuals seeking help and also the preferred "talking" method of treatment for clinicians including psychologists, psychiatrists, counsellors, therapists and a range of health care practitioners. It is interesting that cognitive therapy like many of the other psychotherapies of which there were well over 150 at the last count is referred to as a "talking" therapy. Whilst we cannot doubt that talking *per se* is an essential component of this and most other forms of psychological interventions, one may want to argue that "listening" is perhaps more of a primary component of the so called "talking" therapies as it is by listening to a patient/client that we begin to gather the rich information that will hopefully allow us to gain insight and help us to begin to develop a "picture" of what difficulties the individual is experiencing and perhaps some of the reasons as to why they are experiencing these difficulties. Naturally the aim of this book is not to have a philosophical discussion as to whether a therapy is to be termed a "talking" therapy or a "listening" therapy, the fact of the matter is that both are inextricably linked and combine to become an essential part of any psychotherapeutic process that is likely to lead to some kind of intervention. Just to stay with the semantic debate for a moment, I feel it is also essential to point out that the term *'psychotherapy'*, whilst conjuring up all manner of intellectual and philosophical thoughts is, as I understand just a general term for someone who works in a listening and talking capacity with someone in order to help them overcome or work through their emotional or psychological difficulties. Its dictionary definition from The Dictionary of Psychology (Reber, A. S. 1985) reads *"Psychotherapy – In the most inclusive sense, the use of absolutely any technique or procedure that has palliative or curative effects upon any mental, emotional or behavioural disorder"*. Psychotherapy therefore can include informal talks with religious ministers, counsellors, psychologists and even trusting close friends or strangers for that matter (NB. the stranger on the train phenomenon). In general the psychotherapeutic process involves using various informal or formal psychological methods of influence and techniques of behaviour change to help a person change some aspect of the way they may be thinking or feeling. This description actually encapsulates some of the very essence of cognitive therapy and in particular the importance of a person's thoughts, emotions (feelings) and behaviour, each of which will be discussed in great detail in the following chapters.

The terms psychotherapy and psychotherapist are interesting because in general they conjure up a certain amount of mysticism and intrigue. Indeed, I think many of the psychological therapies are partly intended to give this impression as if they are something "magical" that only a few extremely well trained and extremely insightful and intelligent individuals can possibly understand and practice. Despite the assumed complexity, I tend to think that gaining a basic understanding of an individual is not as complex as sometimes we all like to think in the world of mental health and beyond. That is not to say that it is a simple matter. However if we have a basic understanding of human development and certain pathological processes then the understanding part is far easier than many would let you know or have you believe. Indeed, having recently read a couple of "cutting edge" mental health books aimed at a similar reading audience, I was amazed by the complexity of the words used and the unconscious (or conscious) reluctance to explain in more simpler terms and grammar what exactly they were trying to convey. I have little doubt that there remains a reluctance to demystify the psychological language, perhaps in order to retain the mysticism and the perceived complexity that is the precious art of working in a psychological fashion. Bearing these factors in mind however, cognitive therapies have a greater advantage in the fact that they are relatively easy to understand and have a more "concrete" and empirical rationale. The concepts are not therefore "woolly" but tangible and relevant. To this extent, I believe they are perhaps more honest than those "other" secretive and very "specialist" therapies that perhaps only those very "intelligent" and insightful people can practice. As an example of this I will recall a conference I was invited to just over a year ago. The conference focus was on the more psychodynamic and interpretive therapies (more interesting words). One of the key speakers at the front started talking about how he went about his business of practicing his therapy and I was a little surprised when he said that he didn't assess people who were referred to him. After he finished speaking he invited questions from the audience (largely devotees of what he was "preaching") of about 200 and naturally (being the devils' advocate) I put my hand up and said that I considered it was impossible not to assess someone when they are referred to you. He smiled politely in a rather patronising way and said that he was non-judgemental in his approach and this was an integral part of his practice as it was with many others at the conference. He then asked me to comment on this to which I said, *"the human state does not allow for non-judgemental, for example since the 200 or so individuals walked into this room, everyone has looked at each other and made judgements based on gender, dress, accent etc. Indeed, as I speak people are making judgements both for, against and neutral. Therefore, it is impossible not to make a judgement".* He then became a little less patronising and sort of specialist and said that perhaps he might say to the client that they were looking anxious. Ah! I said you've just assessed them. Many of the audience laughed and I could see that my comments were perhaps a little challenging and thought provoking and apparently controversial. I thought that I was only making a rather obvious comment surely.

There are a couple of key points of note by this experience. One is that I believe the cognitive therapies have a degree of honesty that is "up front" if you like and this in my view is something that does not exist in other therapies. The cognitive therapies are not as mystical and they are perhaps less impressive to describe if one is at a dinner party. For example, what would sound the most interesting, I'm a cognitive therapist, I am an analytical psychotherapist or I am a psychodynamic psychoanalytical psychotherapist. So what is the relevance of all this to cognitive therapy? The relevance is that the discipline is relatively straightforward with a degree of pragmatism and honesty that is seldom seen in other therapies. This approach is appealing to clients/patients who become increasingly insightful and engaged in their own therapeutic process. That is not to say that the other therapeutic approaches have little use however, far from it, and I see the key components of cognitive therapy as being able to contribute greatly to those other "non-judgemental" types of therapy. Conversely, cognitive therapy can also learn from the concepts greatly acknowledged by the more person-centred approaches, particularly with regard to the dynamics of the clinical relationship.

As mentioned in the introduction the relatively uncomplicated nature of cognitive therapy is best illustrated in the title of an article that appeared in the British Medical Journal in 1997. As a keen campaigner for demystifying the psychological jargon that so often accompanies this type of text the title appealed to me as it simply read, *"Talk that works"*. The article itself reviewed a number of therapeutic approaches for working with individuals with a range of emotional and psychological problems and as outlined previously those therapies that had a cognitive approach as their empirical basis came out on top with the article illustrating that it is the more cognitive therapies that have been effective for treating among other problems, depression, panic disorder, generalised anxiety, health anxiety and obsessive-compulsive disorder. So much for its success and its apparent honesty, then what actually is cognitive therapy and how does one go about understanding the theoretical perspective and clinical application? In essence, how does it work?

In order to begin to understand what cognitive therapy is one must first of all put away any pre-conceived prejudices (assuming some of you have them?) with regard to how one proceeds within a cognitive and behavioural framework. I feel this is necessary as I am still amazed and quite saddened by the continuous resistance by many therapists and counsellors alike when they are discussing cognitive therapy or pure behaviour therapy in its own right. Indeed, without both these concepts we may well not have one-to-one therapies within the healthcare setting and/or beyond. I also find that many therapists and well meant practitioners actually do not understand some of the basic concepts of cognitive therapy yet they are happy to put up their *"defences"* and criticise the process before they have allowed themselves to have a good look at what the treatment and clinical rationale entails. Indeed, at the very least I would argue that a basic understanding of cognitive therapy will undoubtedly enrich and inform anyone's clinical practice, whether they are a consultant psychiatrist, nurse, psychotherapist or generic counsellor. Therefore, the first point I want to make is please allow yourself to read through the book, put your preconceived ideas to one side, and put some of the basic concepts into practice. Having spent the last 15 years working with 100s of people both in primary care and in private practice I am well aware and well qualified to state that this stuff actually works very well. If one can combine good interpersonal skills with the following concepts then I believe this will provide the foundation for one to become a far more effective therapist. Furthermore, given that the World Health Organisation (WHO) has recently estimated that by 2020 depression will be among the main contributors to overall morbidity, those who can grasp and develop the principles of cognitive therapy will have a significant contribution to make for the health and well-being of many suffering with emotional and psychological distress in the future. Surely, the WHO estimate should act as a powerful motivation in itself for those working in the caring professions.

2 – Short-term/ Long term therapy– Comparative Dominant Values

Cognitive behaviour therapy is a relatively short-term psychotherapy that was initially developed by Aaron Beck in the 1960's. Today treatment will often take between 6-12 sessions depending on the problem being presented and the clients' psychological resources. The 6-12 session model is not set in "stone" but perhaps best describes the main aims of this book which are generally concerned with the primary care setting such as the GP surgery and for counsellors and therapists in general working within other formal and informal or private settings. One of the many advantages of cognitive therapy as will become evident throughout the book is that whilst assessing salient historical factors that are relevant and pertinent for the client/patient, the approach in general maintains a clear focus on actual current difficulties being experienced in the "here and now" so to speak. The approach however, whilst pragmatic in nature, is still fundamentally built upon an understanding and mutually respectful relationship between the therapist and client/patient. This relationship remains a fundamental and essential part of cognitive therapy and this area is perhaps sometimes a little misunderstood by those not wholly familiar with the approach. Indeed, whilst the clinical components are the *"nuts and bolts"* of the therapy, the quality of the therapeutic relationship will affect how these *"nuts and bolts"* are *"tightened"* or *"loosened"* whatever the case may be. The therapeutic relationship will be discussed in more depth later in the book, however when a respectful and supportive clinical alliance is established, the client/patient is more likely to be able to explore certain difficulties and perhaps feel more "secure" when alluding to some of the reasons as to why they are struggling. If this process is managed carefully with sensitivity and skill then an agreeable, succinct and clear clinical rationale can be mutually arrived at. To the client this provides insight, structure and reason, which are factors that can actually bring about clinical gain and reassurance. Together the clinician and client will then begin to look about how best to address each of the key components that have been highlighted during their discussions. Coming back to the clinical relationship, I am always fascinated by the assumption that the more psychodynamic type of therapist with their "non-judgemental" approach is naively assumed to be "warmer" and perhaps more caring than the cognitive or behaviour therapist. I am well aware that this kind of stereotype exists and was even more fascinated to discover the outcomes of research carried out by person-centred academics into how clients/patients perceived their respective therapist based on their clinical orientation. In essence would they perceive the psychodynamic, person-centred, "non-judgemental" clinician as being "warmer" than the cognitive therapist? As the outcomes were read out at a person centred conference by those who practiced in the person-centred manner the findings revealed that it was the cognitive therapists that came out as being perceived as more "warmer" and "genuine"(Bohart et al 2002). The source of this finding surely lends a significant amount of credence to these outcomes. I feel the outcomes also reflect what I alluded to earlier that there is something in the honesty and the pragmatism of cognitive therapy that is likely to appeal to clients and patients alike. Indeed, I am aware that clients and patients "know where they are" so to speak when visiting a cognitive therapist. This is because the rationale is explained in clear and understandable terms rather than just passively reflecting or interpreting on what the client has said.

Prior to elaborating on some of the rubrics of Beck's initial cognitive therapy it is essential to highlight some of the main practical and philosophical differences between what we often refer to as either a *"short-term"* or a *"long-term"* therapy. These distinctions in themselves should set the reader on the right path to what this book is trying to achieve and an understanding of the comparative dominant values of the short-term and long-term therapist provide considerable insight in themselves to the political and philosophical differences. As previously mentioned, whilst we retain the view that short-term therapy is generally between 6-12 sessions this does not mean to say that it is fixed and rigid. Indeed, there remains a great deal of flexibility and for some difficulties such as moderate-severe obsessive-compulsive difficulties, traumatic sexual abuse or post-traumatic stress, up to 20 sessions has been deemed as being appropriate. However, this is still well within the remit of short-term therapy and hence an understanding of the differing dominant values should provide additional insight into the differing therapeutic approaches and values.

Comparative Dominant Values of short-term and long-term therapy

Short-term therapist	**Long-term therapist**
i) Prefers pragmatism and least radical intervention. Does not believe in notion of "cure".	i) Seeks change in basic character.
ii) Maintains an adult developmental perspective from which significant psychological change is viewed as inevitable.	ii) Believes that significant psychological change is unlikely in everyday life.
iii) Emphasizes patient's strengths and resources and presenting problems are taken seriously (although occasionally not necessarily at face value).	iii) Sees presenting problems as reflecting more basic pathology.
iv) Accepts that many changes will occur "after therapy" and will not be observable to therapist.	iv) Wants to "be there" as patient makes significant changes.
v) Does not accept the timelessness of some models of therapy.	v) Sees therapy as having a timeless quality and is patient and willing to wait for change.
vi) Views psychotherapy as being sometimes harmful.	vi) Views psychotherapy as almost always benign and useful.
vii) Sees being in the world as more important than being in therapy.	vii) Sees patient's as being in therapy as the most important part of a patient's life.

Adapted from Budman & Gurman (1988)

The different values and clinical orientations outlined above are clear and perhaps need no further elaboration other than to say that the short-term therapist believes that changes in one area of psychological functioning may have a positive "knock-on" effect in other areas. A general example of this is when an individual who has experienced a lot of negativity and/or emotional abuse as a child growing up starts to perceive themselves a little more differently and in a less negative fashion. As a consequence of this change of perception and feeling they may move from the position of being a "victim" to one of a "survivor" and this in turn may well help that person to increase their confidence and subsequently their self-esteem and general view of themselves. When this starts to occur the world around them starts to change for the better, as they will now start to perceive things in a different manner. I do not want the above example to sound overly simplistic and similar situations will be discussed throughout the book and will highlight the positive gain that can be achieved when an individual starts to change the way they see themselves and the world around them so that they move away from their previous negative position to one that is more balanced than positive but far healthier and more realistic. The changes can be quite dramatic and they can take some time to "sink in" for the individual in question before they are actually willing to accept things for the better.

What Beck and many others have managed to achieve over the past 3 decades is to alter our view of psychological problems so that a greater emphasis is given to the thought process of the individual who is suffering. In essence, whilst it was commonly held that gloomy or negative thoughts were secondary to depression Beck proposed that negative thinking (depressive cognitions) might actually be involved in the actual cause of the depression. Beck therefore, proposed that crucial underlying factors such depressive cognitions are a kind of "*schema*", or a "mental map" of life characterised by a negative view of the self, the world and the future. Therefore, Beck initially proposed that negative thinking is not simply a symptom of depression, but one of the primary contributing and maintaining factors. Perhaps Beck was elaborating on the familiar philosophical statement by Descartes' and that cognitive therapy has as one its main tenets an emphasis on the statement, '*I think therefore I am*'. Indeed, this is a valid argument and out of these early meanderings came a treatment method that has been shown to be empirically valid and robust. Cognitive therapy therefore went on to illustrate that whilst the initial depression and/or anxiety was a problem in itself, it was generally the unwittingly destructive management of the problem that helped to maintain and further develop and deepen the psychological discomfort.

Whilst the general focus throughout cognitive therapy is on the here and now and current problems, cognitive therapy is not conducted without a thorough understanding of the individuals history and those pertinent factors that may have helped shape ones personality and ones general view of the world and the "self" or ones *"schemas"* to use the appropriate psychological term. Remember *schemas* are just mental maps and impressions that we store in our unconscious. They are largely formed by our initial experiences and are reinforced by our way of thinking and behaving from these experiences. To give a simplistic example, if as a child on our paper round we are confronted by a growling and ferocious German Shepherd dog and become extremely anxious, then our *schema* in the future in relation to German Shepherds' may be one of fear and dread. This may generalise to other dogs depending on how it is reinforced. Therefore, the *schema* remains the mental representation and it can represent an event a situation or a person such as a friend or a parent.

The therapy's attention to the *schema* of each individual is fundamental to our understanding of how and why that individual has come to experience the negative emotion that is currently impacting on him or her. From a cognitive perspective there are a number of crucial areas of personality development that are likely to have impacted on the individual and they are likely to follow a pattern similar to that outlined below.

The development of early schemas and mental representations

Early experiences
Information about a person's early life experiences and relationships that have had a significant psychological impact on the individual in question.

Typical Examples
Negative parenting, failing the 11 plus exam, being ridiculed in school.

Development of core beliefs about self, others and general view of world
"I am a failure, I am worthless, and others are clever and see me as inadequate

Formation of core schemata
The early thoughts become embedded like granite into the individual's personality and "I think therefore I am" becomes justified, perceived failures are magnified and any successes are put down to luck or someone was feeling sorry for them.

Negative Automatic Thoughts
The result of the above is a continuous experience and bias towards negative automatic thoughts that further reinforce the negativity and the feelings of depression and/or anxiety.

With regard to core beliefs one must never underestimate the emotional power that the individual almost fixates to when it comes to a core belief. I have witnessed these negative core beliefs among some of the cleverest and most intelligent of individuals that I have worked with. Each of them will "believe" the core belief as opposed to the "objective" evidence. The person with two university degrees will see themselves as a failure as a result of the way they were parented, the intelligent cabinet maker with dyslexia who was continuously put in the lowest class throughout school and told he would achieve nothing retains the core belief that he is worthless, the woman married to the man who has continuously bombarded her with negative input for 30 years sees herself as weak and hopeless. Yet in all these "real" case examples the objective evidence was that these were people who were thoughtful sensitive and intelligent. Examples such as these overwhelmingly reinforce the tremendous power of our social engineering and experience. Just to briefly touch on the case of the young man with dyslexia. He was actually unaware that he had dyslexia and hence he was placed in the lowest class and perceived as being "thick" (his words) and stupid. His sadness and frustration was immense. When he presented before me all I could see was an extremely handsome young man who was courteous, he presented well, was polite, intelligent and thoughtful. At this initial assessment he was actually unaware that he had dyslexia although he knew that he had some difficulties reading etc and he talked of his embarrassment at pricing work for people. His work was of a very high standard and he was reasonably comfortable with this. However, he couldn't write out the price for the job and had to make it up and pretend he was writing. As a psychologist I was almost instantly aware that some things were not adding up and we agreed that we should administer a test that would help to reveal if indeed he had dyslexia. The outcome was that he had a gross level of dyslexia and his low verbal ratings were in complete contrast to his ratings on other items of the assessment. Therefore, as a young child and adolescent this man's *schemas* had been largely formed on the basis of factors such as he couldn't read and he was "thick". He tried numerous strategies to hide his "weakness" but he knew deep down that he had a difficulty. His situation was further reinforced by teachers who informed him that he would not amount to anything. There was a period of rebellion which was in total contrast to his personality but perhaps understandable under the circumstances. Indeed, it is difficult to imagine how this young must have felt "trapped" and inadequate with little compassion or understanding. The dyslexia test however took that personal responsibility away from him as it went some way to illustrating that his deficits were not as a result of the fact that that he had a low IQ or was intellectually inadequate. This finding in itself had a significant bearing on how he re-evaluated himself and went about his business. Instead of hiding his dyslexia he became far more open about it and found that people were understanding and non-judgemental, as he had previously assumed from his position of low self-esteem. He began to perceive himself from a more balanced and rational perspective and this went a great way to helping him manage his pervasive depression and his life in general. Unfortunately, I am aware that there are still many young children in our schools who suffer with dyslexia, which continues to give them difficulties that generally go unnoticed.

This remains a travesty, as many schools still do not formally recognise these problems. Many of these individuals therefore, are likely to experience low self-esteem and self-worth and may well present with mild to moderate depression in the future. The case however illustrates how one factor can consume an individual's overall perception of themselves to such an extent that they feel worthless and inadequate.

As briefly outlined above the core understanding of cognitive therapy emanates from the premise that the way we think is likely to affect the way we feel and subsequently the way we behave. These *thoughts, emotions and behaviour* are the fundamental principles of cognitive therapy and within these components lay the blueprints as to how we are likely to function from day to day. It is essential however, not to see these principles as simplistic and crude as I am well aware that if we tell someone with depression to think differently then they are unlikely to feel any better. I am certain that this naïve assumption is sometimes why therapists put up their *defences* and naively assume that this is all there is to cognitive therapy. However, the thoughts, emotions and behaviour are the "scaffolding" of cognitive therapy and as such they each need defining and explaining. Indeed, I once asked a counsellor about cognitive therapy and he said that he used it in everyday clinical practice. Naturally I was a little impressed and reassured. When I asked about what sort of cognitive processes he was familiar with he became a little hesitant and shirked the question. I honestly wasn't trying to attack him but was just interested in discussing cognitive psychotherapy. Cognitive processes are actually made up of factors such as attention, perception, concentration and short-term memory. In and of themselves one may argue that these factors have little significance, particularly with regard to how we think about ourselves and the world around us. However, when you begin to understand the primary role they play in our happiness and indeed our sadness then you may want to reconsider their significance in the future. Suffice to say, a good understanding of cognitive therapy and its associated components will not of course just help those who are suffering, it should naturally help you understand yourself better (warts and all). Just to illustrate how these factors are inextricably linked, and to reinforce the point, I remember just starting out on my clinical venture and taking my first clinical post in a GP practice. Six months into my post in which I believed I had established a reasonable working relationship with the GP's and had experienced some good clinical feedback, the senior partner at the practice managed to catch me as I came into the surgery at about 8.30am and said *"Chris, I'd like to have a word with you sometime today."* My immediate cognitive (*thoughts*) response was *"yes no problem, how about 1 pm"* and that was agreed. My emotional (*emotions*) response however said something else as all of a sudden I had become quite anxious. This in turn affected the way I was thinking and from then on I experienced a mild array of worrying thoughts. The *behaviour* in this example is not that relevant as I was "trapped" and had to see the morning clinic through. The thoughts and emotions nonetheless are indicative of how we begin to operate when we perceive ourselves as being under some imagined pressure and/or criticism. My irrational thinking began to suggest that I could always work somewhere else if this GP had a problem with me and this was probably accompanied by a million and one other negative or irrational thoughts such as I could always go back to working in a sports centre and perhaps this psychology stuff is a load of rubbish anyway (these *irrational* thoughts will be elaborated on later). The crux of the situation here however, is that someone had said they wanted a word with me and I had already convinced myself they were not going to be very pleasant come 1 pm. In essence, 1 pm came and I confidently (faked it) marched upstairs and said hello Dr. Mathews after which he said *"oh thanks for popping up, I just haven't had a chance to have a chat lately and I just wanted to say how positive the feedback has been since you joined the practice 6 months ago".* This is an actual story that occurred to me and I think it greatly illustrates the importance of cognition, emotion and behaviour. Those emotional feelings were real and uncomfortable yet those thoughts were completely irrational. The crucial point here is that we must never underestimate the subtle impact that an individual can have on ourselves or that we ourselves can have by just thinking in a particular manner. Today if someone wants to have a chat with me I usually wait to see what he or she wants before pressing the panic button. This does however need practice. I was greatly enlightened one day whilst working at the pain clinic at City Hospital Truro when using a cognitive approach to treat patients with chronic pain. Clinical practice often means taking the theory and applying it and sometimes it needs an analogy or a statement many of which I will use in this book. On this day however, I was handed a "gem" by a woman in her late 60's who came out with an old Cornish saying when she said, *"don't worry worry until worry worries you."* I believe this must have been one of the earliest cognitive strategies used yet the meaning and rationale are quite simple and it would have been useful if I had known it before starting my clinical practice and feeling summoned to speak to the GP.

As previously mentioned the core components of cognitive behaviour therapy are entrenched in *thoughts, emotions and behaviour*. All these factors are inextricably linked and combine in a manner that either allows an individual to think, feel, act, and respond in a manner that is either constructive or destructive depending on their schematic view of themselves and those around them. At its simplest level the components of cognitive therapy are best illustrated by looking at what happens when an individual becomes anxious in a given situation such as when out shopping or at a restaurant. The anxious feelings (*emotions*) are more often than not accompanied with *thoughts* such as "I'm going to faint, make a fool of myself and/or I can't cope. The thinking further exacerbates the way the individual is feeling and a vicious cycle is set in motion. The classic *behaviour*, which is this instance may be the final piece of the jigsaw, is for the individual to leave the given situation and run out of the shopping store or make an excuse (usually a physical one such as an headache, or upset stomach which is far more acceptable) and either leave the shop or restaurant early or avoid it altogether. In these instances therefore, the individual has suffered with anxiety and the "fear" has resulted in a barrage of irrational thinking that has magnified the effect to such an extent that the individual has had to leave the given situation and has subsequently returned home feeling rather dreadful and possibly a little upset (although ultimately relieved no doubt as they have avoided the situation). This is a very real example of how individuals can often function when anxiety rears its head for no obvious reason. This type of anxiety and irrational thinking has no boundaries and I have sat opposite enlightened and well-educated individuals and other "competent" adults from all avenues of life who sit there and explain that when anxiety *"grips"* and the real feelings take hold, all manner of rational thinking is lost. Indeed, there may be some relationship here in the saying that *"the first casualty of war is the truth"* for that is exactly what is happening to these individuals. In essence, they are sitting in a nice restaurant with friends, yet the anxiety grips and the thinking that accompanies this is in essence a "lie" because no actual harm is going to come to them as a result of being in the restaurant. Indeed, it is a *"false alarm"*, but they continue to act as if it is real, the fear and anxiety continue to rise and they are forced to flee and hence they have missed an opportunity of learning to adapt to what, in real terms is a pleasant situation. What may appear quite trivial in this example can significantly affect the quality of a person's life and also their relationship, particularly where the other partner may be becoming a little frustrated at not being able to take his or her partner out to dinner. Many social engagements with friends are lost and this may be the tip of the iceberg before the individual with anxiety begins to lose confidence and starts to withdraw further and further. All this can take time but it can slowly erode ones confidence totally.

The point being emphasised here is that many individuals from all walks of life will experience the above and they are increasingly unlikely to go back to that shop or restaurant. Furthermore, they may even be likely to begin to develop a type of phobia as a result of this. Interestingly, there always remains a part of this scenario that never ceases to amaze me and this is that most individuals know that no harm is going to come to them in a shop and/or a restaurant. They understand that there are no killer tins of beans waiting to shoot them as they glide through the aisles at Asda, they are also aware that eating out is a very pleasurable activity. Indeed, they used to do it all the time but they now avoid it and try to rationalise out the avoidance by saying things such as "I don't feel like eating out anymore and we enjoy eating in and it's not what it used to be" all irrational lies of course but if it helps convince them then so be it.

3 – The Cognitive Bias

The cognitive bias is yet another one of the key components of cognitive therapy and as such it is a factor that needs to be fully understood in order to comprehend how it operates in clinical practice. Whilst the title uses the term *cognitive bias*, this can and will come under a number of different guises including, *maladaptive thinking, cognitive distortions, irrational thinking* and so forth. This list is by no means exhaustive but it will hopefully help the reader identify that they all mean relatively the same thing and that is that this type of thinking is generally emotionally driven and that it tends to result in a way of thinking that is not balanced and true and hence it does not reflect the given situation. Such thinking was alluded to earlier in the brief examples of panic and anxiety in the restaurant situation. In the restaurant there was little evidence of any harm that was going to occur yet the irrational bias towards *fear driven* thinking was evident.

> *"My life has been full of terrible misfortunes,*
> *most of which never happened"*
> *Montaigne*

From those practicing in a more psychodynamic or psychoanalytical manner there still remains a certain amount of resistance with regard to some of the key components of cognitive therapy such as the components associated with the cognitive bias or irrational thinking. This still surprises me because of the considerable empirical evidence into factors such as the cognitive bias. Yet some therapists are still reluctant to accept that "irrational or maladaptive" thinking, if not playing a causal role in ones depression and/or anxiety is certainly likely to have an impact on the maintenance of the problem. I think this is best illustrated by using a "real" life example from an experience I had with a patient some 5 or 6 years ago. I would like to think that it also illustrates how creative a clinician can be using the cognitive approach to "test" out areas of maladaptive or biased thinking. The example involved a woman who was referred suffering with a relatively long-standing and pervasive depression. The depression had been intermittent and had lasted over a number of years. Following an initial assessment, the woman had the courage and hopefully the trust following our discussions to disclose that she had been sexually abused as a young child.

We are unlikely to do the clinical process of this case justice here, as the main aim is to illustrate the nature of the cognitive bias in practice. Therefore, I do not feel it is relevant to go into the case in any depth, as these types of issues will be addressed later in the book. It is essential therefore, for the reader not to get embroiled in the emotionally charged nature of the sexual abuse and to stand back and look at how this affected the person in question with regard to how she thought about her life in general and those around her. As clinicians the main issue for our present purposes is that the woman had been abused as a young child and from a cognitive and therapeutic perspective we would perhaps initially anticipate that this might have affected the way that she saw herself and the world around her (after all the science and empirical evidence would suggest this, what we have to do is to try to "*test*" this out). After an assessment period and in order to "test" out my initial hypothesis (idea/assumption), I remembered that on the wall of the office where I was working within the surgery was a sensitive and rather warming picture (in my mind anyway and with the schemata I had developed over the years) of a proud father naked from the waist up having just seemingly come out of the bath, holding his relatively new born baby in what appeared to be a protective and loving caress. There are many pictures such as this around and they have grown since the 1980s and form part of that "new man" myth. So there was the picture with the dad holding his baby proudly. To test my hypothesis I asked the woman what she saw when she looked at that picture? I was not surprised to see a sad and mildly animated look on her face before she said, *"all I can see is a paedophile".* The clinical relationship was safe and trusting enough to test this out and there was good congruence in the clinical process. Again, it might seem a little contrived when written in this manner so again I would urge the reader just to try to stick with the "facts" of the case rather than try to second guess the inappropriateness or whatever. We elaborated on her view of the picture and her subsequent comments and she confessed to how she saw men in general and in particular when she associated them with young children. The cognitive bias here is that as a result of her own experiences she had developed a maladaptive way of thinking that served to reinforce her own experience and subsequently contribute to her depression. Much of this reinforcement would have occurred quite innocently and unwittingly over a long period of time. There would have been some situations that would have helped reinforce this such as increasing news and media stories that over recent years have tended to focus on child abuse and paedophilia. Many individuals who have had to endure such horrendous experiences often point out that it is *"all around them"*, on the news, in the papers and even locally. Individuals suffering these experiences will tend to notice these factors far more and they will tend to magnify them as they have a significant emotive component. I have witnessed many such cases where the individual in question has managed to live a functional life without too much difficulty, repressing the experience/s in order to live as best they can. Repression is a useful *defence mechanism* that serves to protect our psyche as such. However, the increasing coverage interferes with the repressing and individuals start to become more *affected* often becoming mildly depressed to begin with. This often leads to behavioural avoidance as people find it increasingly harder to cope outside. For those who have struggled to cope with the experience it can further serve to reinforce the maladaptive way that they have come to perceive the world. The cognitive bias in this case was that this woman for many years had associated nearly every man with a child as being a paedophile. Likewise she had avoided relationships to "protect" her own children. Individuals who are suffering like this will tend to have a kind of *selective attention* whereby they will focus on and magnify those factors that reinforce their position and actually disqualify and/or minimise those other factors that may go against their position.

In the case example outlined above, the woman in question eventually discovered that she could accept on a basic rational level that her thinking was biased and that her dreadful experience had lead her to not trust men in general particularly where children were concerned. Over time using largely a cognitive approach based on a secure and trusting therapeutic relationship this woman eventually went on to manage her difficulties far better, right down to having a relationship of her own. Her journey will be a long one but at last she has been guided onto the right road and she has accepted how she was affected by the dreadful experience. To this extent, she has gained insight into her own bias that was tending to make her situation worse or at the very least helping to maintain it. In this instance the woman was also able to analyse her own thinking process to such an extent that she may not be able to stop the initial irrational thinking, however she is able to give herself time to look over a given situation in order to see if she has reacted appropriately. This will subsequently affect how she will then behave and hopefully this behaviour will now be more adaptive and she can go on to live with a greater degree of insight and understanding with regard to her own life. This illustrates the importance of psycho-education during the therapeutic process whereby the client/patient is helped to understand how and why we think, feel and behave in the way we do. Indeed, as one psychologist has put it, potentially we are all our own psychologists or therapists at the end of the day and an understanding of how we operate can only help us in the long run. This also has tremendous potential for the positive maintenance of good therapeutic gain.

The clinical process in this instance also enabled the woman to move from a *victim* status to a *survivor* and beyond. Hopefully, this illustrates just one example of how a cognitive bias can develop and grow immeasurably until it can consume one's life to such an extent that it actually becomes that persons' life with all the irrational and maladaptive thinking and subsequent behaviour that accompanies it. To most people the picture of the father caressing his baby would have conjured up warm thoughts (putting the new man myth aside of course), however to this woman this innocent picture only served to further her angst. One can only imagine how this angst had probably been reinforced in many subtle ways over the previous years.

There are many therapies that would accept the idea that irrational beliefs are at the core of most psychological problems. We could also call these beliefs unrealistic, incorrect, or maladaptive as previously mentioned. Whatever we choose to call these errors of thought there is now overwhelming evidence to support the fact that they can play a significant role in the development, and perhaps more significantly the maintenance of depression and anxiety. In my own clinical practice I tend to refer to this cognitive bias as, *"emotional thinking"*, Therefore, when we tend to think in an emotional fashion then more often than not, we tend to think in an irrational fashion. Each of us should be able to test this out quite reasonably. Using a non-clinical example I am always amazed to see football and rugby fans among others shout and yell about a situation when the evidence totally contradicts the context they have witnessed. The key here is that these supporters are *emotionally charged*. I remember being a spectator at a rugby match when one player actually head-butted the other, the crowd were incensed and one chap said, (and at the time he meant it), *"he didn't mean to do it"*. The referee (Mr Rational) thought otherwise. Recently, I have heard referees actually say to players, *"watch the replay on the video"*. What the referee is of course doing in this case without probably being aware of it is asking the player/s to look at the actual scene with less emotion so that they can actually access their rational side and view it in a more balanced way. Yes, I am aware that even referees get it wrong on occasion but that is a different matter not for discussion here.

Emotional thinking and how it appears in all its guises will become increasingly evident throughout the book. Indeed, it will be part of a continuous theme that will help the reader understand how and why many psychological problems develop and persist until they finally become all consuming. Many psychologists have suggested that emotional thinking is irrational because it is simply not logical (there is no evidence for the emotional thought), or they are based on false assumptions. Albert Ellis, a significant contributor to cognitive therapy and therapy in general identified what he and his colleagues saw as ten common irrational beliefs which, if held too rigidly, are likely to lead to emotional and/or psychological distress. As outlined above, these beliefs are often learned early in life and they can form a significant part of our *core beliefs* from which our thinking pattern further develops. These beliefs are outlined below and whilst they appear quite "dry" in theory and in written form they are not to be frowned upon and each individual will be affected to a greater or lesser degree depending on a number of crucial factors. These crucial factors include one's **personality** that will incorporate elements such as the individuals **coping style** and **emotional resilience.** I like to use the term *emotional resilience* as it can be a significant factor involved in whether one becomes a victim or a survivor and it can help explain, to some extent why some people function better after suffering with problems such as post-traumatic stress, abuse and many other psychological problems. These elements will combine to develop what we call the individuals, *"attributional style"*, which in essence refers to whether the individual will attribute the cause of their difficulties to internal factors (blame themselves) or external factors (other people or the situation itself) This is a crude description and attributional style will be elaborated on later in the book.

Ten Common Irrational Beliefs

---

1 – I must be liked or accepted by every important person in my life for almost everything I do.

2 – I must be successful, competent and achieving in everything I do if I'm to consider myself worthwhile.

3 – It is awful and terrible when things are not the way I would like them to be. Things should be different.

4 – I must feel anxious, upset and preoccupied if something is, or may be, dangerous.

5 – Human unhappiness is caused by events beyond our control so people have little or no ability to control their negative feelings.

6 – It is easier to avoid facing many of life's difficulties and responsibilities than to face them.

7 – The past is all-important, so if something once strongly affected one's life, it cannot be altered.

8 – When people act badly, inadequately or unfairly, I blame them, and view them as completely bad or pathetic – including myself.

9 – Maximum happiness can be achieved by inertia and inaction, or by passively enjoying oneself.

10 – Everyone should be dependent on others and I need someone stronger than myself on whom I can rely.

Adapted from Powell (2001)

As Powell (2001) points out, "what makes these ideas irrational, or maladaptive, is the belief that they are always correct". Of course, working hard will increase your chances for success, but success is not guaranteed. Similarly, there are times when we do everything right, and we still don't get what we want. For some people, this can lead to the conclusion and belief that they are incompetent, stupid, or the world is against them and they are just meant to fail in most of the things that they do. The result can be a loss of self-esteem and/or self-worth accompanied by a lowering of the mood and possibly a mild depressive episode. Therefore, one of the primary aims of cognitive therapy is to help the client/patient begin to understand how and why they may be thinking in a biased fashion and to help them identify their irrational or emotional ideas and thoughts. If this is done in a skilful and supportive manner then most individuals are eventually able to differentiate between those thoughts that are likely to be biased and subsequently maladaptive and those that are more balanced and realistic. Further along in the therapeutic process the emotional and irrational ideas need to be challenged and changed to reflect the "real" world. An illustration of this bias would have been how the woman in the example outlined above whom, having been abused as a child could only see the doting father holding his baby in a loving caress as a paedophile. Again without going into extensive detail at this stage, the woman in question was actually able to significantly move forward with her thinking and her subsequent behaviour to such an extent that she was able to re-examine the way she thought about herself and the world around her so that she became more balanced, rational and less self-defeating in her thinking. In essence, this meant that she was less *affected* by her dreadful experience. One of the key points here however, is as a result of her change in thinking came a change in her behaviour and it is the change in the behaviour that completed the "chain" of thought-emotion-behaviour into a more adaptive and constructive pattern as opposed to a destructive pattern.

It is difficult to illustrate just in words, how significant and subtle these thinking and behavioural changes are and how they greatly affect our lives. Hopefully when we look at depression and some more "real" life examples more extensively will the reader gain a greater understanding of how our mood can be significantly affected by our way of thinking to such an extent that we tend to only see things that tend to confirm our "fixed" and "affected" patterns of thought. It is also difficult to describe the richness of the therapeutic process that allowed for the above change. However, it is true that the person in question was able to begin having a healthy relationship and she re-learned to trust men in a far more adaptive and balanced fashion. Admittedly, she had difficulties; however she eventually arrived at a situation where if there was no "real" hard evidence that the man in question, whether he was the milkman, postman or whatever was an abuser, then she really had to trust this feeling, however uncomfortable. Again, she was able to do this in a manner that showed courage and belief in the therapeutic process. Her move towards a more balanced and adaptive way of thinking lead to a subsequent change in her behaviour and interaction that served to help her overcome her bias further. The subtle result of this of course was that she had more positive experiences on a daily basis. Again, the subtleties involved here cannot be underestimated and these clinical components will be further highlighted in more detail when we look at some other clinical case examples of therapy in action.

Hopefully we have now established how the cognitive bias comes into play in the onset and certainly in the maintenance of problems. Indeed, when all is considered it is something that we all suffer from to a more or lesser extent and there are numerous examples that I am sure we can all think of when we have thought emotionally and irrationally, only to be proven wrong. Those with the powerful bias will even deny that they are wrong when they are faced with contradictory evidence and this occurs a great deal throughout the clinical process. For example, clients will hold rigid beliefs about themselves and the world around them to such an extent that they cannot be flexible enough in their thinking to contemplate that there may be other reasons as to why an event occurred. It still never ceases to amaze me how "fixed" these thoughts can be. I have seen men and women suffering with depression attend college courses and night classes of varying degrees and in general they have been very successful in their studies. Indeed, I am a great believer that education in itself is sometimes the best kind of *"therapy"* as it is something that is achieved solely by the individual and as such can greatly enhance their self-worth. Undoubtedly, this is the thrust behind some classic films such as "Educating Rita" and "Shirley Valentine", which despite their mass appeal for obvious reasons actually reflects "real" life situations that occur on a daily basis. However, education alone is sometimes not enough when someone has such a low opinion of themselves that it grossly biases their thinking. Indeed, I can recall one patient who actually topped the class and was on for a first class degree. I would ask this individual to bring along some marked assignments for us to discuss. In essence this person was achieving between 70% and 80% for her assignments. When asked how she felt about this she responded by saying, *"well its ok but they are probably taking a little pity on me when they are marking as I am a mature student and I think they know I suffer with depression"*. This scenario happens time and time again with individuals who have grown up with low self-esteem and a mild-moderate depression. What we have here therefore is an example of this persons *"attributional style"* that has become fixed as part of her schemata. Attributional style is based on *"attribution theory"* which suggests that certain individuals who have a low opinion of themselves are more likely to attribute the cause of success to reasons outside their control such as luck and chance or people taking pity on them. Conversely, when it comes to failure these individuals are far more likely to attribute this failure to themselves for not being good enough or being stupid. A more balanced way of thinking if one achieved excellent marks on their course work would be something on the lines of, *"well it was worth putting all that effort and revision in, I guess I deserved my success"*.

It would appear that there is a large body of research that suggests that we tend to think about situations in a manner that is congruent with our mood. Therefore, if we are in a low mood then this will affect the way we experience everyday events and again this can be seen as a cognitive bias or an error in the way we are thinking. For example, we may watch a film when feeling low and therefore our account of it to our friends is more likely to be that the film was not very good. Conversely, we may have had some fantastic news and gone on to watch a dreadful film, have a poor meal, yet come home saying that we had a great night out. This might seem rather bizarre and simplistic, yet I can assure you that if we are honest with ourselves and are self-aware this is actually something that happens on a rather regular basis. Naturally, this thought-mood-behaviour pattern has greater significance when transferred into subtle everyday experiences and suggests that the person with little confidence is likely to suffer even further in all manner of situations. This often leads to a great deal of *"avoidance behaviour"* that in turn is likely to lower the mood even further. Cognitive therapy has many ways of looking at the way we think and some of the more common terms given to some of the biased and negative thinking are outlined below. A useful exercise would be to read through each of the emotional thinking styles and try to identify, either in a clinical context or in a non-clinical context examples that you are familiar with.

Styles of Emotional/Irrational Thinking

Dichotomous Thinking:

Also known as Polarized, All-or-Nothing or Black-&-White Thinking. Thinking in extremes, it's either right or wrong, with no possibility of any grey areas in between.

Filtering:

A tendency to focus on the negative details of a situation whilst ignoring the positive. People will also tend to magnify the negative aspects. In situations that involve both positive and negative elements, people tend to filter out information in a biased fashion.

Discounting:

Downplaying and disregarding the positive, phrases like: 'That doesn't count,' 'That wasn't good enough,' or 'anyone could have done it.' Sometimes humour or sarcasm is used to downplay what one feels uncomfortable about.

Catastrophizing:

Expecting disaster, the person becomes full of emotionally driven "what ifs" and has a tendency to expect the worst possible outcome. Exaggerating the importance of problems, shortcomings, and minor annoyances. Something minor goes wrong and the assumption is that it is a major problem. In essence, we will make a drama out of a crisis.

Mind-Reading:

Assuming you know what the other person is thinking and feeling about you or your situation. As well as reading into their motivation and intention. A common style of thinking when someone is depressed or anxious, this is something we are all guilty of.

Emotional Reasoning:

Believing that what you feel is the way things really are automatically. Assuming that because you feel a certain way, that is the truth. 'I feel stupid, boring so I am stupid or boring.' A rather "fixed" and negative attributional style probably formed early on in life as a result of poor interpersonal experience and/or criticism.

'Shoulds' and 'Should-nots':

"Rules" that everyone in the world and their families should live by. Also statements with 'must' 'ought to' and 'have to'. You may feel enraged when others break those rules and guilt/shame when you break them.

As should be apparent by now cognitive biases and distortions are another way of describing the irrational thoughts and the over-generalizing of simple mistakes so that individuals end up developing *"false assumptions"* about the way they think about themselves and what other people think about them, or expect from them. When this is achieved it is akin to turning black into white and white into black. In essence we are distorting reality by the way we are evaluating a situation. Studies have revealed that when people are depressed or anxious then they are more likely to recall events that are congruent with their mood. A simple study using a number of groups of individuals suffering with depression and/or anxiety illustrated this point quite emphatically. Groups of 50 individuals ranging from depression, anxiety, "normal" and a control group were asked to look at fifty positive words such as happy, sunshine, holiday etc, following this they were asked to look at fifty negative words such as dark, sad, bleak etc. They were each given a simple task and then asked to recall as many words as they could. The outcomes were interesting as they revealed that those suffering with anxiety and/or depression recalled four times as many negative words than the control group and the "normal" group. In essence this illustrates how biased towards the negative we become when we are anxious or depressed. Similarly, Willner (1990) and colleagues using the *Depressive Attributional Style Questionnaire* (Peterson et al, 1982) discovered that depressed patients had higher internal (blame themselves) and stable (consistently) scores for negative attributions. What this means is that these patients were more willing to attribute negative consequences to themselves in a consistent fashion. The results therefore suggest that the *'depressive attributional style'* may be specific to depressed or anxious patients. Clinically therefore this should be an integral part of the therapeutic process. Helping the individual to gain insight and understanding into how they are construing life in general in what might be a self-defeating and destructive manner that unwittingly fuels their anxious/depressed state.

The concept of emotional thinking or attributional biases highlights the importance of individuals' perceptions, assumptions and judgments in coping with the world. Therapists can help determine what evaluations are distortions by providing objective feedback about individuals' evaluations of the world, and by working in a supportive alliance in order to facilitate a process that will enable the individual to change the way they perceive themselves and problems in the future. This in turn will help them change the way they think and subsequently the way they behave so that they are able to live in a far more adaptive fashion.

Part 2: Depression

1 – What is Depression?

As mentioned earlier in the introduction, depression in the western world appears to be on the increase with the World Health Organisation (WHO) estimating that it is likely to be one of the major causes of overall morbidity by 2020. Interestingly, the highest prevalence rates tend to be found among those aged between 18 and 30 years of age with rates tending to drop with increasing age. Research suggests that estimates of depression actually reflect a true increase, rather than better recognition or other extraneous factors. The increase is however, likely to be related to a number of issues including political, social and psychological factors such as differing personal expectations and the breakdown of the family and society in general. Whatever the reasons, and the debate would fill a book in itself, depression appears to be something that is here to stay and for the moment is unfortunately increasing.

Whilst most of us will have a general idea of what depression entails or what feeling depressed is like the actual clinical depression that often presents in primary care can be a debilitating and pervasive problem for the individual in question. Whether, the presenting depression is categorised as mild, moderate or severe it is crucial that the depression is assessed and treated in the most comprehensive manner. This can only be achieved by fully understanding the rubrics of depression itself and how we have come to define and subsequently assess individuals who are suffering with depression. Additionally, the care and sensitivity with which this investigation is carried out will inevitably remain essential as the presenting individual is likely to be feeling vulnerable, alone and isolated with their problem. This is often the case when individuals appear to have supportive families and work colleagues. Indeed, despite these "protective" elements, many individuals often describe their situation where, despite the presence of many supportive family and friends they still feel isolated and alone. This remains an interesting situation to say the least and some of the likely reasons for this will be discussed later.

One of the important points here is that whilst most of us may feel a little low or even mildly depressed on occasion, we should not confuse this with the type of depressed state that we as clinicians and therapists alike are going to face. I stress this point as I have witnessed many well-meant counsellors and therapists unwittingly and often unknowingly project their own experiences on to the client/patient without actually giving the individual the time and space to express their own thoughts and feelings. Therefore, whilst empathy and a degree of validation may be an important part of the clinical alliance between therapist and patient it is important that this does not overlap to the extent that the clinician is over-identifying with the individual. If this occurs then the client is likely to assume that the therapist is not listening. Alternatively, if the therapist is able to illustrate a comprehensive understanding of depression and how it is defined then this can only help the clinical relationship and the therapeutic process in general by helping to establish the therapists' clinical credibility.

So what is depression? In general depression is a problem characterised by a persistent and prolonged low mood that affects the individuals' ability to think and behave with clarity to such an extent that they are unable to carry out relatively simple every day activities that they would have previously taken for granted. Often people will say things like, *"I can't remember the simplest of things"*. For example, they may find themselves walking upstairs only to forget what they actually went up for. Similarly, many report putting things in the wrong place such as the milk in the cupboard and the cereal box in the fridge. These daily episodes are likely to further compound the depressed mood and further deepen the depressed state. As one can imagine, for many individuals who may be over a certain age suffering with depression can arouse all manner of irrational thoughts which can be frightening in themselves. For example, many individuals will put the forgetting aspect of memory down to their age and this is inevitably interlinked to the thought that they must be experiencing the early onset of a significant degenerative disease such as Alzheimer's. Naturally, these have to be ruled out, but in general the GP would have assessed these issues and hence it is important to reassure the client that factors such as attention and concentration (which actually feed into short-term memory and are therefore essential prerequisites of short-term memory) are affected by our mood, particularly when we are feeling low. This can actually be reassuring in itself depending on the level of confusion. If however, you are unsure about whether the cognitive difficulties such as attention, concentration and short-term memory are perhaps not wholly related to the depression then it is wise to have the individual re-assessed by someone so that we can be absolutely certain that the problems presented are of a *functional* (depression) rather than an *organic* nature.

Depression can consume the whole person in such a manner that the individual is likely to have little interest and motivation. To this extent, basic every day functioning is likely to be slowed down with the individual "drifting" from day to day in a rather disconnected fashion. There will be a loss of interest in previous enjoyable activities and a gradual withdrawal is likely to take place with individuals continuing to isolate themselves by avoiding social and recreational situations.

At present, informed estimates suggest that depression actually affects about 5%-20% of the population at some time in their lives with the illness being generally more common among women than men. The reasons for this gender difference are somewhat unclear. However it is likely that these gender differences are somewhat biased by factors such as health seeking behaviour itself and general coping differences such as the ability to express emotion. Indeed, these and other factors are likely to play a significant role in why these statistical gender differences for depression exist.

With regard to defining and observing depression it is important that the therapist has a general understanding of some of the mental health definitions associated with the American Psychiatric Association's *Diagnostic and Statistical Manual* (DSM-IV) (APA DSM-IV). The DSM-IV is now recognised as the prime definition of how to recognise and assess depression. Indeed, DSM-IV definitions are closely linked to those in the World Health Organisations' "*International Classification of Diseases*" (ICD-10), which is the other universally, recognised mental health definition manual. However it is now generally accepted that the DSM-IV now "drives" the ICD-10 making an understanding of the DSM-IV criteria even more relevant. Indeed, this understanding of the leading definitions should be a fundamental and integral part of any therapists' repertoire. There are many other very useful and relatively simple diagnostic tools such as *The Hospital Anxiety and Depression Scale (Zigmond & Snaith – 1974)* that will be discussed later, however the DSM-IV criteria should be the *"benchmark"* for observing and understanding depression. When observing the following criteria we must always keep in mind that individuals will suffer to differing degrees usually ranging from mild to moderate to severe as previously suggested.

The DSM-IV outlines nine distinct criterions related to depression and naturally they range from criterion A1 to A9 respectively. It is important to acknowledge that not all of the criterion need to be present for a diagnosis of depression and naturally each criterion, depending on the individual in question may vary in its severity and intensity. Below is a general outline of each criterion, which should give the reader some idea of how depression is being conceptualised.

APA (DSM-IV) – Criteria for Depression – Criterions A1-A9

Criterion A1 refers to the mood in general that is often described by the individual as being sad and hopeless with general feelings of pessimism and despair. Many individuals will complain of a kind of "emotional numbness" that they are experiencing whereby they have little or no emotional feelings. The presence of a depressed mood can often be inferred from the person's body language and in particular facial expression and/or general demeanour. Some individuals however are more likely to emphasise somatic complaints for example such as bodily aches and pains rather than reporting feelings of sadness. Therefore it is always wise to keep a careful note of not only what is being described but how it is being described.

Criterion A2 generally refers to a loss of interest or pleasure that is nearly always present. Individuals may report feeling less interested in hobbies for example with the previously avid gardener now resigned to the house not having the inclination and/or motivation to go out. There are generally numerous excuses for this and these often serve to "rationalise" out the reasons why the individual is avoiding things that they used to enjoy. It should be good practice for the therapist to "test" out each criterion as he or she assesses an individual. Therefore, taking a clinical history can also involve just generally enquiring as to what they are interested in such as music, gardening, sport etc. This is also a good opportunity to reflect back to the client and hence establish additional rapport at what is generally looked upon as a crucial stage in the therapeutic process.

Criterion A3 in the DSM-IV refers to appetite that is usually reduced, although some individuals may actually have an increased appetite (possibly comfort eating). Therefore, there may be either a significant weight gain or loss depending on how the individual is coping. This may be relevant for the fatigue that often accompanies depression, as food of course is one of our main sources of energy.

Criterion A4 refers to sleep disturbance with the most common sleep disturbance being a lack of sleep, commonly referred to as insomnia. Again, this loss of sleep is likely to affect one's ability to function well from day to day with the individual suffering with depression feeling tired and lethargic with little or no energy to think or engage in any kind of activity. Just a few of the above criterion already illustrate how inextricably linked each component of depression is and it should be relatively easy to see how a "vicious cycle" is set in motion. Interestingly, with regard to criterion A4 there are instances with regard to sleeping that include a number of individuals who actually present with oversleeping (hypersomnia). Indeed, I have witnessed this hypersomnia on many occasions in the primary care setting and would consider it a form of "escape" from the "troubled" and "tortured" world that is depression. I consider this hypersomnia as an attempt to gain some respite from the depression itself. Having witnessed many individuals suffering with depression it is easy to understand the temptation to just withdraw and isolate themselves away from the world and their depressive thoughts. Whether this is a conscious decision or not remains unclear, however it is clear to see why one would want to just sleep when the world "outside" appears negative and bleak. Indeed, I have often heard individuals around Xmas time in particular (a very difficult period for those suffering with depression) say, *"I wish I could go to sleep and wake up when it's (Xmas) all over".* This statement probably touches a nerve in most individuals, even those fortunate enough not to experience depression. With regard to the sleeping difficulties associated with criterion A4 it is common that the individual will present to the GP seeking help just for the disturbed sleeping problem itself. Therefore, it is always important to keep in mind the constellation of symptoms that make up depression as the initial stages of the illness may be so subtle on occasion that some individuals may not actually see themselves as being depressed. Indeed, when we briefly touched on gender differences and depression earlier it may well be the case that a female is more likely to express her emotions to her GP far better than her male counterpart. Therefore, the GP is more likely to rightly diagnose the female as suffering with a mild or whatever form of depression. Alternatively, the male may walk into the surgery and just state that, *"I'm not sleeping that well Doc"*. Given this presentation and the time involved the male may be just given some general advice to drink a little less at night and/or some temporary sleeping tablets to be used in the short-term. I appreciate that this is a rather simplistic example but hopefully it should serve to illustrate a point. Naturally, GP's and other interested parties are also likely to have varying degrees of time and skill when it comes to identifying and treating depression, although most are far more skilled in this area than some would think. Indeed, as the first line of approach it is the GP and primary care team that often treat most of the depression within the primary care setting, particularly as access to good psychological and therapeutic intervention may be unavailable. Thankfully, in recent years this situation has been greatly improved with far greater attention now being given to individuals presenting with depression and anxiety; however there is still some considerable improvement to be made.

Following on with the rubrics of depression, *criterion A5* refers to general psychomotor changes which include an inability to sit still and relax and a general feeling of increased irritability, or being "on edge" as the individual will often describe. Conversely, there may be a slowing down and a general retardation associated with the depression, this can also include slowed speech, thinking and body movements. Although the *speeding-up* and the *slowing down* may appear contradictory descriptions it is the fact that both components appear to be extreme when someone is suffering with depression. Many will say that it feels like they are *"wading through treacle"* and that their head feels as if it is in *"cotton wool"*. It is quite surprising how individuals suffering with depression use the same descriptions and a *"woolly"* and/or *"fuzzy"* feeling in the head are common words that I have heard time and time again to describe the feelings associated with being depressed.

Criterion A6 is perhaps a natural follow-on with the individual feeling as if they are slowed down with decreased energy, tiredness and fatigue being the most common symptoms.

Criterion A7 tends to be more related to the way the individual is thinking often with a sense of worthlessness or guilt associated with a depressive episode. This is also likely to include a number of unrealistic negative evaluations of one's worth and/or guilty preoccupations or ruminations over minor experiences. These areas were briefly alluded to in the cognitive therapy section and as we proceed hopefully a continued "picture" will begin to evolve linking the overall cognitive processes and functions to the depression itself.

Criterion A8 refers to the situation whereby many individuals report an impaired ability to think, concentrate and/or make decisions. Again, they may appear easily distracted or complain of memory difficulties. One of the most common reports by people suffering with depression is that they can't make decisions. Even the simplest of decisions remains difficult if not impossible and again this can illustrate just how a problem in one of the criterion can lead to a gradual build-up of difficulties that might eventually become overbearing. The individual for example who cannot make a decision is likely to not involve him/herself in previous activities. They may do this quite unknowingly and feel they do not have the energy to make the decision, however the end result is that they are likely to become increasingly disconnected on a social level and this is generally not good for their depression or general well-being.

Finally we come to *Criterion A9* that includes thoughts of death and/or suicidal ideation. There may even be a suicide attempt either recent or in the past, which is commonly referred to as a *para-suicide*. If indeed, there has been a suicide attempt in the past then naturally this has to be given careful consideration and one should involve other professionals in the assessment process before agreeing a course of therapeutic action. Interestingly, suicidal ideation is not considered a necessary condition for the diagnosis of depression, and in other depressive states it may not actually feature at all.

DSM-IV

Depression - Criterion A1-A9

A1 - Depressed mood, sadness, pessimistic

A2 - Loss of interest in previously enjoyable activities

A3 - Appetite, weight gain or possible loss,

A4 - Sleep disturbances, insomnia and occasionally hypersomnia

A5 - Increased irritability cannot sit still and relax

A6 - Decreased energy, tiredness and fatigue

A7 - A sense of worthlessness and/or guilt that may include unrealistic negative evaluations of one's worth and/or negative ruminations over the past.

A8 - Impaired ability to think, concentrate or make decisions, easily distracted.

A9 - There may be thoughts of death and/or suicidal ideation.

For a diagnosis of a major depression:

1 - At least 5 of the DSM-IV symptoms must be present.

2 - These symptoms must be present during the same 2-week period.

3 - These symptoms must represent a change from a previous level of functioning

When someone has five or more of these symptoms most of the time for a period of 2 weeks or longer then we would consider that this person is likely to be suffering with depression. This may sound a little obvious, however there are many times when individuals may get down for 2-3 weeks at a time but we wouldn't consider them as suffering with depression unless they "fitted" the criteria outlined above. There are other times when people go through certain periods where these symptoms are really intense; times when these same feelings could be present and persist at a lower level for longer periods, sometimes even for a number of years. Conversely, some people may have just one episode of depression, or they may go on to have many more after feeling quite well for a while. The permutations are numerous and the very nature of being human is that we have the potential to evolve and adapt sometimes for the better and perhaps sometimes not. To this extent, we may grow as individuals to become more resilient to depression and other emotional difficulties. Alternatively, there will be others who may become more vulnerable as time goes on. There are of course many reasons for these scenarios and much will depend on the personality of the individual, the amount of stress they may have been exposed to over the years and the experiences they have faced which have psychologically "shaped" them in a certain way. I recall an example from "real life" where an experienced fireman was called out to a horrific road traffic accident. Despite his years of experience and previous resilient psychological demeanour the individual in question was so affected by what he witnessed that he continued to suffer with a major depression for many years after. The depression itself was severe with most if not all of the criteria outlined above. This example, extreme yet true, hopefully serves to highlight some of the factors that surround the potential onset of depression. Therefore, depending on one's experiences it is evident that even the strongest can suffer with major depression if certain circumstances combine. As we shall see later there are common criteria that contribute to these depressive feelings and they will include loss, separation and marital discord to name but a few.

Despite the potential complexity associated with depression and the numerous variables, there are often clear indicators as to why someone has become depressed. It is therefore important during the assessment process that all the significant factors are addressed and carefully "teased" out so that we can begin to build a "picture". Often it may well be an *exogenous (reactive)* depression as a result of an event in their life that has gone on to significantly affect their mood such as the case of the fireman described above. Alternatively it may be more of an *endogenous* depression. This term is seldom used these days but I still feel it is a useful word used to describe a depression that is more related to the individual and hence it may be a personality variable or have a genetic or biological component. To this extent it may well be more akin to a depressive personality or a personality type that is more vulnerable to suffering with emotional distress and depression. I feel using the terms *exogenous (reactive)* and *endogenous* at least can give us a general guide as to what has contributed to the depressive episode. In general exogenous depression has been seen as being less severe and endogenous more severe. However, these conditions are now understood to be more complex in their causation. For example, life events such as bereavement, unemployment, moving house and the break-up of relationships can act as *"triggers"* to what would previously have been seen as a biological or severe type of depression. Equally, some people who encounter adversity in their lives get depressed while others seem to cope with all circumstances no matter what they are faced with. Having just written that sentence the name Nelson Mandela came into my mind and it is difficult to think of a more appropriate example of someone who coped with such adversity. I am however unaware as to whether he suffered with depression or not.

The permutations triggering the onset of depression are numerous and naturally there will be those persons who may have vulnerable personalities who have also been exposed to an event that has caused them to become severely depressed. This scenario will place even greater demands on the therapist and the assessment process. However, for the purposes of understanding depression the terms endogenous and exogenous or reactive will be used and as previously suggested, at the very least they will serve as a general guide for our learning purposes.

The above description of different types of onset also illustrates the importance of trying to keep an open mind for all possible contributing factors when it comes to assessing the person who may be experiencing depression. Furthermore, it reinforces the fundamental importance of taking a comprehensive history when assessing a client/patient. Indeed, I will always maintain that the reasons for the depression are often revealed in the history taking and that the subsequent treatment that follows will only be successful if the assessment has been comprehensive, thorough and relevant. Despite this description of the assessment that may sound a little daunting, I believe that most if not all assessments can be achieved in far less than 1 hour. Naturally, a lot of factors will feed into this such as the motivation and co-operation of the client/patient and the referral factors and symptoms themselves. However, in general 1 hour should be more than enough for a thorough assessment that should result in an eventual formulation of the problem and a subsequent working hypothesis.

2 – Why do people become depressed?

As outlined earlier, there are both predisposing and precipitating factors that can contribute to the onset of depression. Predisposing factors are features of one's personality or even one's lifestyle that may make one increasingly susceptible to depression. These may be related to genetic factors, to early lifetime experiences, or to social circumstances. This has been referred to as an endogenous depression. Precipitating factors are "triggers" that directly lead to the episode of depression and this is more of the exogenous type of depression. For example, stressful life events such as the loss of a job or the end of a relationship can trigger an episode of depression. Indeed, there are many factors that can contribute to depression and these include particular life events, medical conditions and the absence of good social supports.

Evaluation of Life Experiences

When depressed, a person will tend to focus on minor negative aspects of what was otherwise a positive life experience. For example, after a vacation at the beach, the depressed person will remember the one day it rained, rather than the six days of sunshine. If anything goes wrong, the depressed person evaluates the entire experience as a failure, or as a negative life experience. As a result, memories are almost always negative. This is indicative of selective memory attention that is mood driven. The problems here are self-evident as the depressed person reinforces a vicious cycle of negativity that is likely to maintain the depressive mood.

Nothing in life ever works out just as you want. If we expect perfection, we will always be disappointed. Many Psychologists help people to develop *realistic expectations* about life, and help to determine what people need as opposed to what they want. After all, most of the things that don't work out are little things. And even when important problems develop, we can either resolve the problem or regroup, recover, and start again, with hope for a better future. In depression however, the hope is missing.

What risk factors play a role in depression?

In general and at a simplistic level the risk factors that contribute to depression are akin to a math formula: for example, a person is more at risk of becoming depressed if he or she:

- Feels a lot of pressure for any reason, plus
- Has no one to share worries or concerns, plus
- Lacks practical and/or interpersonal support.

Feeling connected to others in our daily lives makes an enormous difference in ones ability to survive the kinds of stress that trigger depression. Generally speaking, people who feel unknown or unseen, or who avoid the support and comfort of others, risk depression and depressive disorders.

What kinds of events and experiences increase the risk of depression?

Depression can be the outcome of many different kinds of experiences in a person's life, from early childhood to later life events. Some examples of events or experiences that can lead to depression are:

- **Chaotic, unsafe or dangerous environments** (for example, living in a violent home, or living in a house with little heat and little room).
- **Early life serious losses or traumas** (such as the death of a parent in childhood, or being abused or neglected)
- **Loss of social support** (due to the death of a loved one, divorce, moving away from friends and family, break up of a relationship, loss of a job, or loss of trust)
- **Unhealthy social conditions** (such as poverty, homelessness, and community violence)
- **Experiences that undermine self-confidence** (such as social or work related failures)
- **Learned helplessness and negative thought patterns** (chronic or repeated stressful events leading to the belief of helplessness, reinforced by lack of control over the situation)
- **Chronic illness** (such as heart disease, stroke, HIV, Parkinson's, cancer, or diabetes) that seriously restrict activity
- **Side effects of medications** (for example, blood pressure medications and numerous other drugs)
- **Hormonal changes** (stage of life adjustments, such as the onset or end of menstruation that affect mood)
- **Substance abuse**: alcohol and some drugs are known to have depressive effects, and the negative social and personal consequences of substance abuse can also be a contributing factor to depression (however, it may not be clear which comes first-depression and attempts control it with substances, or the use of substances that then cause depression)
- **Genetic causes**: people with close family members who suffer from depression are more prone to depression (however, since no gene for depression has been found, this could also be environmental rather than genetic)
- **Biochemical causes** (an imbalance of neurotransmitters such as seretonin is known to affect the processing of thoughts and emotions)

The above are by no means exclusive and hopefully illustrate some of the more common factors associated with depression. Of course, these factors alone are often not enough to result in depression and it is how these factors interact with other components that will affect whether one will suffer with a depressive episode or not. Some of the key factors are outlined below.

Key factors in the onset of depression

- Personality – resilient/vulnerable (Endogenous type of depression)
- Event – (Reactive type of depression)
- Cumulative events (Reactive type of depression)

Given the above information it is likely that those individuals who have a vulnerable personality are more likely to suffer to a greater degree when they are exposed to a potential traumatic event. However, it is generally accepted that there is no actual single cause for depression and as mentioned many factors play a role including genetics, environment, life events, and certain thinking patterns that affect a person's reaction to events. Indeed, research has revealed that depression often runs in families and suggests that some people inherit genes that make it more likely for them to get depressed. However, not everyone who has the genetic "makeup" for depression actually gets depression. Conversely many people who have no relevant family history of depression will still suffer with the condition. Despite this obvious conundrum it is the wise therapist who becomes increasingly aware of some of the main patterns and variables involved in the onset of depression.

Perhaps understandably, our family and social environment are likely to play a role in the onset of depression and this may depend on the family values and structure to some extent. For some teenagers for example, a negative, stressful, and/or unhappy family atmosphere can affect their self-esteem and self-worth and lead to depression. Given the increase in divorce and separation this area is likely to be of increasing concern in the future. Additionally, there are economic factors and social conditions such as poverty and homelessness that can make it more likely for people to become depressed. Outside of the genetic, social and psychological factors there are also certain medical conditions to consider that can affect hormone balance and therefore have an effect on mood. Some conditions, such as *hypothyroidism* for example, are known to cause a depressed mood in some people. When these medical conditions are diagnosed and treated the depression usually disappears.

Life events for example, such as the death of a close family member or friend can go beyond what one would consider as "normal" grief on occasion and this can sometimes lead to depression. The well documented Holmes and Rahe rating scale (1967) is a useful tool that enables us to look at some of the more significant and common difficulties such as loss, divorce, change and increased debt that have been shown to have contributory influences with regard to the onset of depression. Noticeably, whilst a singular major event can be enough to cause depression it is also evident that depression can also result from a cumulative effect of negative events which in and of themselves may not appear that distressing. The cumulative effect however, as the name suggests can act like a "dripping tap", with each drip having little impact until eventually the "drips" amount to something more significant and we can become overwhelmed.

Holmes and Rahe's Study of stress and life events

Originally, Holmes and Rahe set out to investigate whether life events cause stress and if so does this then lead to any physical illness? Holmes and Rahe examined the medical records of 5000 patients that had recently suffered illnesses. They then asked the patients whether they had experienced any significant life events preceding the illness. Patients were subsequently asked to rate these events with a score. Interestingly, it was found that many participants in the original study had suffered major life events preceding their illness. These events as such have been further elaborated on and are considered to be some of the most significant contributing factors involved with regard to people suffering with emotional distress.

What are life events?

These are changes that occur suddenly in someone's life. Interestingly, they don't necessarily have to be bad, and so can be viewed as being either desirable or undesirable. Life events have been classified according to how stressful they are. Holmes and Rahe's original scale consisted of over 40 classes of life event and included stressful life events such as the death of a spouse, divorce and marital separation. Other stressful events included redundancy and retirement.

Why are life events so important?

There is good evidence to link life events with the onset of both psychological illness and physical illness. Physical illnesses for example have included abdominal pain, which can lead to the removal of a healthy appendix if the psychosomatic nature is not adequately investigated. Psychological illnesses that can be associated with life events include anxiety, depression and obsessive-compulsive disorder. It is, however, often difficult to decide whether life events are dependent or independent. Dependent life events for example may be secondary to depression, for example someone may lose their job because they are not working as efficiently due to deterioration in their attention and concentration as a result of depression. Other, independent life events, on the other hand, do not occur as a result of symptoms of an illness. Losing your job as a result of cost saving measures would be a simple example of this and there are many others that one can imagine.

Depression and life events

Interestingly, an excess of life events of the above nature have been shown to occur in the three months prior to an episode of depression. Furthermore, it has been suggested that the risk of depression can increase six-fold in the six months after experiencing markedly threatening life events. As outlined earlier various life changes could also cause changes in behaviour. For example, if a couple are separating, one might start drinking heavily, which increases the risk of being ill. Any change in the routine of our lives is potentially difficult and even welcome ones can be stressful, both in terms of the way in which we perceive them and in terms of the increased incidence of physical illness and death that occur during the following 12 months. The Holmes-Rahe Scale assigns values attributed by a sample of 394 individuals to the life events concerned and whilst the research behind the scale is correlational rather than experimental the data nonetheless gives us some insight into some of the major influences that can have a detrimental effect on our mood.

The Holmes-Rahe Social Adjustment Scale

Events	Scale of Impact
Death of spouse	100
Divorce	75
Marital separation	65
Jail term	63
Death of a close family member	63
Personal injury or illness	53
Marriage	50
Dismissal from work	47
Marital reconciliation	45
Retirement	45
Change in health of family member	44
Pregnancy	40
Sex difficulties	39
Gain of new family member	39
Business readjustment	39
Change in financial state	38
Death of close friend	37
Change to different line of work	36
Number of arguments with spouse	36
Major mortgage	31
Foreclosure of mortgage or loan	30
Change in responsibilities at work	29
Son or daughter leaving home	29
Trouble with in-laws	29
Outstanding personal achievement	28
Partner begins or stops work	26
Begin or end school	26
Change in living conditions	25
Revision of personal habits	24

Trouble with boss	23
Change in work hours or conditions	20
Change in residence	20
	20
Change in schools	20
Change in social activities	17
Mortgage or loan	16
Change in sleeping/eating habits	16
Change in family get-togethers	13
Vacation	
Christmas	13
Minor violations of the law	
	12

It is probably futile to attempt to add up a 'score' on this scale. The values are there simply to show the *relative* impact of stressful events and to give some indication of the wide range of stressors in our lives. The list is by no means exhaustive and as society changes so do those things that are likely to impact on our mood. Indeed, a useful exercise would be to think of what changes have occurred since the inception of the original scale that might play a part in our mood swings. I'm sure technology will have something to answer for in amongst your suggestions along with everyday traffic perhaps!

What Happens in the Brain When Someone Is Depressed?

Whilst as therapists and practicing clinicians we may feel that an understanding of the brain in depression is not part of our remit so to speak, it is nonetheless useful to briefly look at the role of neurotransmitters and the biological influences in relation to depression. Inevitably, depression involves the brain's delicate chemistry - specifically, it involves chemicals called **neurotransmitters**. These chemicals assist in transmitting messages between nerve cells in the brain. Certain neurotransmitters regulate mood and when they are not available in sufficient quantities, the result can be depression. The brain's response to stressful events, such as those described above, may alter the balance of neurotransmitters and result in mood swings and/or depression. Sometimes, a person may experience depression without any particular sad or stressful event that they can point to. People who have a genetic predisposition to depression for example may be more prone to the imbalance of neurotransmitter activity that is part of depression. Medications used to treat depression work by helping to restore the proper balance of neurotransmitters.

Types of Depression & Terminology

For some people, depression can be intense and occur in bouts that last for weeks at a time. For others, depression can be less severe but can linger at a low level for years. Doctors who treat depression often distinguish between these two forms, diagnosing the more severe, short-lasting form as **major depression**, and the longer-lasting but less severe form as **dysthymia**. Dysthymia (the Greek roots of the word mean "bad state of mind" or "ill humor") is a disorder with similar but longer-lasting and milder symptoms than clinical depression. By the standard psychiatric definition, this disorder lasts for at least two years, but is less disabling than major depression. For example, patients are usually able to go on working and do not need to be hospitalised. About 3% of the population will suffer from dysthymia at some time - a rate slightly lower than the rate of major depression. Like major depression however, dysthymia occurs twice as often in women as it does in men. It is also more common among the poor and the unmarried. The symptoms usually appear in adolescence or young adulthood but in some cases do not emerge until middle age.

The warning signs of dysthymia are:

- Poor school/work performance
- Social withdrawal
- Shyness
- Irritable hostility
- Conflicts with family and friends
- Physiological abnormalities
- Sleep irregularities
- Parents with major depression

A third form of depression that may be diagnosed is called **adjustment disorder with depressed mood**. This refers to a depressive reaction to a specific life event such as a death, or a divorce when the adjustment to the loss takes longer than the normally expected time frame or is more severe than expected and interferes with the person's daily activities. Much of this has been alluded to previously.

Everyone has some ups and downs, and we must always be aware that occasional sadness is a "normal" emotion and even an essential one so that we may adapt and move on rather than trying to pathologically "block" things out. The normal stresses of life can cause teens to feel sad every once in a while. Things like an argument with a friend, a break-up, doing poorly on a test, not being chosen for a sport, a best friend moving out of town, or the death of a loved one can lead to feelings of sadness, hurt, disappointment and grief. These reactions are usually brief and go away with a little time and care. It is still wise however to acknowledge these "normal" reactions so that they do not have the opportunity to become more sinister. Depression however in its more pure guise is more than feeling blue, sad, or down in the dumps once in a while. Depression is a strong mood involving sadness, discouragement, despair, or hopelessness that lasts for weeks, months, or even longer, and interferes with a person's ability to participate in their normal activities.

We should now be well aware that depression affects a person's thoughts, outlook, and behaviour as well as their mood. In addition to a depressed mood, a person with depression may also experience other symptoms like tiredness, irritability, and appetite changes. When a person experiences depression, the world looks bleak, and the person's thoughts reflect the hopelessness and helplessness they feel. People with depression tend to have negative and self-critical thoughts. Depression can cloud everything, making even small problems seem overwhelming. People who are depressed can't see any future ahead and feel powerless to change things for the better. They may feel like giving up. They may cry at small things or cry for no apparent reason at all. As a consequence of their deep feelings of sadness and their low energy, people with depression sometimes pull away from people around them or from activities they once enjoyed. This however, only causes them to feel more lonely and isolated, making the depression worse and even more pervasive.

3 – The Cognitive Model of Depression

Whether you believe that you can do a thing or you can't

you are probably right

Henry Ford

The experience of depression is amorphous, like a thick dark fog where direction is lost and motivation is muted. In cognitive therapy however, depression is broken down into its symptom categories so that the tangible aspects can be identified. As you will see, preventing certain depressive symptoms from maintaining the depressive state is what cognitive therapy is all about. Below are the general symptom areas of depression.

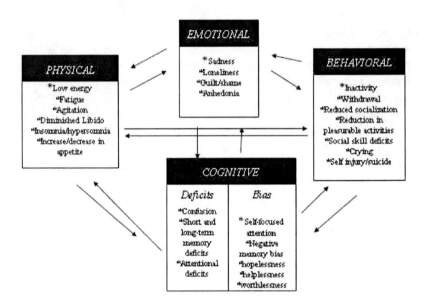

Each of the above components remains inextricably linked with each having the potential to significantly impact on the other. Our mood therefore can impact on the way we think and behave and this can subsequently affect our physical demeanour. Each interacts with the other often in subtle ways that are undetectable, hence a great deal of self-awareness is a useful attribute to acquire so that we can become increasingly aware of what situations and/or events are likely to impact on us in a particular way. Whilst we are mainly focussing on depression and anxiety here, there is of course another (opposite) side to the story whereby certain situations and events will result in us having a very positive and happy experience. These factors will equally interact with each other in a positive and adaptive fashion. This positive interaction cycle has been shown to bode well for one's health and well-being in general and particularly where depression is concerned and perhaps sometimes we need to log into our memory those elements of our lifestyle that are likely to enhance the way we feel.

Depressive symptoms however have the potential to "feed" one another, and this inextricable link can set off a serious chain reaction of doom and pessimism that can prolong and maintain a depressive episode. Consider the following relatively simple example of an applicant who is turned down after a job interview and comes to the following conclusions: *"I'm a loser, I'm unemployable"*, *"what's the point"*? These self-statements will certainly make him/her feel sad and frustrated (emotional), which in turn may lead to a lethargic, listless physical state (physical), to which he/she might elect to spend all day in bed (behavioural), leading to insomnia that night (physical). During the wakeful hours of darkness and silence, he/she has other thoughts like *"I can't do anything with my life"* (cognitive) and to conjure ugly memories of past failures (cognitive). They will undoubtedly have decreased energy the next day (physical) and find it hard to concentrate (cognitive). They may elect to cancel a lunch date with a friend (behavioural) then think thoughts like *"my whole life is falling apart,"* (cognitive). This, in turn, will add anxiety to her experience (emotional) which will add increasing restlessness to her fatigue, (physical), which may lead to the decision to cancel another scheduled job interview the following day (behavioural) and so on and on… The example is relatively simplistic, and I am sure that most of us are familiar with similar situations that eventually subside and we begin to pick up. For those who are prone to depression however the vicious cycle remains and can begin to take on a life of its own.

As we have seen, depression is a mood state with many causes: negative life events such as divorce or cumulative stressors at work are perhaps reactive examples. Depression also involves biological changes, as is the case with postpartum depression and bipolar illness and on occasion these can be considered more endogenous although there always remains a "chicken and egg" element here. The presence of dysfunctional thoughts and beliefs only serve to cause and maintain a depressive state which then begins to magnify any negative or even neutral event or situation. As we can begin to imagine, what remains particularly insidious about depression is that when the symptoms are allowed to cycle automatically and the state can maintain itself for weeks, months and even years.

Consider the downward spiral depicted in the figure below:

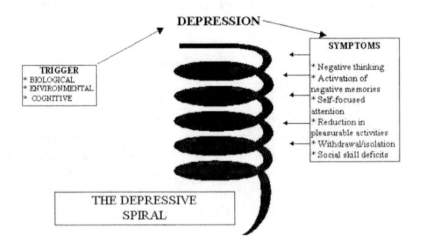

The figure illustrates how symptoms of depression are not simply by-products of the problem itself. Indeed, they actually serve to strengthen and prolong the depressive state. This may seem like a very discouraging model, but it also offers the logical conclusion that if depressive symptoms perpetuate depression, the reduction of these symptoms should weaken the state and this is exactly what research has shown. Though depression is a self-fuelling state, the cognitive and behavioural symptoms that worsen the state are tangible, and when modified will weaken it.

Many people in the throes of clinical depression don't think that their mood varies much and that it is always pretty much at the same miserable level. This is actually not true and even very depressed people experience changes in their mood throughout the day. The periods of reduced depression are far from insignificant; they are periods when the depression is actually weakening or distracted by cognitive and behavioural factors such as having to concentrate on something else or having to do a particular chore. Whilst the depression and mood in these instances changes somewhat these changes remain temporary and as such will not result in any consistent lasting improvement of mood.

Furthermore, most behaviours and attitudes associated with temporary relief tend to be those that counter the aforementioned behavioural and cognitive symptoms of depression (i.e., withdrawal, reduction of pleasurable activities, inactivity, hopelessness, helplessness and worthlessness). Recovery from depression occurs gradually as people challenge these sorts of feelings and begin to modify their negative thinking. For example, instead of withdrawing further individuals may find the strength and insight through therapy to re-engage gradually with some of the previous activities that they used to enjoy, whether it is a swim or walking the dog it can be a start on the way to recovery or better management and this is likely to impact on their thinking in general.

4 – The Assessment – Depression

There are numerous facets involved in becoming a competent and effective therapist. However, of all the key components', being able to conduct an appropriate assessment remains vital if one is to operate effectively as a skilled clinician. Indeed this should be true of any healthcare practitioner. One of the key components therefore revolves around being able to assess a client or patient appropriately. Furthermore, I would go as far as to say that the assessment process is probably the most important component of therapy. For example, if we get the assessment wrong then naturally we will start off on the wrong foot and no matter what clinical skill follows it is likely to be futile as we have begun our clinical journey down the wrong path. To highlight the importance of the assessment I can recall a useful example that occurred some 9 years ago when I was referred a young professional woman in her early 30s. The woman in question had been suffering with depression since the birth of her first child and despite help from her GP, mid-wife and supporting team she had continued to experience a persistent and rather pervasive depression resulting in a significant loss of confidence that for the woman in question was extremely unusual. Gradually over a period of time, she had become increasingly tearful, agitated and emotionally vulnerable. Indeed, during my assessment, and perhaps being a successful professional in her own right the woman actually banged the desk with her fist and said something along the lines of *"why is this happening to me, I am an intelligent woman"*. Suffice to say that I did not mention that even intelligent women (and men for that matter) become depressed on times. The GP and mid-wife had perhaps naturally referred her because she was suffering with post-natal depression. She wasn't depressed before she had the baby and she is depressed now so there we have it, cause and effect all neatly formulated. This case is an excellent learning example as it illustrates to me just how simple it is to get things right with a relatively basic straightforward structured assessment. As I have alluded to already, if we take a comprehensive assessment then we are likely to have the most relevant clinical information to hand. Of course that is only half the battle, but it is an important half. The next half of course is the treatment and we will come on to that later. Back to the professional woman suffering with post-natal depression, after gathering some basic information I proceeded to ask Mrs X about her family and she briefly described a happy marriage to Mr X and she was happy with baby X. She described some classic depressive and anxious symptoms, particularly those of increasing vulnerability that interested me and also a degree of avoidance behaviour. She actually described how she had become so vulnerable on occasion that she had resorted to calling in to see relatives on the way to important meetings. She reluctantly acknowledged her vulnerability and the fact that her confidence had began to drain away. She couldn't understand why she had started to do this other than she felt the "need" and it helped to reassure her in some way. After looking at her immediate family I asked her about her parents and whether there were any siblings. Mrs X informed me that her dad lived close and they had a good relationship. When asked about mum Mrs X paused and then said that mum had died about 15 years ago of cancer when Mrs X was 19 years of age. There was a pause and her bottom lip gave a slight quiver (naturally my immediate thought is that I need to keep this in mind just to test out, it may be something or nothing). Mrs X went on further to say that she had a sister who was 2 years younger than her. Naturally, I went on to ask her what sort of relationship she had with her mother and she said quite categorically that they were inseparable and that they had enjoyed a close and loving relationship. I then asked her how she coped around the time that mum passed away. Her response was interesting and to the trained clinician perhaps a little revealing as she said, *"I sailed through it without too many problems"*. Of course it is easy in hindsight to see a picture building here but this is relatively basic information that no one had picked up on. Now however, the assessment, which was the first meeting, was beginning to reveal the rich and appropriate clinical information. So here was Mrs X who had a close and loving relationship with her mum up until mum died when Mrs X was only 19 years of age. How did she cope with such a devastating loss? She *"sailed through it"*. Something doesn't quite add up, does it? At this juncture it would be interesting for the reader to pause and try to begin to think of all the possible permutations. However, whilst it is important to "test" out possible influences it is essential that we don't immediately infer cause and effect just as those professionals who had assumed that it was post-natal depression had done as a consequence of the depression appearing to follow the birth of her first child. I went on to ask her why she sailed through the loss of her mum and she responded by saying, *"well I had to, I had a younger sister to look after and my father wasn't coping very well."* This is probably the most revealing information. Here was a young woman who had lost what was probably the most important emotional figure in her life yet because she had a younger sister who was suffering and a father whom she adored was not coping, she repressed her own grief to help get her family through this awful period. As many therapists and clinicians would have come to know one of the most interesting questions we can ask ourselves when we have someone in front of us who is suffering is, **why now?** The why now refers to why is it now that the person in question has sought help and why is it now that they are struggling. With regard to Mrs X the answer was relatively simple (generally it always is if you have done your groundwork with the assessment), Mrs X had become depressed following the birth of her child. She had lost her mum over 10 years previous but had kept the family together. The trigger for her depression and loss of confidence was actually the baby. This however was nothing to do with post-natal depression. The question we should ask ourselves in this case is when is a young extremely capable woman most likely to need her mother? The answer of course is when she is giving birth to her first child. Mrs X had repressed her grief and her loss for many years and as a point of information grief can be repressed for decades before it surfaces and then it can appear as if the grief had happened only yesterday with the depth and grieving associated with such a loss. About 25 minutes into the assessment Mrs X started to cry and she then said through her tears, "*I knew it was going to be about this*" (referring to the loss of her mum). We elaborated on this further and Mrs X continued to talk through her grieving tears. She had fought against facing up to this loss for many years but the repression had finally been shattered by the birth of her child. Over the following weeks Mrs X was able to work through her loss and gain a far better understanding of her whole circumstance. Eventually, she went on to continue her successful career and enjoy her family life without the "need" to call on others for reassurance.

There are many examples within just this one case and again it is difficult, if not impossible to do justice to the richness of the clinical assessment and the therapeutic process by just using the written word. However the case hopefully serves to highlight the importance of asking certain relatively basic questions. It was also interesting to note that because Mrs X was so capable that this appeared to cause her more frustration as if she should be able to just "pull herself together" and get on. It was therefore quite easy to understand why she had taken on the predominant caring role when her mum had died. She was after all the "strong one" and as such had put her own emotional feelings "on hold" so that she could care for those she loved around her.

Whilst the above example involving Mrs X and the loss of her mum may appear relatively easy following the assessment (hindsight is a great thing), there is little doubt that the actual assessment process involves a high degree of both skill and knowledge. Whilst the skill is likely to come with experience, the knowledge should be ready to hand and *if there is one thing I would want all readers to gain from this book then it would be how to best assess the individual sitting in front of you*. I have heard countless arguments from the non-directive and more person-centred therapists that they *do not assess* clients. In this day and age I find this extremely difficult to comprehend and actually impossible to carry out in practice as the human condition does not allow for "not assessing". For example, we are constantly making judgements about individuals on a day to day basis and these judgements are usually subjective and based on our own experiences and the limited information we have whether the judgements are based on age, gender, race or colour of hair it is something we all do. Whilst it is important to be dynamic and open during all stages of the therapeutic process the clinical assessment does need to have a certain amount of structure. At the same time, it does not have to be too restrictive or reductionist. There should be room to gather both *quantitative* and *qualitative* information that should provide the therapist with a good idea of what is going on for the person in question and why this is happening to begin with. Additionally, the assessment should provide us with some idea as to the extent to which the person is suffering. Without sounding contradictory, I much prefer the assessment process to be more dynamic than rigid and I believe this can be achieved despite the fact that we have to ask a series of questions at the earlier stages of the therapeutic alliance. Indeed, in my experience of assessing many hundreds of individuals I have seldom had difficulty with the more direct aspect of the assessment getting in the way of the therapeutic process or the assessment in general. I do believe however, that the dynamism I refer to during the assessment and therapeutic process is largely related to the confidence and interpersonal skill that the therapist has. This may be something that the therapist can develop over time, although some will be naturally far more skilled than others when it comes to the dynamic aspect which I believe is greatly related to core personality traits and interpersonal skills. With this dynamism in mind however, the subheadings below are intended to act as a general guide. If however, a therapist feels unable to carry them out as the individual may appear to be too upset or disinterested then it would be more appropriate to make good eye contact, remain congruent and address the more immediate difficulties the individual may be exhibiting. We can then come back to the much-needed information at a later time in the session when the client/patient is feeling more comfortable.

Key information for the Assessment

Basic Information

I have used the term basic information as this generally refers to factors such as name (what do they prefer to be called), I actually spent 4 sessions calling a gentleman George when he eventually told me that he went by his middle name of Peter so don't forget the basics. Similar to the case of Mrs X, I would want to know if the person was married and/or in a relationship whether they have children and if so their names and ages. I would want to know if he or she had any siblings and the type of relationship they have. Naturally I would ask about parents and again the nature of the relationship. This would also be true of the parents of the spouse or partner. What we are trying to do here is build up a general "picture" of the immediate family, the dynamics of the family and where the potential support networks are. The information gained from this type of assessment is paramount and having the family layout in front of you can be extremely revealing. Naturally, to the insightful clinician gathering this information may reveal more about the dynamics and nature of each relationship. Therefore a therapist needs to be "tuned in" not just to what is being said and/or described but also to **how** this is being described. Hence we need to be acutely aware at this stage of the therapeutic process and the demeanour of what is being said along with any non-verbal cues that may be apparent. For example, the young woman who had presented with "post-natal depression" described her relationship with her mum prior to her loss as, *"we were inseparable"* with little or no emotion, conversely, when probed a little more her bottom lip gave way a little. These are non-verbal factors that can be extremely revealing during an assessment.

I feel D. W. Winnicott, an eminent analyst who was world famous for his work with disturbed children, illustrates the importance of the family, which of course plays a significant part in our development, quite aptly in the title of one of his many books. The book was simply entitled, *"Home is where we start from"*. Sometimes the simplest of titles are also the most powerful and this I believe is a case in hand.

Whilst most of the above information is likely to be at hand in a referral letter of some kind I still feel it is important to ask the questions as this "gets the ball rolling" and if executed with skill and sensitivity it can serve to establish an initial clinical rapport. This will also help to make the client/patient feel more at ease with the process. Therefore, even if the information you have implies that he or she has 2 children and her parents are divorced you should still cover this ground with some general questioning. I explain this to each person and have never had any difficulty, indeed, I get the impression that it is actually what the client/patient is expecting.

Social Circumstances

This might appear quite insignificant or even invasive, however in my experience asking such questions seldom, if ever presents as a problem and the more information we are able to gain from the individual then the better position we are in to be able to understand their difficulties. I do believe that some therapists consider themselves to be a little "precious" and on the wrong side of political correctness on occasion. The fact is that the more information we have to hand then the better position we are in to be able to understand the problem. For those who like to "tip toe" around clients and patients my advice would be "get over it" and gather information that is likely to be crucial to the therapeutic process and never overlook the obvious. This is your opportunity to establish a clinical rapport so be both professional and compassionate when asking questions. Social circumstances would generally refer to things such as housing, employment and finance. Believe it or not, it doesn't actually help if someone is experiencing stress within the workplace if they are also £10000 in debt; hence asking an individual if there are financial pressures would seem reasonable and therefore, it is useful information to have to hand. It is one thing having wonderful therapeutic techniques, however if there are more immediate worries and concerns then they need to be acknowledged.

Presenting Problems in practice

The presenting problems can be placed into three categories, (i) general signs and symptoms, (ii) psychological symptoms and (iii) physical or somatic symptoms as they are often referred to. Most of these of course will have been outlined in the DSM-IV-R criteria and below are some of the general terms that we are likely to come across when faced with someone suffering with depression.

(i)   Signs and Symptoms - General Terms

The signs and symptoms generally refer to a loss of interest and dissatisfaction with life. The individual may talk about how they have become more withdrawn and isolated. It is useful of course to ask about how they were prior to feeling depressed and what sorts of things they were involved in. For example, they may have lead busy lives with lots of interests or they may have had a more sedentary but content existence. This will then act as a kind of baseline or template from which we can invisibly measure where they are in the future. Try to get them to be as explicit as possible. Some people are often amazed at how much of life they have gradually avoided over a period of years to a point that their lifestyle is almost unrecognisable to what it used to be. I can recall one gentleman who was referred suffering with a low level yet pervasive depression. The gentleman in question was in his mid 50s and was a person who perhaps didn't fit the "stereotype" of someone who would suffer in this way. When taking a history and asking some relatively basic questions about his life he informed me that he was a passionate sailor and had always had a boat, he went on further to say that he had been a keen rugby player all his life and had enjoyed coaching the youngsters when he could no longer play. He was happily married with a couple of kids who had been to university and he was financially solvent. Without going into further detail about the depression itself the gentleman was amazed when he talked about his sailing and his rugby as both these integral factors had slowly disappeared from his life. This had probably been a gradual withdrawal as the depression had subtly and slowly began to take control of his life. He came out with classical excuses such as he didn't have the time and he was too tired. However, when probing a little deeper he realised that these were just excuses and he actually started laughing at himself. This "real" life example briefly serves to illustrate just how easy it is to gradually withdraw and become depressed. To begin with, the changes would have been unnoticeable but as they progressed his whole life started to take on a different meaning. Again, this process can take so much time to evolve that we hardly notice the changes which are so subtle, indeed we actually justify them or rationalise out with sayings such as *"I'm a little old for that now"*, or *"I don't feel like doing that anymore"* or, *"I think I'd prefer to stay in"*.

> **"Action may not always bring happiness, but there is no happiness without action"**
>
> *Benjamin Disraeli*

Many individuals will often state that they do not have the energy any more to get involved with "things". They may talk further of their disinterest in most if not all things including hobbies, interests and also their friends. Eating becomes more of a chore than a pleasure and often where depression has taken a hold and eating becomes a significant problem, I will encourage people to just see food as a means of refuelling to begin with just to ensure that they are getting enough to eat so that they can at least have some energy to go about their business. Again, basic nutritional factors should never be overlooked and asking someone how they are eating, sleeping and feeling in general should be the *"bread and butter"* of assessment.

(ii)   Psychological symptoms: feelings, thoughts and behaviours

When we refer to psychological symptoms we tend to look at things such as negative thinking with the individual likely to be feeling sad or hopeless for most of the day. There may well be a tendency for the person not to be able to think of anything that is positive or enjoyable in their life. We must remember at this stage that this thinking is more than likely to be the depression talking rather than the individual; however it is important that we don't challenge this at this acute stage. Many well meant therapists might be tempted to say something on the lines of, *"that's only how your feeling at the moment, things may seem a little different before long"*, I appreciate this is not the best example but hopefully it illustrates a point. It's a bit like trying to console someone who's just had very bad news, it doesn't work and it isn't going to work so just "be there" and resist any temptation to directly address the thoughts and feelings at this stage. The individual may be experiencing feelings of excessive guilt, particularly if they have a young family. Additionally, there may well be recurrent thoughts of ending one's own life, with or without a specific plan.

Understandably the skill of the therapist is paramount at this stage and it will be of great benefit for the therapist to have the requisite knowledge that is crucial if one is to develop excellent clinical and listening skills at this stage of the assessment. The listening skills themselves will be discussed later but they remain an essential component right through from assessment to treatment. This may also be the most vulnerable stage of the process for the individual as it may be the first time that they have actually voiced aloud how they are actually feeling. This may result in them becoming tearful upset and possibly angry. If the therapist can allow for this and handle this period with great care, respect and dignity then it may have a tremendous therapeutic effect in itself and it will no doubt have a significant impact on how the therapeutic process progresses. Indeed, just voicing their distress in a safe environment can lead to some therapeutic gain of a cathartic nature and perhaps some optimism. Interestingly it is often said that the modern day therapist is akin to the priest of latter days (and probably today) whereby individuals talk about their private thoughts and feelings in a manner akin to the confession. On a positive level this can lead to a type of catharsis as mentioned above and may help, at least in some part to release the individual from the depressive burden they are carrying.

(iii)   Physical or "Somatic symptoms

As mentioned previously, many individuals suffering with depression will initially present to their GP's with physical problems. These physical problems are likely to include weight gain and/or loss as a result of difficulties with appetite, e.g., *"I just don't feel hungry"* or conversely the classic *"comfort eating"* scenario. Headaches are also common and may be related to problems associated with attention, concentration and general overall anxiety. Fatigue and loss of energy are also classic physical symptoms as is a loss of libido and sexual drive.

Brief Family History

As with the example of Mrs X, the family history is often where we find the most revealing information. Equally, it may well be from within the family network that we discover certain strengths that may act as a support at this difficult time. Alternatively, the opposite may also be true and the family may hold the causal or contributing key to the depression. Therefore, when asking about the immediate family it is important to ask about the relationships and dynamics within the family from the clients' perspective. This would include the individuals' relationships with their partner, siblings, parents and in-laws. It would be appropriate to elaborate on each a little and ask questions relating to how close they are, who can they turn to and whom do they find is supportive. Does the family actually know that you are suffering? Often, of course there will be separations and divorces involved and there will be second families where children will have a step-mother or father. Despite these variables the assessment remains the same although a little more comprehensive, as we may have to take a number of x partners and stepchildren into account. Despite these additional permutations the assessment of the family does not have to be a complex and long drawn out process. Indeed, as the therapist becomes more experienced then he or she will learn to perceptively focus on the presentation of the information so that less time may be spent asking about people who may have little or no bearing on the situation in hand. The therapist is therefore then able to concentrate and focus in on the relevant "players" from within the family context.

All of the above information can be achieved within 30-45 minutes and often far less

---

Simple Family Assessment

Clients' parents		Partners parents
	(How long together)	
Clients' Siblings	Client – Partner	Partners Siblings
	Child 1 (age) – Child 2 (age) – Child 3 (age)	

Personal History

As the title implies a personal history is related solely to the client presenting for assessment/treatment. We would want to know about any childhood anxieties and schooling in general, academic and social progress, bullying etc. Any significant school changes, relationships within and outside the family, relationships with parents and other siblings. Most of the above is general and again the information can be achieved in an economical fashion. After all, the client/patient is unlikely to go over material that is relatively insignificant, although one should be aware of any avoidant material when discussing the presenting problem.

Formal Assessment of Depression

The assessment interview and the relevant questions are there to help us gather rich and relevant information that will hopefully help us to understand how and why the individual in question is experiencing difficulties. To compliment this qualitative assessment process it is also useful to use a more formal instrument to measure the level of distress currently being experienced. There are a number of extremely useful assessment tools that help to quantify the assessment process. By the word quantify we mean they can help to give us an indication of the type of problem the person is suffering with and the extent and severity of that problem. As an example I have outlined the Hospital Anxiety & Depression Scale (HADS) below, which I feel, is an excellent assessment tool. The HADS should also serve as a good learning instrument when helping us to understand how to quantify the assessment process. I believe this is an area that is still greatly missed on many clinical and counselling training courses, although I am reassured that there are now steps to re-dress what I see as a gross omission.

The Hospital Anxiety and Depression Scales were originally developed to detect anxiety and depression in a non-psychiatric hospital setting. The scale originated from the work of Zigmond and Snaith (1983). Having used the HADS on many occasions I consider it to be an excellent instrument for assessment purposes and for monitoring progress or otherwise. The HADS actually separates out Depression and Anxiety and questions relating more to anxiety are indicated by an 'A' while those relating to depression are subsequently shown by a 'D'. Scores of 0-7 in respective subscales are considered "normal", with 8-10 borderline and 11 or over indicating clinical. These ratings can help the therapist to assess to what degree a person is suffering, with the categories in general ranging from *Normal-Mild-Moderate and Severe.* I also feel that using the HADS or a similar assessment tool gives the impression that the clinician actually knows what they are doing. I believe by formalising the assessment process we are helping to formalise the therapeutic process itself and this can only impart a degree of knowledge to the client/patient and further add to the clinician's credibility, which in turn should help make the client/patient feel more secure in the therapeutic process.

Hospital Anxiety and Depression Scale (HADS)

(Zigmond and Snaith, 1983)

I feel tense or 'wound up':	A	I feel as if I am slowed down:	D
Most of the time	3	Nearly all of the time	3
A lot of the time	2	Very often	2
Time to time, occasionally	1	Sometimes	1
Not at all	0	Not at all	0
I still enjoy the things I used	D	I get a sort of frightened feeling like 'butterflies in the	A

to enjoy:		stomach':	
Definitely as much	0	Not at all	0
Not quite so much	1	Occasionally	1
Only a little	2	Quite often	2
Not at all	3	Very often	3

I get a sort of frightened feeling like something awful is about to happen:	A	I have lost interest in my appearance:	D
Very definitely and quite badly	3	Definitely	3
Yes, but not too badly	2	I don't take as much care as I should	2
A little, but it doesn't worry me	1	I may not take quite as much care	1
Not at all	0	I take just as much care as ever	0

I can laugh and see the funny side of things:	D	I feel restless as if I have to be on the move:	A
As much as I always could	0	Very much indeed	3
Not quite so much now	1	Quite a lot	2
Definitely not so much now	2	Not very much	1
Not al all	3	Not at all	0

Worrying thoughts go through my mind:	A	I look forward with enjoyment to things:	D

A great deal of the time	3	A much as I ever did	0
A lot of the time	2	Rather less than I used to	1
From time to time but not too often	1	Definitely less than I used to	3
Only occasionally	0	Hardly at all	2
I feel cheerful:	D	I get sudden feelings of panic:	A
Not at all	3	Very often indeed	3
Not often	2	Quite often	2
Sometimes	1	Not very often	1
Most of the time	0	Not at all	0
I can sit at ease and feel relaxed:	A	I can enjoy a good book or radio or TV programme:	D
Definitely	0	Often	0
Usually	1	Sometimes	1
Not often	2	Not often	2
Not at all	3	Very seldom	3

The HADS only takes a minute or two to complete and if need be the form itself can be filled in prior to the assessment interview. Clients are asked to read each item first and then place a firm tick in the box opposite the reply that comes closest to how they have been feeling in the past week. Clients are encouraged not to take too long over their replies as it is commonly accepted that an individuals' immediate reaction to each item will probably be more accurate than a long thought out response. As previously mentioned, the HADS is an excellent tool for separating out Depression from Anxiety and whilst we have yet to look at the symptoms associated with anxiety, the HADS never ceases to amaze me by just how accurately it can make this distinction. In essence the main clinical and symptomatic differences between depression and anxiety concern problems associated with *autonomic arousal*. For example, whereby autonomic arousal remains an integral part of anxiety it is generally more or less absent when someone is suffering with depression. As a crude but general guide - the physiological "system" of the body speeds up during anxiety and slows down during depression. Autonomic responses characterised by increased autonomic arousal include sweaty hands, dry mouth, cold feet, tense muscles and accelerated heart rate and the full extent of these factors will be addressed later when we take a closer look at anxiety in all its guises.

5 – Treating Depression

It is always difficult to do justice to the treatment process when writing about depression and particularly to the creativity and dynamism that is an integral part of the therapeutic process itself. However, I am sure it has been said somewhere that good therapy is a combination of both "science" and "art", if this hasn't been said before then I am claiming it as I feel they are both components that compliment the therapeutic process. This may sound a little strange to some as I have repeatedly described the empirical (scientific) basis of the cognitive approach and hence this "art" aspect may appear a little contradictory. However, what I am referring to with the word "art" is something akin to the fact that if the "science" is the "paint" then it is how we apply this that matters and to this extent I feel this is the "art". Again the richness of the therapeutic process is likely to be lost in the following descriptions, however it is up to the reader to conceptualise what is being said in relation to what has been described. It is then up to the reader to then use his or her intuitive skill along with the science to assimilate this information and eventually start to begin putting it into practice.

Explaining Cognitive Therapy to the Patient/Client – A Brief Outline

As should be apparent by now, the approach involves a significant psych-educational component and despite common misunderstandings, often by more person-centred therapists, the therapeutic relationship is a significant component with appropriate levels of empathy and understanding being an integral part of the therapeutic process. Empathy for example, is often illustrated when the therapist is able to understand how the client/patient feels and is able to subtly communicate this back to the client/patient. This can also act as a means of "checking out" that the therapist is actually on the right lines with what the client or patient has been talking about.

A crucial part of any type of therapy is naturally the first meeting between therapist and client/patient. The first *"bite of the cherry"* if you like. This is generally an anxious moment for the person sitting opposite the therapist and a great deal of interpersonal skill is often required. The first session of therapy will tend to focus on those variables that will enable the therapist and the individual to develop a shared understanding of the problem in question. These variables *per se* are those briefly discussed above and relate to the assessment process in particular. Throughout the therapeutic process clients are generally expected to be active participants. Therefore, throughout the clinical alliance clients and therapists often work together to identify and understand problems in terms of the relationship between thoughts, feelings and behaviour (these are usually in relation the clients' history and/or a significant causal event). If this process is managed successfully then it can lead to a better understanding of some of the antecedent factors (historical factors) that have contributed to the difficulties being experienced. If these essential antecedents are mutually agreed by therapist and client/patient then this will lead to the next stage, which is the identification of the respective clinical goals and strategies required to bring about clinical gain. In simple terms, for one client a specific goal initially may mean that they begin to stop avoiding some of the situations that have resulted in them withdrawing and isolating themselves from their family, friends and society in general. Naturally, this will be agreed with an understanding of some of the possible anxieties that may occur and strategies for coping with irrational negative thoughts and physiological changes would have been discussed well in advance so that the client feels that he or she is armed with certain "skills" to help them cope. A comprehensive understanding of anxiety and the associated physiology is discussed later in the book and it will form an integral part of most therapeutic procedures. Following this, the core elements relating to *thoughts, emotions and behaviour* will be continually monitored and re-evaluated as therapy progresses and each session will provide an opportunity to "test" out these goals and strategies. Indeed, goal setting in this instance is not just a practical exercise but it is a creative clinical aspect that looks at how the individual is functioning in day-to-day life. For example, if a person is avoiding situations and is aware of this then I want some real life examples of avoidance in the assessment phase and we may then agree to try to re-examine this in-between sessions. This is likely to be just one aspect of the therapeutic process but again it is integral and gets the individual thinking and behaving in a different manner

Each session may last between 40-50 minutes and typically a session of therapy occurs once a week or a fortnight when plans are established, although this remains flexible and is largely dependent on the type of problem being presented. It is not inappropriate for treatment to occur every 2 weeks and eventually longer as any clinical change that is going to occur will happen outside the treatment room and not inside it.

"If clinical change is going to occur as a result of the treatment, process, then it will largely occur outside the treatment room and not inside it".

That is not to say that there will be key moments within the therapeutic context, however the "real" change is going to happen well away from the room and where it really matters in the "real" world. Most courses of cognitive therapy last for several weeks and it is common to have anything between 6 and 20 sessions, depending on the nature and severity of the condition. As a general rule, the more specific the problem, the more likely cognitive therapy may help and most courses of treatment are generally below 10 sessions.

What are the goals of Cognitive Behavioural Therapy?

In essence the goals of therapy are generally to facilitate change in the way a person is thinking, feeling and behaving. For example, following an initial assessment we may want to involve the individual in a process of cognitive restructuring which will mainly focus on the thought aspect and in particular the clients' values, perceptions and beliefs. A change here can result in adaptive and constructive behavioural and emotional change. During therapy, coping skills and abilities are also re-assessed and re-evaluated to the extent that they are geared in a more adaptive fashion where need be. To begin to achieve this however we need to allow the individual to gain increasing insight into their difficulty and this is likely to be the first step followed by a continuous process of psycho-education. The following is a typical case example of someone suffering with depression. We shall use this example to draw out some of the relevant points that have been highlighted to date. As mentioned, it can be difficult to do justice by just using the written word, however by utilising "real" case examples and materials it should hopefully at least provide a degree of validity to the clinical process.

Case example – Depression:

The referral:

Therapists work in many different environments including the private, voluntary and public sector. For our purposes however we shall use a relatively typical public sector (NHS) GP type referral to illustrate the rubrics of the referral process and the subsequent assessment to treatment path. Outlined below is a "typical" referral letter, albeit slightly modified for reasons of confidentiality. We shall take up the case from here followed by some illustrations of cognitive therapy "in action" so to speak. Again, whilst reading through the following example one must understand the inherent difficulties when explaining a case such as this which cannot do complete justice to the actual "richness" of the therapeutic process. Therefore, I would urge the reader to try to resist the temptation to fill in gaps or wonder how certain ideas were arrived at. The emphasis therefore is to use the following example as a general teaching aid, as a full and comprehensive discussion of the case from start to finish would be enough to fill a book in itself.

Typical referral letter:

Dear Ms/Mr Therapist/Counsellor,

RE: Ivor Problem – DOB: 06/04/1961
7 Depressive Avenue
Milton Avoidance

Thank you for seeing Mr Problem who presented in my surgery today in floods of tears. I have known this gentleman for many years and I have never seen him present in such a state. Indeed, I have always had the impression that he was a rather stable conscientious and well-balanced chap. He has been an accountant for some 15 years or so and appears to be happily married with 2 children. To my knowledge there are no financial problems although he admitted to some stresses at work and some problems with his sleep. I am reluctant to prescribe any anti-depressants at present and would appreciate your assessment in the hope that you may be able to help him with his difficulties. Best wishes.

Yours sincerely

Dr John Caring-Insightful

This is a very typical referral letter and sometimes GP's or other referrers will go into great detail and other times there will be little relevant information, as they will be leaving it up to the therapist to assess more comprehensively. I am always happy with the briefest referral information (unless there is something very obvious that I need to know) as we can begin the important aspect of gathering relevant information at the first session.

Initial Assessment

As previously mentioned, prior to starting a course of cognitive therapy a person is likely to be asked to complete a formal assessment such as the Hospital Anxiety and Depression Scales outlined earlier. The scales usually reflect the level of depression and/or anxiety and will also reflect the individuals' general health in relation to their emotional distress. Having some advance awareness of the responses to these questions gives the therapist some insight into how the person is feeling and the types of symptoms they are likely to be experiencing. This gives the therapist a *"head start"* if you like and provides some rich information prior to the actual clinical discussion. That is why it may be useful on occasion to send out such a form for return prior to seeing a client/patient. This also starts the clinical process far earlier. The ratings on the scales themselves will also help to quantify (measure) what is happening and are of course useful to evaluate the therapeutic process as it progresses, particularly later at the end of therapy.

Mr Problem presented reasonably well during his first appointment, he was smartly dressed and he communicated quite eloquently during the first 15-20 minutes with little, if any show of emotion, he was a little nervous but this would have been expected under the circumstances. Initially, I explained that his GP had referred him as he was a little concerned about his mood and I then went on to briefly explain the HAD and the reasons for using it (keeping this fairly general), he subsequently filled each section in and this took about 2 minutes. I then put this to one side and explained that I would now ask some brief questions to get some idea of his family and social situation. These questions serve a number of functions and perhaps one of the most important is that they give the client/patient the opportunity to build an impression of the therapist as he or she goes about their task. This I feel helps to "smooth" the way for the clinical alliance to begin and for initial trust to develop.

From the initial assessment Mr Problem revealed that he was happily married and that he had a supportive wife. They had 2 children, a boy aged 12 and a girl aged 13 and there appeared to be no difficulties here. Mr Problem went on to describe his childhood, which appeared rather idyllic, being brought up by his father who was a successful accountant and his mother who looked after the house with Mr Problem and his younger brother. He described his father as a little strict but reasonably fair and his mother as loving and very supportive. He confessed to being closer to his mother but this did not appear to pose any particular problem. He was fond of his brother who was a graphic designer but he did confess to being a little jealous of him. There appeared to be some strains when he was talking about his father and I paused and said something that I often do when I feel it is appropriate and that was that, *"Sometimes I believe most people I see are actually aware of the root cause of their problems or difficulties"*. He paused and smiled in a defeatist sort of way and went on to describe how he had always felt pressure to follow in his fathers' footsteps and become a successful accountant. He confessed to feeling restricted when growing up and that whilst he presented very well, underneath he had little confidence and felt a complete "fraud". When asked why this was, he said, *"I always wanted to go into the arts but I was afraid what my father would say"*. He then started sobbing and started apologising. He talked further about how he felt his life had been a farce and that he had regretted taking the "expected" route rather than the desired one. He felt resentment towards his father and jealousy towards his younger brother who was actually doing something he envied. He also felt quite guilty about this aspect, as he loved his brother very much. When asked if his wife was aware of this he said, *"I think so"*. His wife was perceptive and as is the case in most relationships the other partner is more often or not aware of things even if they are not voiced. He had generally avoided talking about this situation for fear of embarrassment and he generally avoided anything to do with it because it made him more depressed. When asked about his work, he suggested that there were lots of areas that he liked with regard to his work, however he was now beginning to feel more and more resentful and less happy within the workplace and this was causing him to become increasingly low until eventually he plucked up enough courage to go and see his GP.

Without going into further detail at present, Mr Problem had described the very early impressionable stages of his life where he had begun to form certain *"schemas"* about himself and the world around him. Going back to our previous chapter on how these "schemas" are formed we can begin to build a picture of how he has found himself in this position. Earlier we described how cognitive therapy operates largely in the *"here and now"* and looks at current problems. However, initially the primary focus of cognitive therapy is concerned with gaining a thorough understanding of the individuals history and those pertinent factors (in this case Mr Problems view of his father) that may have helped shape a clients' personality and their general view of the world and the "self" or ones *"schemas"* to use the appropriate psychological term.

Remember *schemas* are largely formed by our initial experiences and are reinforced by our way of thinking and behaving from these experiences. In the above situation Mr Problem had felt emotionally and morally obligated to follow the route of the accountant. Indeed, our following discussions revealed that his parents thought that this is what he had wanted for himself. By broaching this issue with him he agreed that it would be useful to discuss his concerns with his family in a constructive and warm manner. Having found the courage to discuss some of these issues with his parents and partner he was more able to see that it was actually his lack of assertion that had lead him on to the path of accountancy as he had been afraid to voice his initial concern about accountancy as a career. He did admit that it wasn't all negative to begin with and there were parts of becoming an accountant that had been attractive, however, he maintained that it was still largely against the grain for him.

From the above outline there are numerous cognitive and behavioural factors that have emerged that have been alluded to in previous chapters. For example:

1 – Fear of father resulted in *"must become accountant"* – This was largely a cognitive error based on his view of his father who was strict but actually quite fair when we discussed things in more depth. As discussed in the cognitive bias section these errors in thinking can significantly affect the way we behave. The result of this is that we tend to develop a set of *"false assumptions"* about the way we think about ourselves and others and subsequently what we expect from them. Mr Problem had developed a set of *"false assumptions"* and these were elaborated on during the following sessions. Mr Problem had lived by these "fixed" and invisible set of "rules", which if broken would result in guilt, shame and embarrassment. Indeed, just by initially going to discuss his problems he felt a degree of failure and shame.

2 – A number of irrational "beliefs" eventually surfaced similar to those discussed in the previous chapters. In the following sessions these beliefs were discussed in more depth and these discussions resulted in a great deal of cognitive restructuring and as a result of this there was a psychological "shift" that produced behavioural and emotional changes in his life. This resulted in Mr Problem actually taking more responsibility for his situation which resulted in him feeling less resentful toward his brother. This improved what was a very good relationship and for the first time he actually found himself asking his brother about his job and what it entailed. He had previously avoided all types of discussions around this as it aroused his angst and created a great deal of conflict. The conflict and guilt were all that more significant because (as should now be apparent) Mr Problem was actually a very kind and sensitive (albeit too passive as is usually the case with this "profile") individual. Further work therefore looked at his passivity and again this resulted in significant clinical gain.

We must remember that therapy's attention to the *schemata* of each individual is fundamental to our *understanding* how and why that individual has come to experience the negative emotion that is currently impacting on him or her. We can outline the subheadings below and it should be relatively easy for the clinician to get an impression of what was happening for Mr Problem from an early age and how this in turn helped "shape" his life and chosen career path.

The development of early schemas and mental representations

- Early experiences
- Development of core beliefs about self, others and general view of world
- Formation of core schemata
- Negative Automatic Thoughts

Following sessions looked further closer at Mr Problem's lack of assertiveness and how this played a significant role in the fact that he felt unable to do the things he actually wanted to. Throughout each subsequent session Mr Problem gained increasing insight into his difficulties and he began to be more open about his feelings and concerns. He would discuss these issues with his partner who was very supportive and he became increasingly "unburdened" by this openness. During our initial discussions it had become increasingly apparent that he had actually gradually withdrawn from some of the things that he enjoyed such as painting, music, and the garden. He had felt that these creative aspects to his life had started to diminish shortly after the birth of their first child. Not that there were any difficulties with his relationships with the children but it appeared that he had made an unconscious decision to withdraw from his "fun" outlets and take a more "responsible" approach to life. Together we went on to describe this as one of his father's traits, one that produced a lot of conflict for Mr Problem. Was he to carry on with his pastimes and interests whilst his children were very young (something he wrongly imagined his father and others would disapprove of - cognitive error) or should he now act with consummate responsibility for the sake of his wife and young family? All his family wanted of course was for him to be happy.

From this example, it should be relatively easy to see how we can develop and actually nurture our very own neuroses. The early years and parental relationships are often the richest source for this type of information and in particular the formation of those crucial early "schemas" on life. The rest of the therapeutic process that took 9 sessions in all involved some of the following components:

Cognitive:

Helping Mr Problem to think and respond differently to certain situations. This process of cognitive restructuring allowed Mr Problem to look at both himself and the outside world differently. The result of this was a continuous process of restructuring and reconditioning if you like whereby Mr Problems' perception on life was being considerably modified away from an emotionally driven irrational way of thinking to a more balanced and assertive rational view. In retrospect it is also interesting to see how his GP (and probably many others) thought of him as being extremely balanced and a rather solid citizen. In essence, if you don't let people know how you are feeling (passive) then no one is likely to know how you are really "feeling". I appreciate that for many, letting people know how you really feel is not as simple as it sounds and to all intents Mr Problem was actually a pretty solid citizen with an underlying issue that was causing him considerable distress.

- Challenging irrational beliefs
- Self monitoring
- Assertiveness skills training
- Psycho-education – making the links

Behavioural:

The behavioural aspect of therapy is the part where we actually *put everything into practice in everyday, real-life situations.* This of course means, less avoidance and re-engaging in things we used to do. Where guilt is concerned I often ask clients to use the guilt feelings as a barometer that *"I am doing the right thing – I'm just not used to doing it"* and that is why people feel awkward or anxious. This area is usually handled last because we need a strong foundation of cognitive and emotional skills/strategies so that we can begin living and acting differently before we confront real-life challenges. One of the most significant clinical events for Mr Problem was actually sitting down with his parents and having a general discussion about their relationships and his up-bringing (which again wasn't that bad to say the least). From these discussions he realised how loved he was by both parents and how proud they were of him. This made him feel far more secure and happier in every area of his life (parents have a huge impact on our emotional well-being, no matter what age we are). *Pause for thought* – I just remembered that a couple of years ago I spent £60 for Mothers Day by ordering flowers, chocolates and wine as a sort of on-line "package" for the day itself. I will never forget my mothers' call, she was pleased of course – however the main thing I remember for from the call is just before the end she said, *"I thought I would have had a card – you know how much I like a card"*. Bless her! You can't win them all eh! No need to guess what she had the following year and indeed it had the desired affect and saved me about £45. In essence all we want and more often than not need is a sense of ***approval*** from our parents. This remains such an important aspect of our emotional health and those who are unable to receive this will obviously present a different challenge to the therapist. Again, try to remember, if they are not being critical then let's not imagine that they are. Mr Problem had spent most of his life wrongly assuming things (this is not uncommon).

Emotional:

It is important to have some type of relaxation or "de-stress" strategy that is accessible. This may be personal to each individual as different types of things relax different types of people. Interestingly, some of the very things that make some people anxious and/or stressed others find completely relaxing. For example, I have come across numerous situations over the years where the "ironing" for example is a mild-moderate source of stress yet for many I have witnessed; doing the ironing has been found to be therapeutic and relaxing. Therefore, keep an open mind. As for Mr Problem he just went back to being a little creative with his spare time that resulted in him becoming far more relaxed in general. He managed to work through his initial "guilt" at being able to "indulge" in his interests but he soon realised that everyone actually approved of this and subsequently he became far happier.

The more your mind is at peace and relaxed, the easier therapeutic information can be received, retained and processed. The result of this is that we are less likely to then let our anxiety and irrational thinking affect us. Not convinced? Then why do we think in the way that we do when we are on holidays faced with the sea and the sunshine? Being relaxed and rational is simply another way to let the therapeutic process reach your brain and assimilate. For Mr Problem, emotional change came largely as a result of the above cognitive and behavioural changes that he made and hence the positive knock-on effect of those inextricably linked factors that we now know as thoughts emotions and behaviours.

From the above scenario Mr Problem went from an initial HAD rating of 12 for depression (moderate) and 6 for anxiety (within norm) to 4 for depression (norm) and 3 for anxiety (norm). The qualitative aspects were there for all to witness and they revolved around his relationships with his family, friends and work colleagues and his general outlook on life including his behavioural changes. His sleeping improved as did his general quality of life and he had a renewed energy and was able to make the appropriate "connections" relating to his personality and his behaviour. His assertiveness or lack of it was something that would be a continuous factor that he needed to monitor but he nonetheless now had the insight, strategies and techniques to continue this improvement.

Mr Problems' case is one of 100s of clinical cases that could have been chosen, others would have been equally valid examples and hopefully we can now build an impression of how each would have been assessed, managed and treated. Naturally, not all families will be supportive and there may be complexities that differ greatly from the above example. However, some of these will be discussed in more detail in the following chapter when we look at more typical cases of depression.

Treatment Recap

Cognitive therapy does not necessarily aim to solve every problem in a persons' life. Instead, cognitive therapy aims to teach individuals the skills and techniques that come from having an increased level of self-awareness and insight. Armed with these skills clients are far more able to resolve and manage their own problems now, and in to the future. Cognitive therapy largely focuses on the "here and now", although this focus is only achieved after a thorough discussion and understanding of the clients' history and in particular key events and situations that have helped to "shape" the individuals view of themselves and those around them including their immediate family, friends and society at large. Therefore an emphasis on the way a person thinks about everyday life and the attitudes and beliefs they have developed remain essential during the therapeutic process.

Cognitive therapy works by helping individuals identify where their thoughts and actions are unhelpful and self-defeating. Once aware of these issues, a therapist will help the individual to replace these negative thoughts and "bad habits" with more balanced thoughts and more constructive behaviours. There are various strategies for achieving this, including asking for feedback from other people and weighing up the pros and cons of different options. Cognitive therapy remains a collaborative process therefore based on understanding, empathy, support and most importantly, a strong belief that a person can change, for the better as far as their health and well-being are concerned.

People who have completed a course of cognitive therapy often say they feel significantly happier and more able to cope with the problems in their lives. They often report improved relationships and increased productivity. In addition, they frequently state that they have a clearer vision for their lives, as well as a greater sense of confidence that whatever difficulties might arise in the future, they will be able to cope far more constructively than they would have prior to their experience of cognitive therapy.

Part 3: Problems associated with depression

As we have seen from the preceding chapters there are countless variables involved in the onset of depression. Some of these variables may come from the client in question having a difficult childhood or upbringing in general, other variables are likely to include reactions to some distressing situation or event and we have generally referred to this as a reactive type of depression as opposed to a more endogenous type whereby the personality may play more of a prevailing role. This chapter will take a closer look at some of the more "typical" and unfortunately more common problems that one will come across as a practicing therapist. These problems include difficulties associated with loss and in particular bereavement and separation, other areas reviewed will be sexual abuse, confidence and self-esteem. Finally we shall take a brief look at some personality factors associated with depression. Whilst there is often a degree of overlap between these difficulties for example with someone who has been abused likely to be suffering with a degree of low self-esteem, each area will have its unique and distinct profile and it is useful for the reader to become aware of the subtleties involved with each problem. Each problem will largely be described within a cognitive framework and a brief case study from a "real" clinical situation will hopefully help to draw out some of the intimate differences and unique thought and behavioural processes involved in each. Whilst we will look at each of the above areas in detail, the reader should now have a familiarity with regard to both the assessment and the basic cognitive approach to treating or working with each problem. Therefore, we will only briefly touch on these areas as they have been comprehensively covered to date and this should have already provided the reader with more than an idea of how to conduct a thorough assessment and indeed what to look for during an initial interview.

1 – Loss: Bereavement & Separation

2 – Sexual Abuse

3 – Confidence & Self-Esteem

4 – Personality factors in Depression

1 – Loss: Bereavement & Separation

Loss and separation will be divided into two distinct areas; first there is the loss that we associate with death, dying and bereavement. This inevitably involves grief and the grieving process. Secondly, there is the painful loss associated with divorce and separation and the ending of a close relationship. Both are painful processes with unique and distinct factors involved. We will look at each in turn and try to understand the *"mechanics"* of both. An understanding of the processes involved is invaluable for the therapist and sharing this knowledge can be of great clinical benefit to the individual suffering at the time.

Loss & Bereavement

"A thing which has not been understood inevitably reappears; like an unlaid ghost, it cannot rest until the mystery has been solved and the spell broken..."

Sigmund Freud, 1909.

In life there are few things that are inevitable, unfortunately one of those factors that will always remain constant is that sometime in the future we are going to experience the loss of someone we have loved, cherished and depended on. Whether they are family or friends, a loss through death, whilst being a "normal" experience is extremely painful and possibly one of the most emotionally draining experiences we will ever have to endure. Despite the pain, more often than not, bereavement in itself should not require psychological treatment unless it is prolonged, exceptionally intense or complicated. Often, losing someone close to us is going to be an emotionally difficult and stressful experience and to a large extent we may never be the same individuals again. Indeed, depending on the type of loss we may have to re-learn to look at the world in a different light and learn to re-evaluate our own lives and ourselves. Whilst loss is a generic term we remain acutely aware that in general parents losing a young child are likely to suffer a great deal more than the son or daughter of a man in his 90s. Whilst understandably these differences are bound to exist I would want to reinforce that *a general guide to how one suffers and copes with loss will be largely related to the nature and quality of the relationship itself and in particular the emotional dependence associated with the relationship.*

In clinical terms it is useful for the clinician to look at loss and bereavement from a psycho-educative perspective. The prevailing intention here is that we can help the individual by helping them to try to make some kind of sense out of what has happened. Making sense, first of all out of their loss and secondly out of what is now happening to them can provide some guidance and solace at this dark time. There are generally clear physical reasons why someone has died whether it is from natural causes or the fact that there has been an accident. It is important to keep these physical reasons in mind at all times, as it is the actual reason why the person has died. This requires skill and care and we may have to wait a while until we have established a warm and trusting clinical relationship before we can go over the physical reasons for the loss. Naturally, this tends to be an easier process if it is an older person who has died from natural causes in comparison to a child killed in an accident. However, whilst taking that as a general "barometer" to gauge the grief reaction we should never assume that one person will suffer more than another purely based on these factors alone. The key is therefore to wait to see what you are presented with and similar questions associated with the assessment process discussed earlier will be extremely relevant particularly in relation to the nature of the relationship with the person who has died. Again it is important to retain an emphasis at least in the therapists' mind of the physical reasons for the death. The client may want to wander off on many different tangents early on as the disbelief slowly becomes reality. Timing is important and people will need time and space to begin to adjust.

Being able to talk openly about the "mechanics" of loss and bereavement will eventually help individuals to understand both physically and psychologically what is happening to them. This will also involve them having to recognise that certain thoughts and feelings are quite "normal" under the circumstances and as painful as they might be, they will eventually get a little easier to cope with (again this will naturally depend on the type of loss). For the clinician, working with grief can be an emotionally draining process and this needs to be considered, however it can also be extremely rewarding to be there for someone at the most difficult and distressing period in their lives and perhaps this is one of the most intimate privileges involved when working as a therapist. Understanding the "mechanics" and the process that the individual is going through can also help us to remain both objective and understanding at the same time. Just to illustrate the potential complexities of grief and loss, below is just a sample of different types of loss and whilst there are countless other reasons the small list illustrates the uniqueness of loss and some of the potential complicating factors. Loss at sea for example generally means that there is no actual physical body to grieve for, hence the *"letting go"* aspect can be extremely difficult. Under these circumstances many will report that they have seen or heard their loved one as the mind is unwilling to accept the loss and of course there has been no physical evidence to confirm the loss and *trigger* the grieving process. However, whilst each loss is unique in itself they are all linked together by the fact that the individuals who are left are going to have to go through a number of similar phases associated with death and bereavement. It is these phases that we shall concern ourselves with during the therapeutic process.

Types of loss

- Natural causes in later years
- Cancer in mid 30s

- Suicide in early 40s
- Child in accident
- Husband/father lost at sea

The Assessment

The assessment process will remain pretty much the same throughout each difficulty that we are presented with. Where grief is concerned it is useful to look at the impact of the loss on all of those within the family context and not just the client or patient who you happen to be seeing. Loss will naturally have some affect on all within the family context and the dynamics of the family itself are likely to change somewhat. Therefore, whilst focussing on the relationship of the individual who has died it is essential to look how the client/patient now views themselves and others within the family context. For example, if a father has died then the client may want to talk about how her sister or brother is not coping and this may actually be of more concern than the loss itself. In essence, when someone dies the dynamics of the family context change. It is important therefore, not to just purely focus on the individual relationship until you have covered this ground.

The quality and nature of all the relationships within the family context is useful and should be part of the information gathering process itself. People may be very upset at first and it may be important to offer some clinical reassurance at this stage. Their feelings, however distressing are likely to be very "normal" and this may need to be reflected back. Naturally all circumstances will be different, however an initial meeting to discuss ones loss can be very threatening, therefore it is perhaps useful to "tread" just a little more carefully during this type of assessment. The attachment to the lost individual will still remain the key variable with regard to the pain experienced and also the intensity of that pain. However "normal" the process may be it is possibly the most painful to experience. From a cognitive perspective we should be aware that one's mood will have a significant effect on how an individual thinks and behaves. The individual will need to understand these principles eventually and it is important to be bold on times and give directive advice. People may not want to go out and they may not want to talk to anyone or do anything. This however will only prolong the grief of course and fuel the likelihood of depression or anxiety. Courage is needed to face the world and an understanding of what we term "the phases of grief" can help the individual to identify with what is happening and what is likely to happen to them over the coming weeks, months and possibly years.

Measuring/Assessing the depression associated with grief

Alongside the qualitative information we should again look at quantifying how the client is feeling. This would involve something similar to the Hospital Anxiety & Depression scale discussed earlier. However, another useful assessment tool in this context would be The General Health Questionnaire or G.H.Q., as it is often referred to.

The General Health Questionnaire (GHQ) asks 58 standardised questions but is often abbreviated to the following 20 measures of mental distress, with responses of 'more than usual', 'same as usual', 'less than usual' and 'not at all'. Where grief is concerned it is more useful to use the abbreviated form as otherwise it can be overly intrusive and with attention and concentration often at a minimum then the least intrusive measure is usually best. I must point out however, that apart from being able to measure and quantify ones difficulties I always find that where grief is concerned having the client actually see what they are experiencing such as loss of concentration and avoidance in social and other areas can actually provide a clinical "mirror" if you like and this can often prompt the individual into taking a more adaptive stance rather than a depressive and avoidant one. In essence the assessment allows the individual to look at some of the behaviours they are unwittingly engaged in that are likely to prolong their difficulties. Again, this must be viewed from a clinical perspective as there will be countless emotional processes that the client will have to endure and they may need to avoid for a while before being encouraged to gently "come back" into a similar lifestyle prior to the loss.

The General Health Questionnaire (GHQ)

In the last 2 weeks have you:

Been able to concentrate on whatever you were doing?
Lost much sleep over worry?
Been managing to keep yourself busy and occupied?
Been getting out of the house?
Been feeling you were doing things well?
Been satisfied with the way you've carried out your tasks?
Felt that you were playing a useful part in things?
Felt capable of making decisions?
Felt constantly under strain?
Felt that you couldn't overcome your difficulties?
Been able to enjoy normal day-to-day activities?
Been taking things hard?
Been able to face up to your problems?
Found everything getting on top of you?
Been feeling unhappy and depressed?
Been losing confidence in yourself?
Been thinking of yourself as a worthless person?
Been feeling reasonably happy?
Been feeling nervous and strung up all the time?
Found you couldn't do things as your nerves were too bad?

Individuals may be asked specific questions about their general state of health, according to the styles and interest of the therapist and the presenting problem.

PHASES OF GRIEF

The process of bereavement may be described as having four phases:

1. Shock and disbelief:

Initially, there is an overwhelming sense of shock and disbelief and a sense of numbness. Family members may find it difficult to believe the death and they feel stunned and more in shock. This happens immediately following the death and can last for a few hours or several days. Symptoms include feeling emotionally numb and an inability to accept or believe the death.

Symptomatically this may not be the worse period as certain *"defences"* may be keeping the pain at bay temporarily.

2. Yearning and searching:

This is when the emotional difficulty begins to develop and loved ones may begin to experience separation-anxiety as they struggle. Emotionally at this stage they cannot accept the reality of the loss. They try to find and bring back the lost person and feel ongoing frustration and disappointment when this is not possible.

3. Disorganization and despair

The reality of the loss hits home and family members and loved ones feel "depressed" and find it difficult to plan for the future. They are easily distracted and have difficulty concentrating and focusing. On occasion there remains a sense of de-realization as if this is not happening to them.

4. Reorganization or acceptance

This is the final stage of the grieving process. It is perhaps better described as *"recognition of reality"*, as it is arguable whether one is ever able to accept the death of a loved one. For most people the intense symptoms of grief gradually begin to subside approximately six months after the death of a loved one. However, much anger and guilt still looms in the minds of many and often people may feel that they could have done something that would have changed the outcome. Often feelings of anger and guilt block the natural healing process. It is at this stage that practical stress management exercises can be used to help an individual move forward in their lives.

We are all different and it is fair to say that each of us will cope with the loss of someone in many different ways. For some and depending on the nature of the loss the experience may actually lead to personal growth, even though it is an emotionally difficult and trying time. As previously mentioned, the way a person grieves depends largely on the personality of that person and the nature or quality of the relationship with the person who has died. We will often here statements when someone in their 80s dies such as, *"oh he had a good innings"*, and perhaps we can justify this to some extent. However, to the son, daughter and/or friend who had come to rely on that individual the loss can be devastating and extremely distressing. As previously mentioned we must always stand back and observe the reaction of the individual and listen to what they have to say about the nature of the relationship before we are tempted to "jump in". With regard to the clinical work involved it is useful to be explicitly aware of the dynamics of grief itself and the fact that the terms grief, bereavement and mourning, whilst often used interchangeably are actually unique processes in themselves.

Grief is the normal process of reacting to the loss. Grief may be experienced as a mental, physical, social, or emotional reaction. Mental reactions can include anger, guilt, anxiety, sadness, and despair. Physical reactions can include sleeping problems, changes in appetite, physical problems, or illness. Social reactions can include feelings about taking care of others in the family, seeing family or friends, or returning to work. As with bereavement, grief processes depend on the relationship with the person who died, the situation surrounding the death, and the person's attachment to the person who died. Grief may be described as the presence of physical problems and constant thoughts of the person who has died. Guilt and hostility are commonplace and there is likely to be a distinct change in the way the person normally acts.

Bereavement is the period after a loss during which grief is experienced and mourning occurs. The time spent in a period of bereavement again largely depends on how attached the person was to the person who died, and occasionally how much time was spent anticipating the loss (mental preparation).

Mourning is the process by which people adapt to a loss. Cultural customs, rituals, and society's rules for coping with loss also influence mourning. This stage of the grieving process normally begins approximately one week after the death and can last for 6-12 months. Emotional symptoms include feeling sad or depressed, loss of appetite, crying spells, anxiety, anger, poor concentration and feelings of guilt. Some people feel the need to blame themselves, someone else, or some place or thing for the death. Physical symptoms include pains and nausea. Once the reality of the situation *"sinks in"*, a natural reaction is to worry about one's own future and how the loss will affect you. It is common at this stage to feel that you cannot cope with life; negative thoughts flood the mind, remembering experiences shared and grieving for the loss of future experiences that will not be shared. This is particularly true when suffering the pain of losing a child. It is often said that *"one mourns a parent for what they had but one mourns a child for what could have been"*. As the years go by the memories of a lost parent for example become nostalgia; feelings are coupled with warm memories of love. When one loses a child, each celebration of life is coupled with *"our child will never see this"*. The difficulties here are all too evident.

Clinical Skills & Techniques when Working with Loss

Each therapist will develop their own "style" of working with loss and it is important that they develop an approach that they feel comfortable with. However, it remains essential to have a framework from which to work rather than having an open-ended discussion about the loss itself. The therapeutic dialogue therefore, must have a certain amount of structure however "invisible" this may appear. The following sets out some of the therapeutic components that are useful to incorporate when working with this client group.

Grief Counselling & Grief Therapy

Whilst the skills overlap considerably it is useful to separate out grief counselling from grief therapy. In essence grief counselling is a clinical process that may help the normal grief reaction and grief therapy is something involved with working with more complex grief reactions. Both are outlined below along with some useful insights and strategies.

Grief Counselling

Grief counselling helps mourners with normal grief reactions work through the tasks of grieving. Grief counselling can be provided by professionally trained people or in self-help groups where bereaved people help other bereaved people. All of these services may be available in individual or group settings.

The goals of grief counselling include:

- Helping the bereaved to accept the loss by helping him or her to talk about the loss
- Helping the bereaved to identify and express feelings related to the loss (for example, anger, guilt, anxiety, helplessness, and sadness)
- Helping the bereaved to live without the person who died and to make decisions alone
- Helping the bereaved to separate emotionally from the person who died and to begin new relationships
- Providing support and time to focus on grieving at important times such as birthdays and anniversaries

- Describing normal grieving and the differences in grieving among individuals
- Providing continuous support
- Helping the bereaved to understand his or her methods of coping
- Identifying coping problems the bereaved may have and making recommendations for professional grief therapy

Grief Therapy

Grief therapy is used with people who have more serious grief reactions. The goal of grief therapy is to identify and solve problems the mourner may have in separating from the person who died. When separation difficulties occur, they may appear as physical or behaviour problems, delayed or extreme mourning, conflicted or extended grief, or unexpected mourning.

Grief therapy may also be available as individual or group therapy. During grief therapy, the mourner talks about the deceased and tries to recognize whether he or she is experiencing an expected amount of emotion about the death that is in proportion to the loss. Grief therapy may allow the mourner to see that anger, guilt, or other negative or uncomfortable feelings can exist at the same time as more positive feelings about the person who died.

Human beings tend to make strong bonds of affection or attachment with others. When these bonds are broken, as in death, a strong emotional reaction occurs. After a loss occurs, a person must accomplish certain *"tasks"* to complete the process of grief. These basic tasks of mourning include accepting that the loss happened, living with and feeling the physical and emotional pain of grief, adjusting to life without the loved one, and emotionally separating from the loved one and going on with life without him or her. It is important that these tasks are completed before mourning can end.

Complicated grief reactions require more complex therapies than uncomplicated grief reactions. Complicated grief is identified by the extended length of time of the symptoms, the interference caused by the symptoms, or by the intensity of the symptoms. Major depression, agoraphobia and panic attacks are just some of the symptomatic reactions to loss. Occasionally, complicated or unresolved grief may appear as a complete absence of grief and mourning, an ongoing inability to experience normal grief reactions, delayed grief, conflicted grief, or chronic grief. Factors that contribute to the chance that one may experience complicated grief include the suddenness of the death and again the nature of the relationship to the deceased (for example, an intense, extremely close, or very contradictory relationship).

A person, who avoids any reminders of the person who died, who constantly thinks or dreams about the person who died, and who gets scared and panics easily at any reminders of the person who died may be suffering from some form of post-traumatic stress. Alcohol abuse may occur, frequently in an attempt to avoid painful feelings about the loss and symptoms. In this context it is again useful to remind oneself of some of the basic tenets of the cognitive framework looking at thoughts and behaviours that are likely to help and those that are likely to inhibit. Both these adaptive and maladaptive "coping" strategies will significantly affect the clinical outcome here. Therefore, encouraging the individual to be involved more in what we term adaptive strategies can have a positive "knock on" effect. Conversely, drinking and continuous avoidance will significantly prolong any improvement and may lead to further mental health difficulties.

In grief therapy, six tasks may be used to help a mourner work through grief and clients should be encouraged to:

i) Develop the ability to experience, express, and adjust to painful grief related changes

ii) Find effective ways to cope with painful changes.

iii) Establish a continuing relationship with the person who died.

iv) Stay healthy and keep functioning.

v) Re-establish relationships and understand that others may have difficulty empathizing with the grief they experience.

vi) Develop a healthy image of oneself and the world.

Therapeutic work

"Grief work" includes the processes that a mourner needs to complete before resuming daily life in a more functional manner. These processes include *"separating"* from the person who died, readjusting to a world without him or her, and forming new relationships. To separate from the person who died, a person must find another way to redirect the emotional energy that was given to the loved one. This does not mean the person was not loved or should be forgotten, but that the mourner needs to turn to others for emotional satisfaction. The mourner's roles, identity, and skills may need to change to readjust to living in a world without the person who died. Eventually, the mourner may need to give other loved ones the emotional energy that was once given to the person who died in order to redirect this energy. Naturally this will take time and will depend on where the individual is at with regard to adjusting to the loss.

People who are grieving often feel extremely tired because the process of grieving usually requires tremendous emotional and physical energy that is often exhausting. The grief they are feeling may not be just for the person who died, but also for the unfulfilled wishes and plans for the relationship with the person. For some people a death may act as a reminder and it may well act as a trigger for past losses or separations. To this extent, "unfinished business" may surface and will need to be addressed.

Conclusion

Like many other areas of therapeutic work working with loss can be very rewarding for the therapist and of course extremely beneficial for the client as they begin to come to terms with losing a loved one. This can help clients move forward instead of being "stuck" with all the pain and the potential harm that can occur to their general health and well-being. There are important factors to consider, as this work is particularly demanding. In particular we need to be aware of our own losses and how they can impact on the therapeutic process. We have to be compassionate but strong for the client and a great deal of self-awareness is essential. The therapist must also be aware that working in this area can be emotionally demanding and good supervision and a healthy lifestyle are probably as important when working with this client group as with any other as the potential for transference and counter-transference becomes all too evident with so much displaced emotion being expressed. Therefore, proceed with care and compassion.

Divorce & Separation

If you have made mistakes there is always another chance for you.
Indeed, you may have a fresh start at any moment you choose, for this thing we call
"failure" is not the falling down, but the staying down

Mary Pickford – 1893-1979 (Actress)

Divorce and separation have become increasingly more common over the past 30 years. Whilst there are many varying reasons for this, the fact remains that divorce and separation is often a prolonged and painful process. We may forgive ourselves for assuming that at least on one level divorce and separation are perhaps not as painful as the type of loss experienced through the emotional pain associated with death and bereavement outlined above. However, in practice it is again wise to keep any pre-conceived ideas and generalisations to ourselves and judge the level of pain we are presented with as objectively as we can. Indeed, I have heard numerous clients/patients say something in line with the following statement:

"It would have been easier to cope if they had died, the fact that I have to see them, and see them with someone else, knowing I have lost them, is just too painful".

This statement hits home the potential magnitude and devastation associated with divorce and separation. On a very general level, when there is a separation like this there is usually a "winner" and a "loser". That is not to say that the "winner" *per se* does not suffer with guilt and conflict but generally it is the "loser" who is left to pick up the shattered pieces of their lives. I therefore, appreciate that these terms are rather inappropriate and I only use them to illustrate the point. Indeed, using the term "loser" is naturally not the healthiest of all descriptions. To the one left behind however there is likely to be tremendous emotional turmoil as he or she struggles with conflicting feelings of love, hate, anger and worthlessness.

When the love someone had hoped and expected would last forever fails, a persons' world and very reason for existing can be shattered beyond all recognition. Understandably, the most difficult separations occur when a spouse or partner begins to reject the others love and affection. This rejection in itself can be significantly harmful to ones self-worth and self-esteem and it is common for individuals to lose any sort of confidence that they may have previously had. Often the more sudden the separation then the more bewildering it can be.

Whilst there is eventually a "silver lining" to many separations (even for the one left behind), this positive aspect remains too far ahead for many to envisage. Therefore the potentially creative growth experience that is often a by-product of separation for all concerned is not apparent in the short term. Indeed, whilst there may well be benefits to be gained further down the road, losing the most important relationship can crush an individual resulting in sadness, anger and subsequently depression. It can overwhelm a person with frightening emotional and practical changes and decisions involving new responsibilities and economic hardships.

The relationship conflicts may have lasted for months or years before the actual separation. Following the separation however, the emotional distress can last for many months and often years if bitterness and anger ensure and certain issues are not resolved. In fact, although people expect to feel better soon after a separation, in some cases the worst time is about one year after the divorce. Interestingly, during the first year after separating, 73% of women and 60% of men think the divorce might have been a mistake (Hetherington, Cox and Cox, 1985). Yet, half of the men in the above study and two-thirds of the women said that overall they were "more content with life" five years after a divorce than they had been before and that includes those that were left behind. This illustrates how vulnerable all individuals become during the first year of separation and in itself this is probably a significant factor in why so many go on to what we term a *"rebound"* relationship. This is something to be aware of in the clinical setting as a vulnerable individual is likely to be emotionally hurt and needy and unwittingly they are increasingly likely to find themselves in a relationship that superficially "masks" those wounds. This may ease the pain initially but is nonetheless more likely to be inappropriate in the long term. The key is to help the individual work through their pain and to offer insight into how they can rebuild their lives without "diving" back in too quickly – It is however understandable why people have this need following a separation.

Beginnings and endings

Separation and divorce can be seen as a time of both endings and beginnings and the eventual decision to separate is not often a mutual one. This can be a difficult time for everyone, especially where children are involved. Both partners experience a range of emotions, which, as outlined above are likely to include a sense of loss, grief, pain, anger and a sense of failure. It takes time to go through this process and it's important to acknowledge and deal with these uncomfortable feelings. The person who inevitably makes the decision to leave will experience the separation differently to the person who has been "deserted" or left behind. In general, it is the person left behind who will suffer most, although there are occasions when the guilt gets the best of the person who has left and they may well go on to suffer far more in some instances, indeed, this may be the client in front of you – hence keeping an open mind and remaining objective remains the therapists' goal at this stage. In general men and women are likely to experience the separation process differently as outlined below, although again this is a generalisation.

Separation variables to consider

- The partner who chooses to leave may experience more guilt, where as the one that is left can feel rejected.
- Often women feel more fear around their security and financial support where as men can feel more helpless and lonely.
- All these negative emotions can lead to resentment and anger, which of course need to be dealt with constructively.
- For some, separation can be an enormous sense of relief yet it can still produce conflicting emotions that need to be disentangled.

The painful facts of divorce and separation

Supposedly, time heals all wounds, but the pain of divorce and separation may last and last. Indeed, in one particular study researchers discovered that 10 years following separation 40-50% of women and 30-40% of men remained very angry at the former spouse and felt rejected and exploited (Wallerstein, 1986). Females over 40 years of age have an especially hard time with the above study suggesting that females in this bracket have less chance of remarrying (28%), are likely to have an inadequate income (50%), and suffer with loneliness and even clinical depression (50%). After 10 years, in only 10% of divorces was life perceived as being better for *both* partners, in 27% of the cases both had a poorer quality of life, and 63% of the time one partner was better off but the other was unchanged or got worse. In the latter situation, the upbeat spouse is more likely to be the woman (55%), usually in her 20's or 30's. Some researchers have found that women more often report joy as they experience independence and new competencies (Riessman, 1990). However, for the majority, losing love inflicts deep and remarkably lasting wounds. Divorced women, who get custody of the children, also suffer a 33% decline in their standard of living. Men are considered "better off" (except they frequently become responsible for another family). However, only about 50% of divorced fathers pay child support regularly; 25% pay some and 25% pay little or nothing at all. Non-custodial parents (75% are men) are often depressed and anxious because they feel alienated from their children. Maybe people need to look at these long-term statistics before considering divorce or separation or perhaps if they looked at them prior to a relationship they may well stay single for the rest of their days. I make this last comment in a rather "tongue in cheek" fashion and single life for many young adults is often a chosen path rather than a consequence. Maybe this is avoidance behaviour with regard to pain itself or perhaps it is a healthy rational decision. I am sure each reader will have their own view of the changing demographics associated with relationships in the millennium and whilst the above stats can appear contradictory the fact remains that losing someone you have loved will initially send you into emotional turmoil.

Whilst no two separations are alike there are patterns of behaviour that have become familiar during the separation process. For the therapist working in this context it is useful to have an awareness of the most prevailing patterns. Outlined below are some of the more common factors associated with this type of separation. It is useful for the therapist to familiarise themselves with these "stages" and the likely emotional feelings that will be simmering either beneath the surface or on top for all clients going through this difficult time.

The separation process

Stages of divorce adjustment (2-4 years)

1. **Denial**
2. **Recognition** relationship is over–anger
3. **Realisation** of losses–mourning
4. Slow, painful **Readjustment**

Feelings

- Rage/anger
- Failure
- Remorse
- Guilt
- Fear/insecurity
- Abandonment
- Aloneness
- Rejection/being unloved/unwanted
- Incompetence (trying to do things for oneself which partner has always done)
- Finding it hard to let go of the relationship

- Ambivalent/confusion
- Being only half a person/loss of identity

Behaviour

- Mood swings–depression/euphoria
- Paralysis/frenetic action
- Don't eat/eat too much
- Drink more
- Accident prone
- Nightmares
- Don't sleep
- Sudden overwhelming tears

Cumulative losses

- Partner/marriage/children
- Familiar roles/routines
- Full-time parenting role
- Revived memories/pain of earlier loss
- Financial security - anxiety about future
- Less money
- Friends/relations
- May have to move house/home
- Belongings
- Life style
- Self image–success

Clinical Skills & Techniques for Working with Divorce and Separation

Most adults would find the separation process exhausting and emotionally upsetting as they desperately try to rebuild their lives. At the very early stages most cannot rationally handle the complex and emotional consequences of divorce and separation, hence the initial denial process probably serves an important function early on where individuals are unconsciously repressing their pain until they are emotionally strong enough to begin to deal with these consequences. Perhaps understandably, friends are often supportive of whatever they think the individual wants to hear, a sort of *"colluding"* if you like. However, this may only serve to maintain a kind of *"victim"* position, even though the support is well meant. Therefore, during this extremely vulnerable stage it is probably more relevant to try to establish a warm and mutually respectful clinical relationship. If this can be achieved then it will help facilitate the process considerably, particularly where the discussion of painful material is concerned. This may go some way with regard to the vulnerable individual becoming a little less *"defensive"* as they try to cope with their conflict and pain. The following steps are a general guide to working with divorce and separation and again it is important to remember that each situation is unique and that the dynamics of each separation will be different. With those differences in mind however, these guidelines should serve the therapist well, particularly as the therapist should by now have a good understanding of the thought-emotion-behaviour pattern associated with distress and cognitive therapy.

1 - History taking and establishing a therapeutic relationship

The history taking aspect in this context can be more qualitative than quantitative and early on the emphasis should be on developing a trusting and supportive relationship whilst at the same time remaining emotionally strong for the individual in question. Being able to listen and empathise is paramount at this stage; however it is far more beneficial for the client to perceive the therapist as not just being warm and empathic but also strong and secure in their approach.

As we are aware, no separation is alike and it is important to look at the immediate reasons for the separation before going into more depth and looking at the relationship in its entirety. As with all assessments we will need to look at the family and psychosocial dynamics as well as sources of support. Where there are children present we will need to know the arrangements for their care and how the adult is coping with managing the children. We also need to know what the individual is doing on a day to day basis and if things are particularly acute we should ask if they have thought of self-harm and if so enquire about risk as in risk assessment.

2 – Basic health care

Initially the therapist needs to enquire about basic health care such as eating, sleeping and general behaviour. Again most of this would have been covered previously when we looked at depression in general. A depression questionnaire similar to those already discussed will provide some insight into how the individual is functioning and again the usefulness of these assessment tools is illustrated by the fact that it will help reveal some of the maladaptive behaviours that may be occurring. Contrary to popular belief and myth in the therapeutic world these assessment tools are not obtrusive and serve an important part of the therapeutic process, so have the courage to use them and try to see them as an adjunct to your clinical skills.

3 – Psycho-education

By now readers should be aware of how important I feel this factor is. Therefore, helping the individual understand what is happening to them can be of great therapeutic value in itself. Much of the detail outlined above under the sub-heading, *"the separation process"* should be relevant at this stage. This offers the individual increasing insight into why the client may feel like wanting to "harm" their x partner or indeed his/her new partner and the dangers of displacing their emotions all over the place will be all too evident. My direct advice to clients/patients going through this trauma (when the therapeutic relationship is established) is to encourage them to try to **maintain their dignity** in the face of increasing adversity. I also acknowledge that maintaining dignity in the face of adversity is a far easier thing to say than do. However, if the individual can grasp this then it will again help them move away from a position of *"victim"*. I have witnessed many (and again it is understandable) take verbal cheap shots including a barrage of abuse at the x partner and/or their friends and possibly family. Whilst initially this may serve a primal purpose of minimal benefit there is little doubt that shortly after behaving in this manner, the person will feel worse and even more out of control and bereft. Therefore, maintaining ones' dignity should be encouraged as this gives the individual a sense of control and as such it will help them move away from a position of victim. The emotional grieving for the loss can occur alongside this and it should be dealt with appropriately through the mourning for the loss. However, despite the mourning, never underestimate how strong and adaptable people can be. It is important therefore, that we facilitate this message where possible. This message is best facilitated if the therapist can take a strong and secure approach whereby they are appropriately empathic without overly identifying with the clients pain. When this therapeutic stance is maintained clients are far more likely to be able to maintain their dignity and this is then reflected in their behaviour that becomes far more adaptive and appropriate. To some extent, being able to do this actually gives the client the higher moral ground and begins the next stage of helping them re-establish their identity and self-worth. If they are not strong enough to achieve this then they risk displacing their emotions onto most people they come into contact with and this again will not bode well. The classic strategy for example of telling the children how bad their mother or father is (no matter what they may have done) should be avoided at all cost as they then risk alienating and temporarily emotionally "losing" their children as they struggle to cope. Naturally, this is not going to help the children during this difficult period.

4 – Re-establishing identity or "rising from the ashes"

Much of the therapeutic work with regard to helping the individual begin to piece their life together will be discussed when we look at confidence and self-esteem in the following chapters. However, there are factors unique to the separation process that the therapist needs to be aware of and developing self-esteem is an important step in living through separation and divorce. Therapists should encourage clients to focus on personal strengths and not be distracted by situations that decrease confidence. Confidence does not come automatically. It requires a repetition of well-done tasks and it may also depend on how one is able to resist getting involved in maladaptive emotional behaviours that will again hold the person back. I am sure the reader can think of countless behaviours that occur during a divorce and/or separation that in the short-term may bring some sense of primal emotional respite such as sending a vicious text to the x-partners new lover. This type of behaviour however, is to be discouraged and if possible the emotional energy should be re-directed more constructively. Just as a series of failures can destroy a persons' confidence, a series of small successes will help to rebuild it. The individual should therefore, be made aware of the self-critical thoughts that can lead to maladaptive behaviour and self-pity. Mourning is one thing and is often a necessary process, wallowing in self pity however can lead to an increasing depression and therapists need to be strong enough and insightful enough to be able to encourage clients through this difficult period. Again, the quality of the therapeutic relationship will be a significant factor here. Where possible and when appropriate, people should be encouraged not to view divorce as a failure. In time to come they are far more likely to view it as a learning experience. However, even a small success at an acute stage can be of tremendous help. As mentioned previously, one small success may lead to another, and the positive effect on ones self-image is likely to be cumulative and emotionally beneficial.

One should be able to imagine how the cognitive framework is considerably relevant for this type of problem whereby the individual is likely to have a whole range of emotionally driven self-defeating thoughts and cognitions. Their behaviour is likely to be congruent with these feelings and this will serve to reinforce the helpless state. Indeed, one partner often seems to become trapped by perpetuating their low self-esteem. The result is that they are treated the way they allow themselves to be treated, based on how they feel and think about themselves. This is very much the victim stance and whilst it may serve an adaptive function initially, if prolonged it becomes self-destructive and bitter. To reinforce this point and to allow the budding or experienced therapist some insight into how your demeanour will either encourage or discourage the victim stance I will quote a conversation that a colleague had with his solicitor when he was going through the initial stages of separating after 13 years of marriage. We shall call the man separating Mr X and the solicitor Mr Y. Mr X approached the solicitor whom he knew in a social capacity and informed him that his marriage had come to an end he was naturally upset and wanted Mr Y to handle the divorce from a legal perspective. Mr Y's response was (and this is the crucial bit) *"I am sorry to hear that you and Mrs X are separating as I know this can be a difficult time for most people, however, as I know you and the person you are, I will not be feeling sorry for you as I know you will get through this and move forward. I am happy to handle all your affairs in relation to the separation however and am confident we will represent you well."*

I can hear the cries of dissatisfaction from the reader already but "hold on" and try to just think about the point being made. Yes I know the solicitor Mr Y isn't a therapist and yes I know he has some previous knowledge of Mr X. However, the above doesn't do justice to his strong and compassionate approach towards Mr X. The above words actually went some way to stopping Mr X becoming a victim and the initial meeting actually made him stronger. If you are unconvinced, think about the many times you have seen children cope well with adversity. How they cope can be largely related to the initial adult reaction. For example, a 4 year old child falls off their bike and grazes their leg – the adults' reaction will then play a significant part in whether that child is going to become emotional and upset or whether they are going to laugh and jump back on their bike and off they go. I think the reader should now be aware of what is being said here. Therapeutic work should involve helping clients and patients get back on their bikes where need be. The analogy may be weak but hopefully the point being made is strong and understandable and it is this type of strong *"rational compassion"* that I am trying to encourage here.

Simple Case Study

The following is a brief example of a referral following a separation. It will hopefully just highlight some of the main factors outlined above.

Referral: A woman in her late 40s was referred following the sudden ending of a 24-year marriage. The separation had occurred some 4 months previous, however the woman in question was now finding life difficult to cope with and was now off work because of this.

Assessment: – As above initial assessment looked at the rubrics of the separation as well as those closely involved and in particular how she was coping. It was revealed that her husband, who was 8 years older than her had left her for a woman in her late 30s (initial blow to self-worth, self-esteem, security etc). They had 2 sons aged 18 and 16 respectively. The 18 year old was angry with his father and the 16 years old was rather dismissive of most things. The woman in question was a teacher and she had been off work for 4 weeks and was struggling to cope. She had intense feelings of anger towards her x partner and his new partner and she would often vent her anger out on them where possible. She experienced acute anxiety reactions when she came into contact with any of them and/or saw their car or a car that was similar to the one they drove. She was not sleeping well and was not looking after herself in general. Basic advice was given in this context and the emotional reactions were reviewed and re-evaluated.

Subsequent sessions: – These generally revolved around her feelings toward her x partner and how she felt about herself. Initially, there were intense feelings of insecurity with regard to the future; however these appeared to subside quite quickly when financial matters were better understood. To begin with she had great difficulty resisting the urge to be verbally vindictive but when it was appropriately pointed out that she was only harming herself with these actions she eventually managed to cope better with this. To this extent she focussed her energies on things she could influence and these were behaviours that were far more adaptive as opposed to maladaptive. She began to avoid friends less and became more proactive in the things she had previously enjoyed. The pain was still there, however she understood it better and she knew how to manage it when it reared itself. She did go on a couple of "rebound" dates in the early part of the separation and whilst the dangers of these were pointed out she nonetheless felt some benefit from them, at least in the short-term. None of them lasted but they may have served a purpose in this context. Eventually she was able to go back to work and whilst the pain was still evident she began to re-build her life without her x-partner and was able to conduct reasonable conversations with him about the children etc. A number of sessions were spent looking at her own self-worth and confidence and within 4-5 sessions she was beginning to see some positive aspects about the future. Indeed, all of a sudden she had been able to see that she had actually been given an opportunity to some extent (the silver lining was appearing). The future was less certain but it was a little more exciting and she actually acknowledged that she felt a little younger. She did feel less secure but this in itself resulted in action rather than withdrawal. She had moved away from the victim role and whilst life ahead was a little frightening and less predictable this also came with a degree of excitement and autonomy where she had the independence to do what she wanted.

Endings: – 4-5 months and 12 sessions after being referred she was now laughing and joking about the situation although the pain was still there (as one would expect). She was able to work without much difficulty and her daily thoughts no longer focussed on her x-partner and his new lover. Indeed, she was now thinking that they are probably unaware what they have got involved in (often the case and good adaptive thinking) however it shouldn't be focussed on too much. Whilst the immediate future remained a little less secure it nonetheless presented opportunities. The down periods would occur and on occasion she felt lonely, however she was now no victim and her health in general was far better. Just as important was the fact that she believed she now possessed the psychological "tools" and renewed personal insight to cope with the difficulties in the future and she felt strong enough to deal with them.

Summary

Again it is important to reiterate that it is difficult if not impossible to do justice to a case when briefly writing and outlining some of the main issues. In addition, there are so many permutations to consider. For example, the "children" above were 16 and 18 years respectively and the situation is likely to have been different if there were younger children involved. Whilst the "classic" leaving for the younger woman was an issue above, this is only one of many other permutations to consider and hence each situation has to be taken in its own context. With regard to the 12 sessions over a 4-5 month period, they were weekly for the first 4 session's bi-weekly for the next 4 sessions and then monthly as the woman became stronger. This typical format also helps to protect any dependency creeping in at what is a vulnerable time for the individual in question. A particular warning to opposite gender therapists of a similar age to the client (although age may not be relevant on times) is to **be careful** of the potential for transference to occur during these initial sessions. Where there is a vulnerable member of the opposite sex and there is a caring and compassionate therapist there remains great potential for transference issues that will inevitably sabotage any clinical gain and produce complex problems in themselves. Be on guard and maintain your level of self-awareness and objectivity with the help of good supervision.

The children

Whilst the main focus here is the health and well-being of the adults going through separation it would be wrong not to briefly mention the children who will be exposed to the separation process. Indeed, how they cope with the whole event is likely to be inextricably linked to the health and well being of both parents involved. Ideally, children should have equal representation in a divorce. In general, many children, no matter what age, have an intense traumatic response to their parents' conflicts: they fear the "fighting" and worry about possible abandonment; they often *feel they are responsible* for the arguments and for one parent leaving home. What a terrible load for a child to carry and the child or children inevitably long for the missing parent. During and long after the divorce or separation, the children, especially those going through a custody battle, suffer a variety of psychological problems including shock, denial, physical problems, anger, panic, depression, guilt and self-criticism and low self-esteem. The children must therefore, be reassured that *they* aren't being divorced. They have a birthright to two parents, their time, love, and resources. The children will remain "sons" and "daughters" forever with the parents, even though the divorced parents will have no relationship with each other. The most vital decisions in a divorce are about how to continue and enrich each parent-child relationship, not who gets the house and pays the bills. Child custody is an enormous problem. Some of the children's stresses might be lessened if the children were equally cared for by both parents even though the parents are divorced. However, not all joint custody arrangements have worked out well and they can often be a forum for upsetting the other partner. However, there is data to suggest that father custody or joint custody can benefit certain children, especially boys (Warshak, 1992). However, no situation is the same and ultimately the decision must be based on what is best for the children, not on a parent's emotional needs and further research is needed to more fully understand these complex issues. As a society, we must find ways to keep the parent-child relationships strong, in spite of the animosity between the parents. Thus far, we are not doing a particularly good job when it comes to caring for our divorced children although extensive efforts are now being made by courts around the country to get divorcing parents to learn to cooperate effectively in providing two loving and secure homes--Dad's house and Mom's house--to their children.

Conclusion

Separation largely involves a complex and painful "letting go" process and a self-esteem process not usually associated with loss as when someone dies. Indeed, research has shown that both men and women can continue to experience negative effects in emotional and health terms for some years after the divorce or separation. It is therefore important to have some strategies for dealing with the grief and anger of a broken relationship so that the individual is able to envisage a future without the lost partner. Recovery from a divorce and separation can understandably be a long and difficult process. The individuals' sense of self and self-worth is likely to have been inextricably linked within the lost relationship. With the relationship lost the individual becomes emotionally lonely and confused and their whole identity may be lost in the process. The events can be made even more difficult as the individual struggles to come to terms with what they are going through. This aspect again highlights the importance of *psycho-education* as a therapeutic tool. The individual in question may feel anger, hate, and a whole range of distressing emotions. They see each of these separately, as if each emotion had nothing to do with any of the others. Actually, all of these emotions are part of an overall cycle of loss associated with separation and divorce and once people have a little more understanding and insight, life may become just a little bit easier and they may be able to begin to reach a place where they can start to move on.

In the early stages of separation taking physical and emotional care is important, particularly during this acute and often distressing phase when the chaos is only beginning. When there are children involved, ideally, both parents need to be able to help their children through this and be there for them. This is easier said than done depending on the circumstances and close family and social support can be of considerable benefit during this period. Children react differently to situations of change at different stages of their life and development. No matter what age children are, they will to varying degrees, be emotionally affected by separation and divorce. It is important for all adults to be aware of this and that they in turn make sure that they understand their feelings and are there for them.

Those going through an acute depression following separation are likely to want to withdraw and isolate themselves, often alienating themselves from their very own support networks. This will only serve to prolong their agony in the long-term. As difficult as it is and as hard as this may sound, they are not the first to go through this and they will get through it. How they get through this is the key. It is therefore important, where possible to help the client understand that they are not alone and that both family and friends can provide a strong support network at this time. In some cases, the decision to separate or divorce is a mutual one. A couple decides that their relationship has come to an end; they are able to grieve together and move on with their lives. Unfortunately, these couples are in the minority.

2 – Sexual Abuse

Not surprisingly sexual abuse is often associated with a myriad of emotional and psychological problems. As a consequence of these problems psychological treatment of sexual abuse can often be complex, emotionally demanding and time consuming. Taking these factors into account, it remains essential that the therapist working with sexual abuse has a thorough understanding of the likely psychological effects of sexual abuse itself and some of the more common cognitive, emotional and behavioural factors associated with abuse of this nature. Whilst there will inevitably be complexities involved it is crucial that we address what we are presented with and not what we may imagine someone must be experiencing following a traumatic experience. For example, some clients/patients will cope far better with all manner of traumatic experiences; hence whilst we are likely to be presented with a range of psychological difficulties, there will be some who present with relatively mild difficulties despite the awful experience. Conversely, there will be others who exhibit more moderate to severe problems. Whilst the abuse itself may be the causal factor for the depression\anxiety there will be many problems that will be secondary to the abuse and these may include self-harm, eating disorders, sexual difficulties and relationship problems, the list is by no means exhaustive.

The following will briefly outline a number of central principles that are invaluable when working with abuse-related psychological distress. These outlines are intended to further inform the reader before we look more closely at some of the key components involved in the assessment of sexual abuse and the therapeutic process itself.

Problems associated with sexual abuse

- Alcohol and drug abuse.
- Obsessive behaviour.

- Self-harm e.g. cutting, scratching or burning.
- Eating disorders
- Self-confidence, esteem and self-respect.
- Relationship problems – trust/sexual difficulties.
- The ability to trust people.
- The ability to relax and enjoy life.

The list of problems outlined above is by no means exhaustive, however it gives some insight into the consequences of abuse and how damaging it can be for the individual in question. From a therapeutic point of view I will always maintain (and often feed this back to clients and patients) that it takes immense **courage** to seek help and begin to talk about some of the most intimate difficulties that an individual had had to endure. I believe this courage is most evident when clients who have been sexually abused present seeking and asking for help and support with the difficulties they are experiencing.

With regard to the problems outlined above there remains increasing concern with regard to the prevalence rate for mood disturbances, interpersonal problems and sexual dysfunction among previously abused adults. It is common for such clients/patients to experience a range of mixed emotions and cognitions similar to those described in the clinical case earlier whereby the woman could only see paedophiles (male) when she went to the beach. Unfortunately it is common for patients to experience thoughts that include, *self-blame* for the abuse, *self-injurious* impulses, *anger* and *revenge* towards the offender/s and feelings of hostility and betrayal towards parents and family who did not protect them from the abuse or who themselves were the abusers. These are all issues that need to be addressed throughout the therapeutic relationship and some of these thoughts will need to be re-evaluated when the emotive aspect is neutralised or put to one side. There will more than likely be a degree of cognitive restructuring that will hopefully occur when the therapeutic alliance is established and hopefully when the adaptive cognitive, behavioural and emotional changes start to occur.

Ethical Issues

The ethical issues involved in the treatment of abuse survivors are generally the same as those for any other client population. However, these factors may be more salient in work with abuse survivors since sexual abuse can produce a variety of interpersonal difficulties. For example, significant boundary confusion and greater vulnerability to client-therapist dynamics are factors that need to be considered when working with this type of problem. Another important consideration during abuse-focused therapy is that the client should be made aware of therapeutic confidentiality (and its limits) and the potential for treatment to temporarily exacerbate certain symptoms (e.g., post-traumatic stress or depression). As well as having an awareness of these issues, the therapist should also be aware of the limits of his or her expertise in treating abuse survivors, seeking out consultation, supervision, and/or additional training when necessary. Therapeutic interventions should be those accepted by those with knowledge and particular training in the field, and should be appropriate to the survivor's specific and unique difficulties. As outlined above for example, there will be individuals whose suffering can be regarded as reasonably mild and they may therefore be suitable for a therapeutic approach that looks at the issues they appear to be presenting with and some general cognitive therapy over a relatively short period may suffice. They may not want to explore certain issues in depth and this should be respected. **One should always be aware of potentially dismantling clients "defences".** I have witnessed naïve counsellors on many occasions "open up a can of worms" (the easy part by the way) only to be left floundering when the client remains distressed. There remains a naive assumption with some therapists that by talking over all the intimate detail there is somehow going to be a Freudian type catharsis that in itself leads to recovery. This is dangerous and should be guarded against. A good therapist will know his or her boundaries and limits. We all may mean well but we have to sometimes put our desire to want to care and possibly "rescue" to one side as it can potentially be irreparably damaging for the client and "opening up the trauma" is relatively easy, it's what you then do that will either enable the client to cope better or leave them feeling distressed and adrift.

The Therapist

Early on in their work therapists and counsellors alike need to be aware of some of the emotional factors that can impact on them when they are engaged in therapy with certain client and patient populations. For example, working with people who have been sexually abused and listening to traumatic details can place a tremendous emotional burden on the therapist. Indeed, listening to intimate details of abuse is potentially upsetting and distressing and can contribute to emotional "burnout". Therefore, the therapist needs to have considerable self-awareness as well as good supervision where any issues can be addressed and discussed. Indeed, irrespective of self-awareness and clinical experience I have had certain situations impact on me completely "out of the blue", so to speak and this has taken me totally by surprise. So remember, prepare for the unexpected and my advice is to be strong for the client and not to bring your own emotions into the arena, even if they have been "tapped" unexpectedly. I have coined the term *"rational compassion"* which I feel is relevant for all clients that we work with. The *"rational compassion"* I refer to is that of the professional therapist who is able to reasonably identify but not over-identify with what has been happening for the client. This allows the therapist to be both compassionate and objective when working with vulnerable clients.

Disclosure

Disclosure of the abuse is often associated with intense shame and an additional fear of being rejected by the therapist. The sensitivity and care of the therapist in this context remains paramount and should be considered carefully. It is not uncommon for women to be offered female therapists where the client may feel more "comfortable". However the opportunity of working through this with a male therapist should not be overlooked as there may be therapeutic gains to be had if a close professional and trusting clinical relationship can be developed with a positive male or opposite gender role-model as therapist. Where possible, the gender therapist options should be made available and the client/patient can then make the decision for themselves. They should not however, be guided consciously or unconsciously into one particular gender. Unfortunately, I have witnessed this on many occasions and I feel it should be the informed decision of the client or patient where this is possible.

Specific factors relating to the sexual abuse itself will play a significant part in how things will develop from a therapeutic perspective. For example, when exposed to this type of abuse a high degree of psychological damage can occur if the offender makes the victim feel physical pleasure during the actual abuse. This can produce an uncomfortable level of guilt and shame that is extremely powerful in itself. As a result of this the individual may actually be less likely to disclose the abuse to its fullest extent, and if he or she does, they are more likely to minimize certain aspects. This may arise as a consequence of the victim feeling partly to blame for the abuse as a result of the "pleasure" they experienced (this is often a "grooming" technique). As the individual grows older, they may be unable to process the abuse, and continue to blame both themselves as well as the offender. The shame and ambivalence produced can be immense and produce psychological difficulties in itself including, self-harm and other self-destructive behaviours. Over a period of time the person abused may have actually lost a sense of reality on what actually happened and as a result of their low self-worth and esteem may be confused as to whether they were actually willing participants. Again, these are issues to review and re-evaluate during the therapeutic process.

It is useful for the therapist to be aware of issues surrounding the original disclosure of the abuse itself that may have taken place weeks, months or many years prior to coming to seek help. One of the important factors to remember with regard to sexual abuse is that:

"Much, if not most of the emotional and psychological damage someone receives comes not from the assault and sexual abuse itself, but from the post assault reactions from well meant others"

Taking the above statement into account it remains crucial that that those involved following the disclosure of the abuse recognize how their behaviour with the person and their overall interactions can significantly affect both the immediate and long-term ability of that individual to deal with the overall affects of the abuse. Therefore, the first people who come into contact with a victim post assault have an opportunity to set the precedence, through their interpersonal behaviour and reactions. This will go some way to affecting a smooth or complex recovery for the person in question. This also goes for the therapist involved and hence having the clinical knowledge and interpersonal skill, as outlined above remains crucial in this context.

Clinical Skills & Techniques for Working with Sexually Abused Adults

As a result of the many potential psychological difficulties that can arise following sexual abuse the following material will not solely focus on a single case study to highlight specific issues. Instead, the following material will look at some of the key stages in the therapeutic process including the assessment and treatment variables that are likely to be present in most cases. Coupled with the general chapter on cognitive therapy and depression, this should provide an adequate framework for getting to grips with most of the therapeutic factors and variables involved when working with people who have been sexually abused.

Assessment

As should be apparent now, we would want to look at both qualitative and quantitative factors. The general assessment procedures already discussed will be equally relevant here and will give the therapist an idea of what the individual is experiencing and what social supports they may or may not have. With sexual abuse producing a wide variety of symptoms and disorders assessment is especially important if we are to adequately ascertain what specific difficulties the client is experiencing. Not only should we begin with a psychosocial evaluation (qualitative), some form of on-going assessment should be an integral part of the treatment process. This may be true for all problems in general, however it should be explicitly stated with this type of difficulty as symptoms may wax and wane across treatment or they may be affected by initial levels of dissociation and other avoidance responses that decrease as treatment continues, either of which might not be detected if assessment only occurred at the outset of therapy. Therefore, whilst we may engage in an initial assessment similar to that previously discussed we may want to keep an on-going clinical review as things "surface" and symptoms may actually deteriorate to begin with (not uncommon and some therapeutic reassurance wouldn't go amiss here)

When the client is able to tolerate discussion of his or her history, assessment should include a detailed evaluation of the abuse and its characteristics. The presence of other childhood and adult traumas should also be evaluated, since many adults who have been sexually abused may have also suffered with psychological abuse and emotional neglect. They may have also been re-victimized as adults. However, it should not be assumed that any given symptom is the result of sexual abuse, *per se*, as opposed to the many other potentially harmful events and processes that the individual may have experienced.

As previously discussed, people are affected in many different ways following sexual abuse and perhaps most importantly they may want to deal with it in their own personal way (where possible). An example of this occurred some 2-3 years ago when I was referred a woman in her mid- 50s. The referral was rather general and related to some mild depressive symptoms. Having gone over some relatively brief assessment information the lady informed me (about 15 minutes into the session) that when she was a young woman she had been sexually abused. The reason she had presented now was because the man who abused her had recently died and she felt a great need to "offload" what had happened. This woman had been happily married for 30 years and had 3 children and a couple of grand children, yet she had kept this to herself for all these years. She was actually also *"dipping her toe in the water"*. We talked about what had happened and how she had been affected by the events. To a large degree her *"defences"* had worked well in helping her repress the painful memories of the events and now she felt "safe" to disclose what had happened. She did this in a very careful way and again the written word will not do justice to the richness of the therapeutic process in this context. She presented for 4 sessions plus a follow-up and the therapeutic process revolved around some of her avoidance behaviour and her general way of thinking about what had happened and in particular whether she was to blame for it. I informed her that self-blame was common in this type of problem and we discussed the rubrics surrounding how and why people who had been abused might think in this manner. This lead to a process of cognitive restructuring and the woman in question was able to gain a more adaptive view of the events themselves. In this context, the therapeutic process was almost akin to a confessional to a priest. She had been able to "offload" this burden she had been carrying and the cognitive therapy allowed her to move forward in a more adaptive fashion. She had never told anyone about what had happened yet managed to repress things and live a relatively "normal" life. I think there's a lesson there for those who want to just charge in and open up ones *"defences"*. The example serves to illustrate how varied the presentation of sexual abuse can be and I would urge all therapists to wait and see what is being presented before naively "charging" in. This brief example illustrates just one of the many differing presentations that will occur as a consequence of sexual abuse and any overly assertive therapist may well have "frightened" this woman off if they had tried to focus too intimately on the details of the abuse itself.

Therapeutic techniques

The person who has been abused has a tendency to counter abuse related depression with phobic avoidance. It is important therefore that therapeutic interventions proceed slowly and carefully. Taking this into consideration, a primary goal should be to keep from overwhelming the client, either by exposing him or her to unacceptable levels of distress, or by inappropriately discouraging temporary avoidance activities that are governed by the individuals' *defences* (e.g., some level of dissociation). At the same time, however, the clinician must facilitate exposure to traumatic material so that it can be desensitised and integrated. As a result, effective abuse-focused interventions are neither so non-demanding as to be useless, nor so evocative or powerful that the client is re-traumatised. This is where the skill and experience of the therapist is paramount as you balance a fine clinical line.

As briefly mentioned above and as a general guide for both myself and the client I refer to this as clinically, *"dipping your toe in the water"*, in essence the "water" is going to be too hot or just manageable. Our job is to gently get them to go further into the water when they feel strong and safe enough. Such interventions challenge and motivate psychological growth, accommodation, and desensitisation, but do not overwhelm internal protective systems and motivate unwanted avoidance responses. Naturally the above therapeutic process is encouraged when the individual has been well informed. The *"emotional processing"* as it is often referred to can then take place

In addition to balancing challenge with stability, the clinician must work to provide a safe therapeutic environment. In the absence of continuous and reliable safety and support during treatment, the client is unlikely to reduce his or her reliance on avoidance defences, nor attempt the necessary work of forming an open relationship with the therapist. A good therapeutic alliance after all may partially counter-condition anxiety associated with the disclosure (and thus reliving) of traumatic material. The interpersonal skill of the therapist throughout this period is challenged and for those therapists who are able to maintain a sensitive and objective focus the outcomes can be extremely positive and professionally rewarding.

Exploration and Consolidation

Effective therapeutic responses tend to occur on a continuum, with one end anchored in interventions devoted to greater awareness of potentially threatening but therapeutically important material (exploration), and the other constrained to interventions that support and solidify previous progress, or that provide a more secure base from which the survivor can operate without fear (consolidation).

Exploratory interventions typically invite the client to examine or re-experience material related to his or her traumatic history. For example, an exploratory intervention might involve asking the client to describe a specific abuse incident in detail, or to use slightly less dissociation when discussing a painful subject. This process will facilitate the adaptive "emotional processing" of painful thoughts and memories. Consolidation, on the other hand, is less concerned with exposure or processing than with safety and foundation. Such interventions involve activities that reduce arousal and "ground" the client in the "here and now," thus interrupting any escalating internal states and increasing internal stability. In this instance we can perhaps see more of the pure cognitive and behavioural factors that are an integral part of the therapeutic process and for example involve looking at the "here and now" if you like and those relevant thoughts and behaviours in particular. The decision to explore or consolidate at any given moment reflects the therapist's assessment of which direction the client's balance between stresses and resources is tilting. The overwhelmed client, for example, typically requires less exploration and more consolidation, whereas the stable client may benefit most from the opposite.

Emotional thinking

Emotional thinking is largely concerned with the cognitive component of therapy that should be familiar by now. The emotional thinking can occur both in relation to self-attributions (internal) as well as attributions relating to the events themselves and subsequent events since the abuse took place. As discussed in earlier chapters this type of thinking is likely to be have been reinforced over the past months and years until it has become the generally accepted way that the individual tends to see themselves and others in the world around them. Jehu (1988) reports in detail on a range of cognitive approaches to working with the emotional thinking following sexual abuse and below is a summary of Jehu's cognitive-behavioural treatment for mood disturbance and the associated thinking that is a by-product of this.

Provision of information - Information about the prevalence of sexual abuse may help to reduce the client/patient's ideas that he or she is different from the rest of the world. Gil (1984) for example, describes the emotional problems of previously sexually abused adults that can be very helpful for individuals who have been abused and this in itself is a form of psycho-education that will hopefully get the person to think differently about themselves and others. There are now numerous more up to date resources that will serve the same purpose and some of the most useful texts come from the Overcoming Series produced by Constable and Robinson and these are entitled *"Overcoming Childhood Trauma"* and *"Overcoming Traumatic Stress"*. There are others in this series that may also be relevant and they are related to depression, anxiety and eating difficulties.

Logical analysis – Often what is logical for the "lay" person is not for someone suffering with emotional distress. Early on in the book we talked about how the mood can turn black into white and vice versa when it comes to the way we think. This remains even more significant where sexual abuse is concerned and those *"defensive"* thoughts have often been finely tuned over many years. Logical analysis however refers to something on the lines of; **does the evidence necessarily support the victims' conclusion?** – For example, *"if it was his entire fault then what was I doing asking him to come to my bedroom to play with me, I remembered liking him and some of this felt nice"*. The logical analysis from the client's perspective here is that they are partly to blame for what happened. Other conclusions will be offered by the therapist, including, *"what did you really want him to play with you?"* This can be challenging. However the more logical reasons are slowly "teased" out and continuously reviewed and reappraised. There can be an emotive release as the individual actually becomes upset and realises the most rational and logical explanation. Interestingly in this context the maladaptive self-blame strategy has perhaps on one level served to protect the individual from the reality of the circumstances surrounding the abuse and hence the emotional release occurs as that protective "myth" on one level is dismantled.

De-catastrophizing – Someone who has been sexually abused is likely to believe that they have been permanently "damaged" and as such will always be unable to lead a normal life. The process of de-catastrophizing involves challenging this "fixed" position so that they are able to re-learn that many who have experienced quite violent sexual abuse can and do go on to live normal lives. Indeed, many victims of sexual abuse do fully recover. This is not to suggest that they ever forget about what occurred, because they do not. However, they can, with the help of family, friends, and professionals, go on with their lives and be happy again. If catastrophizing can be considered making the worse of the event that has occurred based on a number of false assumptions and emotionally driven cognitions then naturally de-catastrophizing is a reversal of this process.

Distancing – This means making a distinction between *"I believe"* an opinion which is open to dispute, and *"I know"*, an undisputable fact. For example, a person who "knows" that they were to blame for the abuse may be helped to distance themselves from this by hearing the testimonies of other abused individuals who once equally believed that they were to blame. Hence the value of good reading material in relation to sexual abuse can be a great and invaluable adjunct to the more pure traditional therapeutic process.

Re-attribution – This is where the therapist and client review the evidence of the abuse in order to arrive at a more appropriate (rational) assignment of responsibility for the actual abuse itself. This will involve a lot of discussion around the nature of the abuse and in general this leads to a process of *cognitive restructuring* whereby the client is able to look at alternative reasons for the abuse as opposed to persistent self-blaming attributions. The *re-attribution* aspect here is a crucial clinical process and often it will mean that the therapist and client will have to re-visit certain components of the abuse on a number of occasions before the client is able to begin to re-evaluate and re-attribute where the responsibility lies.

Conclusion

Taken together, the approach outlined here allows the therapist to address the irrational thinking, affected or avoidant behaviour and general anxiety and distress common among clients who have been sexually abused. After a secure and safe therapeutic alliance is established (strong and trusting – remember *rational compassion*) the on-going discussion of the painful memories is likely to slowly reduce the client's overall level of psychological distress, although certain disclosures and less avoidance are likely to increase certain anxieties initially. A continuous therapeutic dialogue will however allow the client to address and process increasingly more painful abuse-related material without exceeding their (now greater) self-capacities. This process, under optimal conditions, may continue until substantial symptom resolution has occurred. The process will also enable clients to re-evaluate the abuse itself and the attributional responsibility should be far more rational and hence far more adaptive for the client in question.

Despite the trauma and psychological devastation that can occur as a result of sexual abuse it is always important for the therapist to acknowledge that many people who have been abused actually go on to lead normal, healthy and productive lives. They can learn to let go of the pain, and to increase their self-awareness of how the abuse affected them. Sometimes it takes the right therapist, just the right book, or for some even just time. As a therapist we need to be aware of the therapeutic factors that can facilitate the clients' recovery and subsequently increase the clients' level of functioning. Working in this area, although emotionally challenging, can be rewarding for the therapist who is aware of the most effective way forward and retains an awareness of the potential pitfalls outlined above.

3 – Confidence & Self-Esteem

> *"No one can make you feel inferior without your consent*
>
> *Never give it."*

Eleanor Roosevelt

As the above statement implies our inferiorities are in-built and have probably been *"shaped"* and reinforced since birth via a multitude of differing experiences and perceptions. Despite these ingrained and inferior perceptions, if we are given the opportunity we should be able to re-learn and re-think about our "self" in all its guises. Indeed, if we are able to re-evaluate why we think in this self-defeating and deprecating manner then it is likely to increase both our insight and our general satisfaction with life itself. The key here however, is how we manage "set-backs" or difficult situations. For the individual who lacks confidence and self-esteem these situations are more likely to be fraught with anxiety and anticipation of "failure". As a consequence of this, avoidance and despair are the inevitable and most likely outcomes. As we rush toward the 21st century, our fast-paced ever-changing society places even greater demands on us to be independent. The new social realities imply and often require that you do more for yourself and to some extent rely less on others. Being able to meet the social and psychological demands of society can result in a productive and self-determined way of life. However, for those who lack the confidence and social nous to be able to do this there is likely to be even more avoidance and a continuous feeling of not being worthy. This avoidance can create a vicious cycle often resulting in an increasing lack of self-confidence, an unhappy personal life, and an increasingly distorted view of the self and others. This detrimental cycle will eventually reinforce the low self-esteem, poor self-image and lack of confidence and the individual continues to flounder in an increasing cycle of internal misery, frustration and despair.

Just as the mood in depression can turn light into dark, confidence can open up all manner of avenues leading to a far happier and fulfilling life. Confidence and a healthy amount of self-worth and self-esteem consist of the positive (rational) thoughts and feelings that an individual encompasses as part of their personal repertoire. There is nothing brash in this as people can be quietly confident and content about themselves. However, confidence can and will affect the way an individual is able to think, act, and feel about others, as well as how successful that person is with their own life (we are talking about life not financial rewards and materials here). The acquisition of high self-esteem involves becoming the person that that individual wants to become and this may involve, enjoying others more fully, and offering more outwardly. For others it may just involve a calmer and less critical internal voice that leads to a more content and composed life. High self-esteem is not competitive or comparative, but rather it is the state where a person is at peace with himself or herself. To this extent, it may be different things to different individuals, however the fact remains that without confidence and self-esteem the world can be a daunting and unhappy experience.

What is self-esteem and confidence and where do they come from?

Your self-esteem is something more fundamental than the normal "ups and downs" associated with situational changes. For people with good basic self-esteem, normal "ups and downs" may lead to temporary fluctuations in how they feel about themselves, but only to a limited extent. In contrast, for people with poor basic self-esteem, these "ups and downs" can make a significant difference often leading to moderate and occasionally severe mood swings.

Our self-esteem develops and evolves throughout our lives as we build an image of ourselves through our experiences with different people and different situations. Naturally, our experiences during our childhood play a significant role in the shaping of our basic self-esteem. When we were growing up, our successes (and failures) and how we were treated by the members of our immediate family, our teachers, coaches, and by our peers, all contributed to the creation of our basic self-esteem.

As previously outlined self-esteem and confidence are usually developed early on in a person's life. Whilst there can be genetic overloads it is generally the social and psychological experience of the child that will determine whether the adult will become confident and assertive or perhaps somewhat shy and lacking in general self-worth and self-esteem. Sometimes there are factors beyond social engineering that come into play such as the loss of a parent or a particular traumatic event that has significantly affected the individual. In general however it is the daily social and psychological experience that will determine the health and well-being of the individual in question. As the box below illustrates, childhood experiences such as being exposed to continuous criticism, being ignored or ridiculed or even being expected to be "perfect" at everything, can result in low self-worth and confidence. This is an important point here as the assumption may be that we will be presented with sorry looking individuals who have experienced a negative childhood that has been reinforced through early adulthood. However, there are many other permutations that include the "successful" individual who didn't quite manage to succeed in everything and hence they perceived themselves as "failures". This can occur often in the face of quite remarkable personal achievements. Just writing this has jogged my memory somewhat and taken me back to my summer job when I was 17 years of age. I worked in a sports centre and was on duty during a major swimming tournament between different regions of the country. I remembered a young local boy aged 10 who was quite highly rated and he seemed a polite and rather quiet and shy lad. At the end of the event he had won 4 gold medals and 1 silver from the five events he had entered. You may think what an achievement, as I did. However, his father, a well to do chap came marching down to the pool side and was absolutely disgusted with his son for failing to win the other gold. My heart sank and I remember feeling both sad and angry. The young lad in question went on to swim internationally and not to my surprise later on in life he did not talk to his father. This is a true story and it somehow illustrates how our often fragile development can be "shaped" even in the face of outstanding achievement. Indeed, my own theory is that behind many a successful individual lays someone with a rather low-level of self-esteem and confidence and their continuous striving and achieving is in a way a compensatory method for coping with this. That is not to criticise this way of coping however as it is constructive and to some extent adaptive and therefore should not be totally discouraged.

As we have suggested or implied above, it is generally the early influences that will have a significant impact on our overall confidence and self-esteem.

Healthy Self-Esteem	Low Self-Esteem
Childhood experiences that lead to healthy self-esteem include-	Childhood experiences that lead to low self-esteem include-
Being praised	Being harshly criticized
Being listened to	Being yelled at, or beaten
Being spoken to respectfully	Being ignored, ridiculed or teased
Getting attention and hugs	Being expected to be "perfect" all the time
Experiencing success in sports or school	Experiencing failures in sports or school
Having trustworthy friends	People with low self-esteem were often given messages that failed experiences (losing a game, getting a poor grade, etc.) were failures of their whole self.

Typical signs of low self-esteem and confidence

Whilst the signs can vary the following are generally accepted as those signs most common where self-esteem is concerned. They are equally applicable to both timid individuals and those who may be perceived as bullies. As many of you are aware it is often the "bully" or brash individual who lacks so much confidence and self-esteem that they often resort to maladaptive over-compensatory behaviours as a consequence of their social and psychological inadequacies.

Signs of Low Self-Esteem:

- Feeling not good enough - even if the person is
- Decreased confidence
- Constantly putting themselves down
- Being too scared to try new things
- Unsure of their good qualities
- Making no effort because they expect to mess things up
- Being timid, no assertiveness
- Losing temper

Consequences of Low Self-Esteem:

Low self-esteem can have devastating consequences.

- It can create anxiety, stress, loneliness and increased likelihood for depression.
- It can cause problems with friendships and relationships.
- It can seriously impair academic and job performance.
- It can lead to underachievement and increased vulnerability to drug and alcohol abuse.

Worst of all, these negative consequences themselves reinforce the negative self-image and can take a person into a downward spiral of lower and lower self-esteem and increasingly non-productive or even actively self-destructive behaviour. The above list is by no means exhaustive and it gives further insight into how difficult life becomes for the individual who suffers in this manner.

Clinical Skills & Techniques for Working with Low Self-Esteem and Confidence

Assessment

As for most psychological problems outlined above the assessment will look at both qualitative factors such as family history and general psychosocial history and quantitative components that are useful for, (i) identifying particular weaknesses (and strengths maybe) and (ii) providing a measure from which we may be able to observe improvement or otherwise.

Qualitative assessment: as we have seen throughout the book this will look at the immediate family in particular. We need to look at how the individual was parented and in particular was there any overt or perhaps covert criticism either "real" or "imagined" that may have played some part in the early development of low-self esteem and confidence. We need to briefly look at pre-school relationships and feelings and of course the earliest days of schooling. This is when we begin to develop more of a social sense of *"self"* and this vulnerable stage can be quite revealing. Naturally we go through the individuals' history looking at how they perceived themselves and others and how this in turn affected the way they may have behaved. We need to explore both their thoughts and feelings at this stage without challenging anything.

Quantitative assessment: some of the reasons for quantifying the assessment have been outlined above and in particular the quantitative assessment can act as both a catalyst and a kind of "mirror" that can enable both the therapist and the client to identify patterns of behaviour and thinking that are not helpful. There are numerous measures related to confidence and self-esteem with probably one of the most influential being the, *"The Rosenberg Self-Esteem Scale* (SES)*"*: The SES is scored as a Likert scale and the 10 items are answered on a four point scale ranging from **strongly agree** to **strongly disagree**. Items are rated accordingly and an outcome measure is arrived at.

The Rosenberg Self-Esteem Scale (SES):

		1. STRONGLY AGREE	2 AGREE	3. DISAGREE	4. STRONGLY DISAGREE
1.	I feel that I'm a person of worth, at least on an equal plane with others.	SA	A	D	SD
2.	I feel that I have a number of good qualities.	SA	A	D	SD
3.	All in all, I am inclined to feel that I am a failure.	SA	A	D	SD
4.	I am able to do things as well as most other people.	SA	A	D	SD
5.	I feel I do not have much to be proud of.	SA	A	D	SD
6.	I take a positive attitude toward myself.	SA	A	D	SD

		1. STRONGLY AGREE	2 AGREE	3. DISAGREE	4. STRONGLY DISAGREE
7.	On the whole, I am satisfied with myself.	SA	A	D	SD
8.	I wish I could have more respect for myself.	SA	A	D	SD
9.	I certainly feel useless at times.	SA	A	D	SD
10.	At times I think I am no good at all.	SA	A	D	SD

As should be apparent this type of scale, like many similar can help to start the process itself. In clinical practice I always find that when we administer a quantitative assessment and/or ask someone to fill in some kind of form in relation to his or her difficulties it actually has a positive impact on the client. In general it lets them know that the therapist is knowledgeable and aware of issues surrounding their difficulty and in my experience this has a clinically reassuring affect on the client who feels "safe" that they are with someone with a certain degree of knowledge and professionalism. It suggests to the client that they have begun a process and adding some formalisation to this process in my opinion encourages a pro-active environment. I am aware that there are many therapists who disagree with this and I still find this difficult to understand in clinical practice. At the very least such a scale provides a useful baseline measure at the beginning and further down the process it can act as a useful indicator as to whether the therapeutic process has been successful on some level.

Therapy

Therapy with people who are struggling with confidence and self-esteem should be conducted within the cognitive framework that should be relatively familiar by now. Both the therapist and client will review the historical evidence and look at key developmental factors from both within and outside the family context. There will be a review of any significant events that may have been either causal in nature or just served to reinforce the low self-esteem and lack of confidence. Before an individual can begin to improve their self-esteem they must first believe that they can actually change or modify it. Change doesn't necessarily happen quickly or easily, but it can happen given careful planning and an appropriate amount of motivation, insight and patience. Having reviewed and discussed the historical factors related to the lack of confidence and self-esteem the therapist will sit down and discuss strategies for beginning the change process. This is likely to consist of small "tasks" if you like where the individual will be encouraged to think and behave differently in a given situation. This process will only begin however when the client and therapist have mutually acknowledged what has been discussed and there is a reasonable amount of belief in the assessment and therapeutic process. From then on the client will have an increased awareness of that all too familiar *"inner voice"* that is riddled with self-doubt and criticism. However, from now on the client is encouraged to be aware of that critical voice and is encouraged to develop a more rational internal voice both in given situations and in life in general. This has particular resonance for the way they think about themselves and others. Therefore the first important step in improving self-esteem is to begin to challenge the negative messages of the critical inner voice. Here are some typical examples of the inner critic's voice and how we may begin to help clients counteract that voice. Again the examples here may seem a little "dry", however these are from real case examples and their importance however trivial they may seem should not be underestimated. Remember!, to the casual observer someone with a needle phobia is someone who just has an irrational fear of needles. However, for the person with the needle phobia their whole world can be significantly restricted often leading to bouts of depression and social avoidance. Therefore, what may seem trivial on the outside seldom is and often it may be just the "tip of the iceberg".

Brief case example

A number of years ago I was referred a woman in her mid 50s. Interestingly, the initial referral was concerned about the anxiety the woman was experiencing whenever she had to drive on the motorway or a dual carriageway. Whenever these situations presented themselves she would become consumed with anxiety and this often lead to a great deal of avoidance behaviour. The avoidance behaviour largely meant that she took lots of minor roads so that she did not have to drive on the main dual carriageways. Naturally, this was an inconvenience to say the least and it produced a number of problems including a certain amount of embarrassment and of course more petrol than she would prefer to be paying for as she found her own way of getting to and from her destinations. I found this to be an interesting case and it again will illustrate how we can be consumed by our own self-doubt, even in the face of contradictory evidence. What was interesting about this case was that this woman presented in an immaculate manner, she was extremely well dressed, she spoke with a great deal of intelligence and she held down a responsible job. On the outside therefore, one may be forgiven for assuming that this woman was a rather confident and reliable sort of individual who appeared to be caring, sensitive and in general pretty well together. I will not go through this case with a "tooth comb" so to speak but will just highlight the salient features and scan through the process.

Assessment

During the assessment we discussed her childhood and early family details and there appeared to be nothing significant or out of the ordinary. She enjoyed good relationships with her parents and siblings and she achieved well at the girls Grammar school. She was reasonably reserved and sensitive but not overly shy or passive. She had been married for over 25 years and had 5 children who were all grown up and doing well in their respective lives. She enjoyed very good relationships with all of them and enjoyed their company. Somewhere during the assessment I naturally asked about her driving and she smiled with some embarrassment and a little anxiety. I asked how long she had been driving for and she informed me that it had been nearly 30 years. Naturally I then went on to ask her how many accidents she had had during this time. Perhaps not surprisingly she said that she had never had an accident. OK? – Prior to this I asked about her relationship with her partner to which she responded by saying he had always been extremely critical of her. This had gone on for over 25 years. His criticisms were often apparent when she was driving and she had lost confidence in her ability to drive and her confidence in general was very low despite her excellent presentation. Out of interest (clinical of course) I asked if she and her husband had ever been involved in any road traffic accidents to which she responded by saying, *"Yes, three"*. When I asked who was driving at the time she informed that it had been her husband. This is quite a typical scenario where self-esteem and confidence are concerned. Here was a woman avoiding dual carriageways after being exposed to 25 years + of criticism from her husband who as it turns out was the only one at the drivers' wheel when any accident had occurred. Maybe it was her fault because of the way she was sitting as a passenger? As the reader may be able to imagine, from more of an in-depth discussion about her marriage came the "home truths", the criticisms had often been subtle but they had turned a sensitive and quietly confident woman into someone who had no belief in the way they drove, the way they looked and the way they went about their lives in general. In fact this woman's life could not have been more exemplary both in the way she was as a mother, an employee and as a general human being. In fact I'd go as far as to say that you'd be hard pushed to find a more honest and pleasant person, yet there she was riddled with anxiety and insecurity.

Following sessions

From our following discussions the woman in question gained increasing insight into the factors that had resulted in her losing her confidence and self-esteem. We looked at the driving and we discussed anxiety management principles and what anxiety was and wasn't (detailed discussion on anxiety in next chapter). Following these discussions she managed to quickly understand the principles and after 3-4 months and 8 sessions she was driving on the dual carriageways and was coping much better. A follow-up revealed that all was fine and some of these principles had generalised into her everyday life.

As with most clients/patients I will leave an "open door" policy where appropriate so that if they need a "top up" session or some clarification they can contact me and we can arrange this. Interestingly some 18 months later I was contacted by the woman and we met for an update to which she informed me that she and her husband had separated and she was quite happy (so were the children) despite the obvious "fallout". She was continuing to drive on the carriageways and all was going well. However, she had been asked out by a nice gentleman she had known and this was causing her concern. When I asked what concern, she responded by saying, *"what does he see in me"* and *"what is he after"*. I mention this aspect as it never ceases to amaze me how damaging it can be if someone is exposed to persistent criticism over a period of time. Here was a woman who presented well in all areas and was generally a very decent individual. Her confidence in herself however was minimal to say the least. She described the gentleman in detail and again he appeared a rather genuine chap. I am not going to go into great detail into the above case as previously mentioned, however I will say that eventually this woman ended up living with the gentleman and they decided to pool their resources and move forward. Slowly but gradually she began to see herself for the person she really was and this was probably the best therapy at the end of the day. She had overcome her negative "inner voice" that had tricked her for many years and was now living a more content and fulfilling life.

To try to illustrate some of the thought patterns of low self-esteem I have outlined a number of statements below that this woman talked about during our discussions. Whilst some of these may seem a little trivial for this woman (and many others I'm sure) they were very real and created a great deal of anxiety that further reinforced her low self-esteem and lack of confidence.

Thought Patterns & Low Self-Esteem & More Rational Responses

The familiar Inner Critic's Voice:	The new found voice of reason and change:
Is Unfairly Harsh: I can't even drive on a dual carriageway – I am pretty pathetic. I probably shouldn't even be driving.	**Be Reassuring:** Ok maybe it's just that I'm not confident rather than being a bad driver – I've never had an accident and maybe I'm a little too critical of myself.
Generalizes Unrealistically: I'm always in a fluster when we have guests around – I can never get anything right and I always let my husband down – I would prefer not to have anyone round as it is beginning to make me nervous and on edge.	**Be Specific:** I am actually quite a good cook and I always prepare everything very well – Ok maybe sometimes things don't go according to plan but it doesn't seem to bother anyone – In fact things always seem to go according to plan. Maybe I just need to relax and enjoy the process.

Makes Leaps of Illogic:	Challenge Illogic:
"He is frowning. He didn't say anything, but I know it means that I've done something wrong and he's annoyed with me. I can never get anything right with him. I feel so useless	"O.K. – so now I'm a mind reader – Yes, he appears to be frowning but I don't know why and I haven't done anything wrong or untoward that I am aware of – So why am I acting like a guilty person. It's his frown and he can own it.
Catastrophizes:	**Be Objective:**
I was late for work this morning and I feel embarrassed and inadequate. What are they going to think – they will think I am incompetent and not very considerate – they probably think I'm not good at my job? I probably shouldn't be working at my age anyway. Oh god I can't remember things.	How often am I late? – Never – What do these people think of me – I actually think they like me and are quite fond of me. I have been here 6 years and no one has ever criticised me – except for myself of course – maybe I need to stop doing that – I'll apologise for being late and then move on as I am sure it will be fine

As previously stated (about 100 times so far) it is difficult to do justice to the therapeutic process when describing a case. Hopefully from the above example readers will be able to grasp the "gist" of what is trying to be conveyed. To reiterate, we must never underestimate the impact of low self-esteem on an individual. No matter how successful they are or may appear, deep within is a black voice constantly telling them how useless and worthless they are no matter what the actual evidence suggests.

Some strategies for developing and building self-esteem

- Be aware of the *"black voice"* of doubt and negativity. Learn to understand it and where it has come from. Learn to challenge it and develop the *"real voice"* which is the real <u>you.</u> This voice is nothing special it just allows you to be more rational and balanced in your self-appraisal and the appraisal of those around you. It will take time and patience. Make notes and write down your thoughts after a particular event. Get used to balancing your thinking and not just looking at one possible reason.

- Set achievable goals. (Such an easy thing to say, and so hard to do!) Establish goals on the basis of what you can realistically hope to achieve, and then work step-by-step developing your potential. Do not strive for perfectionism or to be the best.

- Develop the habit of testing your reality. Learn to separate your emotional reactions – all your habitual fears and bad feelings -- from the reality of your current situation. For example, you may be feeling anxious and hopeless about a project that is facing you and appears to be impossible, but if you think about it rationally, you may still have the ability and opportunity to accomplish something and benefit from the experience, even if it is only the knowledge that in the future you have to plan your time better! This applies to any situation in life.

- Create opportunities that will enable you to experience success or at least be able to test out your strategies for living. Probably a better test than success is how you cope when something goes wrong. So what! Everyone gets it wrong on times. Be willing to take chances. All new experiences are potential learning experiences that may help build self-confidence. Expect to make mistakes as part of the learning process. Don't be disappointed if you do not master a new task immediately. Don't be disappointed if you don't do it perfectly right from the start.

- Accept the fact that you have problems in your life. Don't try to constantly avoid your problems, but also don't spend all your time moping over them. Try to identify them, face them, and then find ways either to solve them or cope with living with them. If necessary, seek professional help or the help of loved ones. But remember, if you continually run away from problems you can solve, you seriously threaten your self-confidence and they will catch up with you eventually.

- Get in the habit of making decisions. It is a scary concept at first, but you can do it! Work at practicing making and implementing positive decisions flexibly but firmly, and trust yourself to deal with the consequences. When you assert yourself, you enhance your sense of self, you learn more about yourself, and you increase your self-confidence.

- Learn to rely on your own opinion of yourself. It is good to entertain feedback from others, but don't become totally dependent on their opinions. Trust in your own values when making decisions and deciding how you feel about yourself and what is right for you to do. No one, but no one, knows you as well as you do. And remember what Eleanor Roosevelt said:

"No one can make you feel inferior without your consent

Never give it."

Conclusion

Put simply, your self-esteem is how well you think about yourself compared to other people, such as friends, workmates and even strangers. Low self-esteem means that you think you are a lesser person than others. It can often be traced back to early childhood experiences, such as heavy criticism, being abandoned, and feeling unloved, or being ridiculed or abused. It can also develop in adulthood following certain experiences and in particular if we are exposed to excessive and persistent criticism over a long period of time. It can of course also be a symptom of depression. Short-term cognitive therapy is very helpful for most people. It allows someone to clear out the "cobwebs" and release their inhibitions step by step. Raising self-esteem allows them to feel better about themselves and recognise their good qualities. Their relationships improve, and their overall well-being is greatly enhanced.

4 – Personality factors in Depression

No discussion about depression would be complete without at least a mention of clients/patients who present with personality disorders or personality problems. With this in mind the following is meant to inform readers of some of the likely traits and variables involved when working with personality difficulties and also some of the therapeutic techniques for treating personality difficulties. In particular there will be a look at some of the cognitive variables involved in the treatment process and also a brief look at a treatment known as *Dialectical Behaviour Therapy* or DBT for short. Whilst the following is intended to inform readers, working in this area should ideally require additional training although the basic components for working with mild-moderate personality difficulties should be relatively easy to grasp to the informed and experienced therapist.

Whilst there remains great controversy and debate surrounding the very term "personality disorders" and the "labelling" of such difficulties I feel it is essential for all practicing therapists and clinicians to have some concept of what is meant by personality disorder/difficulty. I would actually go as far as to say that it would be naïve and to a large extent unprofessional for a therapist or clinician not to have at least a basic knowledge of what types of difficulty are likely to present when someone has a personality problem (maybe problem is more politically correct than disorder but it really depends on the range of difficulty being presented). I feel this point is reinforced through clinical experience and in particular where I have witnessed well-meant therapists and counsellors *per se* "treat" someone with a personality difficulty over very long periods of time. For example, a colleague of mine was referred someone who had been seeing a person-centred Counsellor for 2 ½ years, mostly for 2 appointments a week in a different part of the country. When the client moved to our area my colleagues' initial assessment revealed that there were personality issues involved in the process and the client actually agreed with them and a more proactive and collaborative form of treatment took place. In all 12 sessions occurred over a 9-month period that included 2 follow-up sessions. The outcomes in this context were favourable largely as a result of the insight and honesty arriving from the assessment itself. The key here is that both therapist and client arrived at what they both agreed would be realistic outcomes. This is a term that has particular resonance for me as I feel for most therapists and clinicians alike there is an innate desire to want to "help" someone who is experiencing difficulties in their life and on occasion we all need to be realistic about what can be achieved in certain cases. This will be elaborated on further in the book when we look at some of the options available to us when therapy does not work. In the context of the present discussion personality problems discussed here are in relation to those that are largely mild or moderate as opposed to working with severe personality disorders. This should ensure that at the very least the reader becomes more informed with regard to some of the complexities that can occur when working with this client/patient population.

Borderline Personality Disorder

When we are referring to personality problems and depression we are generally referring to Borderline Personality Disorder as defined by the DSM IV.

DSM-IV criteria

The DSM-IV gives the following nine criteria and a full diagnosis requires that the subject presents with at least five of these. Quite frequently people with BPD have a very hard time controlling their emotions and they may often feel ruled by them.

Traits involving emotions:

1. Shifts in mood lasting only a few hours.
2. Anger that is inappropriate, intense or uncontrollable.

Traits involving behaviour:

3. Self-destructive acts, such as self-mutilation or suicidal threats and gestures that happen more than once
4. Two potentially self-damaging impulsive behaviours. These could include alcohol and other drug abuse, compulsive spending, gambling, eating disorders, shoplifting, reckless driving, compulsive sexual behaviour.

Traits involving identity:

5. Marked, persistent identity disturbance shown by uncertainty in at least two areas. These areas can include self-image, sexual orientation, career choice or other long-term goals, friendships, values. People with BPD may not feel like they know who they are, or what they think, or what their opinions are. Instead they may try to be what they think other people want them to be.

6. Chronic feelings of emptiness or boredom.

Traits involving relationships

7. Unstable, chaotic intense relationships often characterized by splitting.
8. Frantic efforts to avoid real or imagined abandonment.

- Splitting: the self and others are viewed as "all good" or "all bad." One phrase that has appeared from someone with BPD is, *"One day I would think my therapist was the best and I loved her, but if she challenged me in any way I hated her"*. There tends to be no or little middle ground where BPD is concerned. Alternating clinging and distancing behaviours (I Hate You, Don't Leave Me).
- Great difficulty trusting people and themselves. Early trust may have been shattered by people who were close to them.
- Extreme sensitivity to criticism or rejection.
- Feeling of "needing" someone else to survive
- Heavy need for affection and reassurance

9. Transient, stress-related paranoid ideation or severe dissociative symptoms

Miscellaneous attributes of people with BPD:

- People with BPD are often bright, witty, funny, life of the party.
- They may have problems with object constancy. When a person leaves (even temporarily), they may have a problem recreating or remembering feelings of love that were present between themselves and the other. Often, BPD patients want to keep something belonging to the loved one around during separations.
- They frequently have difficulty tolerating aloneness, even for short periods of time.
- Their lives may be a chaotic landscape of job losses, interrupted educational pursuits, broken engagements, and hospitalisations.
- Many have a background of childhood physical, sexual, or emotional abuse or physical/emotional neglect.

As one can imagine working with even mild to moderate BPD can be a challenge and keeping realistic goals as well as having an awareness of what can be achieved is essential throughout the whole process. In general BPD is characterized by a pervasive instability in moods, interpersonal relationships, self-image, and behaviour. This instability often disrupts family and work life, long-term planning, and the individual's sense of self-identity. Originally thought to be at the "borderline" of psychosis, people with BPD suffer from a disorder of <u>emotion regulation.</u> BPD is relatively common with 2% of adults, mostly young women experiencing these types of difficulties. There is a high rate of self-harm without suicide intent, as well as a significant rate of suicide attempts and completed suicide in severe cases. Despite the bleak picture, with the appropriate help many (not all) can improve their overall functioning over time and are eventually able to lead more productive lives.

Symptoms

While a person with depression typically endures the same mood for weeks, months and even years, a person with BPD may experience intense bouts of anger, depression and anxiety that may last only hours, or at most a day. These may be associated with episodes of impulsive aggression, self-injury, and drug or alcohol abuse. Distortions in cognition and sense of self can lead to frequent changes in long-term goals, career plans, jobs, friendships, gender identity, and values. Sometimes people with BPD view themselves as fundamentally bad, or unworthy. They may feel unfairly misunderstood or mistreated, bored, empty, and have little idea who they are. Such symptoms are most acute when people with BPD feel isolated and lacking in social support, and may result in frantic efforts to avoid being alone. Indeed, people with BPD often have highly unstable patterns of social relationships. While they can develop intense but stormy attachments, their attitudes towards family, friends, and loved ones may suddenly shift from idealization (great admiration and love) to devaluation (intense anger and dislike). Thus, they may form an immediate attachment and idealize the other person, but when a slight separation or conflict occurs, they switch unexpectedly to the other extreme and angrily accuse the other person of not caring for them at all. Even with family members, individuals with BPD are highly sensitive to rejection, reacting with anger and distress to such mild separations as a vacation, a business trip, or a sudden change in plans. These fears of abandonment often seem to be related to difficulties about feeling emotionally connected to important persons when they are physically absent and this often leaves the individual with BPD feeling lost and increasingly insecure.

Cognitive Therapy & BPD

As we have discussed in previous chapters, cognitive therapy largely focuses on transforming three types of cognitions, (i) automatic thoughts, (ii) underlying assumptions, and (iii) maladaptive schema, and on replacing unsuccessful compensatory strategies with effective life skills. For individuals with borderline personality disorder, the schema level of cognition is the most significant, because these patients usually have deeply held and encompassing beliefs that they are defective, unlovable, dependent and incompetent, and that the world they live in is hostile, untrustworthy, and emotionally depriving. These schemas are represented by words and images, that are likely to be stored and they will evoke extremely painful affective responses.

Such schema can produce significant challenges to the treatment process. For example, *"mistrust schema"* make it particularly difficult for patients to authentically engage and bond with the therapist and because of this, stages of therapy unfold more slowly for these patients. Demanding and challenging behaviour can also threaten the therapeutic alliance. However, empathic acknowledgment of these struggles as they occur in the session lays the groundwork for modifying each schema later in treatment.

The compensatory strategies over-learned in childhood to deal with trauma and overwhelming affect are typically used in a rigid fashion in current situations, often in ineffective and self-defeating ways. Examples include clinging, distancing, manipulation, hostility, aggression, avoidance, and demanding behaviour. More adaptive coping skills, such as self-soothing, which is an aspect of self-regulation and boundary setting, must be learned before the patient can relinquish this limited repertoire of compensatory strategies. Physically self-harming activities, however, must be limited, and alternative tension-reducing activities should be instated from the very beginning of treatment. Later in therapy, more sophisticated communication and problem-solving skills are taught, and continued rehearsal and therapeutic feedback and discussion can help patients incorporate these new skills. This of course is a classic cognitive therapy strategy. This skill training is presented as a way of expanding the patient's options so that incompetence schemas are not inadvertently activated and reinforced.

In the middle stage of therapy, a schema is actually restructured by a process of understanding the schema's genesis, beginning with the less traumatic aspects of childhood, and challenging the schema's appropriateness in current situations. These are typical of the cognitive therapeutic strategies that have been discussed in previous chapters. Patients learn first to identify the triggers that activate particular schema and the person from their past whose voice is echoed in the schema. The patient then learns to examine the veracity of the schema in light of more recent experiences (i.e., with new coping skills patients begin to have more self-esteem and more harmonious experiences with others). The therapist challenges the patient to discriminate "the then from the now" and to assign more adaptive meaning to today's experiences. Imagery, art, and other nonverbal modes of working are also used to modify schemas. As more severely traumatic memories emerge in treatment, the client/patient is taught to pace the work and to use the self-soothing skills learned earlier.

Main goals of therapy

- To help the client to recognise thinking patterns and how they develop and continue to govern much of the individuals life - Trigger-Thought-Feeling-Self talk Behaviours
- To engage the client to recognize and acknowledge negative validating feelings such as (isolation, fear, anger, etc.)
- To help the client acquire skills to recognize triggers for self-defeating thoughts and behaviours and how to de-fuse them.
- Encouraging self-care and self-soothing in positive adaptive ways. Raise awareness of rights and responsibilities or self-care.
- Developing effective interpersonal (non-defensive) communication in order to help develop and build relationships.
- Learning to think creatively to set goals and solve problems.
- Encouraging thoughts and behaviours that will enhance self-esteem, confidence and self-image.

As cognitions are transformed and skills are learned, patients experience a diminution of distressing affect. They come to know themselves (warts and all) and to be themselves as well as being able to appreciate themselves, making the somewhat arduous and challenging process of therapy rewarding for patients and therapists alike.

Dialectical Behaviour Therapy and BPD - (Linehan, M – 1993)

This novel and creative clinical technique for working with BPD was developed by Marsha Linehan at the University of Washington in Seattle and it has produced some favourable outcomes over the years. The following will cover some of the main tenets of this approach; however it is recommended that therapists attend additional training before proceeding with the use of DBT in their clinical practice.

Linehan acknowledges that clients/patients exhibiting features of Borderline Personality Disorder can be notoriously difficult to treat. They are difficult to keep in therapy, frequently fail to respond to therapeutic efforts and make considerable demands on the emotional resources of the therapist. Dialectical Behaviour Therapy or DBT however, is an innovative method that has been developed specifically to treat this difficult group of clients/patients in a way that is both optimistic and forward thinking.

DBT is based on a bio-psychosocial theory of borderline personality disorder and Linehan hypothesises that the disorder is a consequence of an emotionally vulnerable individual growing up within a particular set of environmental circumstances that she refers to as the 'Invalidating Environment'. An 'emotionally vulnerable' person in this sense is someone whose autonomic nervous system reacts excessively to relatively low levels of stress and takes longer than normal to return to baseline once the stress is removed. It is proposed that this is the consequence of a biological diathesis. The term 'Invalidating Environment' refers essentially to a situation in which the personal experiences and responses of the growing child are disqualified or "invalidated" by the significant others in his/her life. The child's personal communications are not accepted as an accurate indication of their true feelings and it is implied that, if they were accurate, then such feelings would not be a valid response to circumstances. Furthermore, an Invalidating Environment is characterised by a tendency to place a high value on self-control and self-reliance. Possible difficulties in these areas are not acknowledged and it is implied that problem solving should be easy given proper motivation. Any failure on the part of the child to perform to the expected standard is therefore ascribed to lack of motivation or some other negative characteristic of the clients' character.

Linehan suggests that an emotionally vulnerable child can be expected to experience particular problems in such an environment. She will neither have the opportunity accurately to label and understand her feelings nor will she learn to trust her own responses to events. Neither is she helped to cope with situations that she may find difficult or stressful, since such problems are not acknowledged. It may be expected then that she will look to other people for indications of how she should be feeling and to solve her problems for her. However, it is in the nature of such an environment that the demands that she is allowed to make on others will tend to be severely restricted. The child's behaviour may then oscillate between opposite poles of emotional inhibition in an attempt to gain acceptance and extreme displays of emotion in order to have her feelings acknowledged. Erratic response to this pattern of behaviour by those in the environment may then create a situation of intermittent reinforcement resulting in the behaviour pattern becoming persistent.

Linehan suggests that a particular consequence of this state of affairs will be a failure to understand and control emotions and a failure to learn the skills required for 'emotion modulation'. Given the emotional vulnerability of these individuals this is postulated to result in a state of *emotional dys-regulation* that combines in a transactional manner with the Invalidating Environment to produce the typical symptoms of Borderline Personality Disorder.

Dialectical Behaviour Therapy

The term 'dialectical' is derived from classical philosophy. It refers to a form of argument in which an assertion is first made about a particular issue (the 'thesis'), the opposing position is then formulated (the 'antithesis') and finally a 'synthesis' is sought between the two extremes, embodying the valuable features of each position and resolving any contradictions between the two. This synthesis then acts as the thesis for the next cycle. In this way truth is seen as a process that develops over time in transactions between people. From this perspective there can be no statement representing absolute truth. Truth is approached as the middle way between extremes. The dialectical approach to understanding and treatment of human problems is therefore non-dogmatic, open and has a systemic and transactional orientation. The dialectical viewpoint underlies the entire structure of therapy, the key dialectic being 'acceptance' on the one hand and 'change' on the other. Thus DBT includes specific techniques of acceptance and validation designed to counter the self-invalidation of the patient. These are balanced by techniques of problem solving to help him/her learn more adaptive ways of dealing with their difficulties and acquire the skills to do so. Dialectical strategies underlie all aspects of treatment to counter the extreme and rigid thinking encountered in these patients. The dialectical world-view is apparent in the three pairs of 'dialectical dilemmas' already described, in the goals of therapy and in the attitudes and communication styles of the therapist that are to be described. The therapy is largely behavioural in that, without ignoring the past, it focuses on present behaviour and the current factors that are controlling that behaviour.

Therapist-client relationship

Throughout DBT the success of the treatment is even more dependent on the quality of the relationship between the patient and therapist than previously discussed. The emphasis is on this being a "real" human relationship in which both members matter and in which the needs of both have to be considered. Linehan is particularly alert to the risks of burnout to therapists treating these patients and therapist support and consultation is an integral and essential part of the treatment. This approach is eminently more traditional psychotherapy than previous approaches, although in essence it is an attempt to synthesize the best of both worlds with a significant emphasis on the therapeutic alliance and its emotional components as well as an adherence to more "concrete" cognitive strategies.

Interestingly, Linehan has a particular dislike for the word "manipulative" as commonly applied to clients suffering with BPD. She makes a very perceptive statement when she points out that: *"Being manipulative implies that they are skilled and as such have control at managing other people when it is precisely the opposite that is true"*. Also the fact that the therapist may feel manipulated does not necessarily imply that this was the intention of the patient. It is more probable that the patient did not have the skills to deal with the situation more effectively. The therapist relates to the patient in two dialectically opposed styles. The primary style of relationship and communication is referred to as 'reciprocal communication', a style involving responsiveness, warmth and genuineness on the part of the therapist. Appropriate self-disclosure is encouraged but always with the interests of the patient in mind. The alternative style is referred to as 'irreverent communication'. This is a more confrontational and challenging style aimed at bringing the patient up with a jolt in order to deal with situations where therapy seems to be stuck or moving in an unhelpful direction. It will be observed that these two communication styles form the opposite ends of another dialectic and therefore should be used in a balanced way as therapy proceeds. The therapist should try to interact with the patient in a way that is:

- Accepting of the patient as he/she is but which encourages change.
- Centred and firm yet flexible when the circumstances require it.
- Nurturing but benevolently demanding.

There is a clear and open emphasis on the limits of behaviour acceptable to the therapist and these are dealt with in a very direct way. The therapist should be clear about his or her personal limits in relation to a particular patient and should as far as possible make these clear to the client from the start. It is openly acknowledged that an unconditional relationship between therapist and patient is not possible and there is always potential for the patient to cause the therapist to reject her if she tries hard enough. It is in the patient's interests therefore to learn to treat her therapist in a way that encourages the therapist to want to continue helping her. It is not in her interests to burn him or her out. This issue is confronted directly and openly in therapy. The therapist helps therapy to survive by consistently bringing it to the patient's attention when limits have been overstepped and then teaching her the skills to deal with the situation more effectively and acceptably. It is made quite clear that the issue is immediately concerned with the legitimate needs of the therapist and only indirectly with the needs of the patient who clearly stands to lose if he/she manages to burn out the therapist. The therapist is asked to adopt a non-defensive posture towards the patient, to accept that therapists are fallible and that mistakes will at times inevitably be made. The honesty and pragmatism engendered in this approach is commendable and I feel it epitomises my early approach in which I referred to the term, *"rational compassion"*.

Throughout DBT there are four modules focusing in turn on four groups of skills:

1. Core mindfulness skills.
2. Interpersonal effectiveness skills.
3. Emotion modulation skills.
4. Distress tolerance skills.

The 'core mindfulness skills' are essentially psychological techniques to enable clients to become more clearly aware of the contents of experience and to develop the ability to stay with that experience in the present moment.

The 'interpersonal effectiveness skills' focus on effective ways of achieving one's objectives with other people: to ask for what one wants effectively, to say no and have it taken seriously, to maintain relationships and to maintain self-esteem in interactions with other people.

'Emotion modulation skills' are ways of changing distressing emotional states and 'Distress tolerance skills' include techniques for putting up with these emotional states if they cannot be changed for the time being.

Stages of therapy and treatment targets

The course of therapy over time is organised into a number of stages and structured in terms of hierarchies of targets at each stage.

PRE-TREATMENT STAGE: focus on assessment, commitment and orientation to therapy.

STAGE 1:

Focus on suicidal or self-harming behaviours, therapy interfering behaviours and behaviours that interfere with the quality of life, together with developing the necessary skills to resolve these problems.

STAGE 2:

More concerned with post-traumatic stress related problems (PTSD).

STAGE 3:

Main concern is with self-esteem and individual treatment goals.

The targeted behaviours of each stage are brought under control before moving on to the next phase. In particular post-traumatic stress related problems such as those related to childhood sexual abuse are not dealt with directly until stage 1 has been successfully completed. To do so would risk an increase in serious self-injury. Therapy at each stage is focused on the specific targets for that stage that are arranged in a definite hierarchy of relative importance. The hierarchy of targets varies between the different modes of therapy but it is essential for therapists working in each mode to be clear what the targets are. An overall goal in every mode of therapy is to increase dialectical thinking.

The hierarchy of targets in individual therapy for example are as follows:

1. Decreasing self-harm behaviours.
2. Decreasing therapy interfering behaviours.
3. Decreasing behaviours that interfere with the quality of life.
4. Increasing behavioural skills.
5. Decreasing behaviours related to post-traumatic stress.
6. Improving self-esteem.

7.   Individual targets negotiated with the patient.

The importance given to 'therapy interfering behaviours' is a particular characteristic of DBT and reflects the difficulty of working with these clients/patients. It is second only to suicidal behaviours in importance. These are any behaviour by the patient or therapist that interfere in any way with the proper conduct of therapy and risk preventing the patient from getting the help they need. They include, for example, failure to attend sessions reliably, failure to keep to contracted agreements, or behaviours that overstep therapist limits (should really be fundamental to most therapeutic approaches).

The patient is required to record instances of targeted behaviours and failure to do so is regarded as therapy interfering behaviour as they are failing to engage in the process itself and this will be an area of discussion in a one-to-one session.

Treatment strategies:

The core strategies in DBT are 'validation' and 'problem solving'. Attempts to facilitate change are surrounded by interventions that validate the patient's behaviour and responses as understandable in relation to their current life situation. Change is further facilitated by illustrating an empathic understanding of their difficulties and suffering.

Problem solving focuses on the establishment of necessary skills. If the client/patient is not dealing with their problems effectively then it is to be anticipated either that they do not have the necessary skills to do so, or does have the skills but is prevented from using them. If they do not have the skills then they will need to learn or re-learn them. This is the purpose of the skills training. Having the skills, they may be prevented from using them in particular situations either because of environmental factors or because of emotional or cognitive problems getting in the way. To deal with these difficulties the following techniques may be applied in the course of therapy:

1.   Contingency management
2.   Cognitive therapy
3.   Exposure based therapies
4.   Pharmacotherapy

Conclusion

Again it is impossible to do justice to the full DBT approach devised by Linehan; however the above should provide enough information for the reader to understand the basic components of DBT and to consider whether they would want to attend further training in this approach. At the very least I feel the above provides a useful framework from which to further develop ones' own therapeutic repertoire as there are components from DBT that are easily transferable to other therapeutic approaches. Indeed, some of the strategies outlined above are likely to compliment and add to the effectiveness of some other therapeutic approaches. The client-patient relationship factor is interesting and one can see that there is an increased potential for transference and counter-transference issues. However, there is a frankness and honesty about the model that is encouraging. DBT is however, specifically designed to meet the needs of patients with Borderline Personality Disorder. It directly addresses the problem of keeping these clients/patients in therapy and is based on a clear theory that encourages a positive and validating attitude to these clients/patients. To this extent it provides structure and hope for problems that have been resistant to more traditional psychotherapeutic approaches.

Part 4: Anxiety

1 – What is anxiety?

Everybody feels anxious from time to time; indeed anxiety is probably the most basic of all emotions and is generally a "normal" human response to a stressful situation. Anxiety is not only experienced by all humans, but anxiety responses have also been found in all species of animal right down to the "lowly" sea slug. Individual experiences of anxiety vary tremendously in their severity from relatively mild uneasiness to extreme terror and panic. Episodes can also vary considerably in their length from a brief, almost fleeting "flash", to a constant and persistent episode. While anxiety by its nature and definition is often a frightening and extremely unpleasant experience, anxiety *per se* and the unpleasant feelings associated with anxiety pose little danger to the individual and indeed no actual harm will arise as a result of the anxiety itself. In general, anxiety is a feeling of intense psychological and physiological unease. Most people will experience this type of anxiety when faced with stressful situations, for example before an important exam, a driving test or an interview. Whilst it remains relatively normal to feel anxious when facing something difficult or dangerous the same cannot be said for 10% of the population in the UK. Indeed, it is estimated that for up to one in ten people in the UK, anxiety becomes a frightening and dreaded experience that can impair everyday functioning to the point where it can leave an individual "frozen" with terror and fear even though as mentioned above, there is little actual harm that is likely to occur. Whilst excessive anxiety is occasionally associated with other psychological conditions, such as depression, it is often just the anxiety itself that can stand-alone and cause insurmountable problems for an individual.

The aim of the following chapter is to help the reader become more familiar with the physical, mental (psychological) and behavioural components of anxiety. A thorough understanding of all these components will help clinicians and therapists alike understand what is happening to the client during such an episode of anxiety and this should go some way to alleviating what in essence remains an "irrational" fear for many sufferers.

The *"Fight or Flight"* Response

In general we experience anxiety in response to some kind of danger or threat. In clinical terms, the response to immediate or short-term anxiety has come to be known as the *"fight or flight response"* and most readers are likely to be familiar with this. It is so named because all of its effects are aimed toward "engineering" the individual to prepare for either "fighting" or "fleeing" the danger. Thus, the number one purpose for anxiety is to actually protect the organism. This is an evolutionary mechanism that has evolved over many hundreds of years. When for example, our ancestors lived in caves, it was essential that when faced with some danger, an automatic response would occur which alerted the individual to take immediate and evasive action, either attack or run. Even in today's hectic world this is a vital mechanism that serves an essential survival function. Just imagine you were crossing a street when a car blasting its horn came speeding towards you. If you experienced no anxiety then the chances are that you would be knocked over and possibly killed. However, more probably your *fight or flight* response would "kick in" and you would be more likely to run and jump out of the way. There are a thousand and one other examples that you can think of where the evolutionary alarm clock if you like goes off and alerts us to danger. The underlying message here however is that the fight or flight response associated with anxiety is there to protect the organism, not to harm it. Indeed, when you think about it, it would be rather perverse and self-defeating for nature to develop a mechanism whose purpose is to protect an organism and yet, in doing so, harms it.

Anxiety generally manifests itself through three systems that remain inextricably linked, often feeding and reinforcing each other. It is important to elaborate and identify each system since each one is capable of being the primary component in any individual person. The three systems are:

- The Physical System – this includes all the physical symptoms such as dizziness, sweating, palpitations, chest pain and breathlessness.
- The Behavioural System – this includes the actual activities such as pacing, foot tapping and general avoidance.
- The Mental System – this includes the actual feelings of nervousness, anxiety and panic and also includes thoughts (usually negative) such as *"there's something wrong"*, and/or *"I'm going to die"*.

During anxiety attacks, the physiology and "mechanics" of the anxiety become the most prevailing factors as they cause the individual to panic further and many individuals' will often assume that these feelings are a consequence of some serious illness and/or disease. A useful initial strategy when describing these systems is to get a client/patient to think of the unpleasant feelings purely in mechanical terms and to reassure clients that this is natures response to coping with adversity. An essential part of psycho-education with the client is the fact that it has as one of its tenets a belief that knowledge is power. Therefore, if an individual can begin to grasp the mechanics of anxiety then he or she is likely to be less fearful to begin with, even though they are still likely to experience the uncomfortable symptoms initially. The knowledge aspect can allow the individual to recognise that despite the intensity and discomfort that arises as a result of anxiety, all these symptoms are actually aimed at getting the organism prepared for immediate action and therefore their purpose is again to actually protect the organism. Going over this time and time again in a relaxed and reassuring manner and having the client/patient *test* this out in everyday life can greatly help the individual to manage their anxiety far better until they eventually develop more specific strategies for dealing with the original anxiety itself. These coping strategies will be discussed further when we look at treating anxiety. This process of psycho-education however, remains a fundamental and key component of good therapy in practice and we shall take a closer look at each of these components.

The Physical System

1 – Nervous and Chemical Effects:
When some sort of danger is perceived or anticipated, the brain will send messages to a section of our nerves called the autonomic nervous system. The autonomic nervous system has two sub-sections or branches called the sympathetic nervous system and the parasympathetic nervous system. It is these two branches of the nervous system that are directly involved in controlling the body's energy levels and preparation for action. Very simply put, the sympathetic nervous system is the *fight or flight* system described earlier which releases energy and gets the body "primed" for action while the parasympathetic nervous system is the system which returns the body to a normal more relaxed state.

One important point to remember is that the sympathetic nervous system tends to be largely an *all or nothing system.* In essence, when it is activated, all of its parts respond and therefore either all symptoms are experienced or no symptoms are experienced at all. It is therefore, rare and extremely unlikely for changes to occur in one part of the body alone and this may help to explain why most panic attacks involve many symptoms and not just one or two.

One of the major effects of the sympathetic nervous system is that it releases two chemicals called adrenalin and noradrenalin from the adrenal glands on the kidneys. These chemicals in turn, are used as messengers by the sympathetic nervous system to continue activity so that once activity in the sympathetic nervous system begins, it often continues and increases for some time. However, for clinicians it is very important to be aware that sympathetic nervous system activity is stopped in two ways. Firstly, the chemical messengers' adrenalin and noradrenalin are eventually destroyed by other chemicals in the body. Secondly, the parasympathetic nervous system (which generally as opposing effects to the sympathetic nervous system) becomes activated and eventually serves to restore a more relaxed feeling. It is very important to realise that the body will eventually have enough of the *fight or flight* response and will activate the parasympathetic nervous system to restore a relaxed feeling. In other words anxiety cannot continue forever unabated, nor can it ever spiral to ever increasing and possibly damaging levels. The parasympathetic nervous system is a built-in counter mechanism that stops the sympathetic nervous system from getting carried away. Another important point is that the chemical messengers, adrenalin and noradrenalin take some time to be destroyed. Thus even after the danger has passed and a person's sympathetic nervous system has stopped responding, an individual is likely to be keyed up and/or apprehensive for some time because the chemicals are still floating around within the individuals system. Again, it is important to remind clients and patients that this is perfectly natural and harmless. In fact, this is actually an adaptive function because, in the wilds so to speak danger often has a habit of returning and it is useful for the organism to be prepared to activate the *fight or flight* response.

2 – Cardiovascular Effects:
Activity in the sympathetic nervous system produces an increase in heart rate and the strength of the heartbeat. This is vital to prepare for activity since it helps speed up the blood flow, thus improving delivery of oxygen to the tissues and removal of waste products from the tissues. In addition to increased activity in the heart, there is also a change in the blood flow. Put simply, blood is redirected away from the places where it is not needed (by tightening the blood vessels) and toward the places where it is needed more (by an expansion of the blood vessels). When you think about it, nature is rather clever and our "systems" *per se* are set up and act in a manner that protects us. For example, blood in this instance is directed away from the skin, fingers and toes which is useful because if the organism is attacked and cut in some way, it is less likely to bleed profusely which may in itself lead to death. Hence, anxiety causes the skin to look pale and feel cold, the fingers and toes become cold and sometimes people may experience numbness and tingling. In addition, the blood is moved to the large muscles such as the thighs and biceps, which help the body to prepare for action.

3 – Respiratory Effects
The *fight or flight* response is associated with an increase in speed and depth of breathing. This has obvious importance for the defence of the organism since the tissues need to get more oxygen in order to prepare for action. The feelings produced by this increase in breathing however, can include breathlessness, choking or smothering feelings such as tightness in the chest as well as pains in the chest. Importantly, a side-effect of increased breathing, especially if no actual activity occurs, is that blood supply to the head is actually decreased. While this is only a small amount and not at all dangerous, it produces a myriad of unpleasant (yet harmless) symptoms including dizziness, blurred vision, confusion, unreality, and hot flushes.

4 – Sweat Gland Effects:
Activation of the *fight or flight* response produces an increase in sweating. This has important adaptive functions such as making the skin more slippery so that it is harder for a predator to grab, and cooling the body to stop it from overheating.

5 – Other physical Effects:
A number of other physical effects are produced by activation of the sympathetic nervous system, none of which is in any way harmful. For example, the pupils widen to let in more light, which may result in blurred vision and spots in front of the eyes. There is a decrease in salivation resulting in dry mouth and there is also a decreased activity within the digestive system. This often produces nausea, a heavy feeling in the stomach and even constipation. Finally, many of the muscle groups tense up in preparation for fight or flight and this often results in subjective feelings of tension, sometimes extending to actual aches and pains as well as trembling and shaking. Overall the *fight or flight* response results in general activation of the metabolism throughout the entire body. Thus one often feels hot and flushed and, because this process takes a lot of energy, a person will naturally feel tired, drained and washed out. It is therefore quite easy to see why an episode of anxiety can be an exhausting experience.

Explaining the above reactions to a client/patient can help them to understand what is happening to them and for some people this may actually be enough as they may have been reassured by what the clinician has explained and their symptoms can be easily corrected with some slower shallower breathing. As we have stated a number of times, no actual harm is likely to occur as a direct consequence of the anxiety itself, yet as we all know too well the symptoms themselves are among the worst that a person can experience and can be extremely distressing and debilitating.

The Behavioural System

As outlined above, the *"fight or flight"* response prepares the body for action, either to attack or to run. Thus, it is no surprise that the overwhelming urges associated with this response are aggression and a desire to escape from wherever you are. When this is not possible (due to social or physical constraints, e.g. at an important meeting, a supermarket or on a plane), the urges will often show through such behaviours as foot tapping, pacing, fidgeting and perhaps "snapping" at people. Overall, feelings of being trapped and needing to escape are produced. In everyday clinical practice I have witnessed people go to all manner of extremes to avoid situations. Sadly, most of these situations would be enjoyable activities such as eating out with friends, going to the cinema or attending a wedding. Interestingly, there always remains a part of them that would love to go, however the anxiety over-rides all rational thought and unfortunately avoidance is the *"safest"* way out and the preferred option at the time. Once this decision to avoid is made it is usually replaced with a huge sense of *relief* initially as the individuals fear is over and they do not have to attend the feared situation. Unfortunately this relief *per se* is quickly replaced with a sense of guilt and failure as the individual comes to terms with the fact that they have avoided yet again and have thus failed to overcome their irrational fears.

The Mental System

The number one effect of the *fight or flight* response is to alert the organism to the possible existence of danger. Thus one of the major effects is an immediate and automatic shift in attention to search the surroundings for potential threat. It therefore, becomes very difficult for people to concentrate on everyday tasks when they are experiencing anxiety. To this extent, people who are anxious often complain that they are easily distracted from everyday activities and they appear unable to concentrate on relatively simple things such as reading the newspaper or making a cup of tea. Most complain of what appear to be significant problems with their memory and particularly their short-term memory. Indeed, I have seen many patients suffering with anxiety who are convinced that they are in the process of some long-term degenerative process, as their short-term memory appears to be failing significantly. They will find themselves going upstairs in the house only to forget what they went up for, they will put the milk in the pantry instead of the fridge and similarly they will forget minor things that cause considerable concern which inevitably exacerbates the anxiety further. When someone is experiencing anxiety some of the most basic yet vital cognitive processes such as *attention, concentration* and *perception* are temporarily affected. All of these factors are essential primary processes for our short-term memory. For example, if we cannot perceive, attend and concentrate on something then we are extremely unlikely to remember it. Therefore, what the individual with anxiety is actually experiencing is a *functional* memory difficulty rather than an *organic* one such as Alzheimer's disease or some other degenerative problem. Again, this can be extremely reassuring for the client/patient and is one of the most common concerns presented in primary care and beyond. Indeed, many of those who are over 50 years of age are only too willing to put their anxiety difficulty down to their age and I am always quick to correct this where appropriate. The attention and concentration problems are actually normal under the circumstances and they are an extremely important part of the *fight or flight* response since its purpose is to stop the individual from attending to ongoing peripheral chores and tasks in order to permit the person to scan their surroundings for possible danger.

Often there is no obvious threat to the individual and this in itself can produce further difficulties that may serve to maintain the anxiety. For example many individuals cannot accept having no "real" explanation for such distressing symptoms. Therefore, in many cases, when people cannot find an explanation for their sensations, they turn their search onto themselves. This results in an irrational barrage of self-statements that again only serve to exacerbate the anxiety. For example, *"I must be dying, losing control, and/or there must be something seriously wrong with me"*. As we have seen however, nothing could actually be further from the truth with regard to these statements since the purpose of the *fight or flight* response is to protect the organism not harm it. Nevertheless, these are understandable thoughts under such difficult circumstances and it will be down to the interpersonal skill of the therapist and the clinical relationship itself to see how these explanations are managed and treated. If one has built a good trusting clinical relationship then the chances of success are greatly increased, particularly where there is a significant amount of anxiety.

Anxiety may manifest or present itself in obvious ways on times but there are occasions when its presentation is more complex. Therefore, an actual definition of anxiety that covers all aspects is very difficult to provide although many of us are somewhat familiar with the feeling that we call anxiety. What is less known however is that sensations such as extreme dizziness, blurring of the eyes, numbness and tingling, stiff almost paralysed muscles, feelings of breathlessness often extending to choking are all components that can be associated with anxiety. When these sensations occur and people do not understand why, then anxiety can increase to levels of extreme panic, especially when people and occasionally other health professionals may assume that they must have something more seriously wrong with them. An example of this occurred a number of years ago when I was rather urgently asked to see a woman in her 50s who was in the general hospital constantly retching and being sick. Her retching was continuous and the staff at the hospital were becoming increasingly concerned for her health and well-being. Without going into excessive detail in this case, the woman's choking and vomiting were revealed to be psychogenic or psychosomatic in nature and were a response to the extreme anxiety the woman was experiencing as a result of her domestic situation. When I talked to the woman about the possible cause of her problem she began to relax and talk openly about her difficulties. The anxiety and subsequent retching subsided and we discussed things further at a number of follow-up appointments. This may sound a bit simplistic when explained in this fashion however, the key here is that anxiety can have a number of different "faces" and the more a therapist understands about the mechanics and general make-up of anxiety, then the better prepared he or she will be when faced with the varying presentation of anxiety.

2 – Formal Definitions of Anxiety

Whilst anxiety has many varying presentations ranging from a relatively mild panic attack to a full-blown acute anxiety attack there are a number of formal categories that need to be understood in order to have a more complete picture of the anxiety "family". The following will outline a more comprehensive view of anxiety and will give the reader an idea of how it is formally categorised and defined in clinical practice. Whilst the word disorders shall be used to describe each category the therapist is more likely to see those at the milder end of the disorder spectrum, although not exclusively and this will of course depend on where one is practicing.

The anxiety disorders are a group of mental disturbances characterized by anxiety as a central or core symptom. Although anxiety is a commonplace experience, not everyone who experiences it has an anxiety disorder. Therefore, there will be individuals suffering with mild to moderate levels of anxiety. They may function reasonably well and hold a job down, however they may be suffering with the occasional panic attack and they are likely to be avoiding situations where they feel their anxiety is going to get worse. Anxiety is also associated with a wide range of physical illnesses, medication side effects, and other psychiatric disorders.

Anxiety is a normal emotion that people experience when facing uncertainty or danger and it is closely related to fear and nervousness. But fear is usually more specific than anxiety. I might be afraid to go to a party because I might meet so and so, while I might be anxious about going to the same party because I might not feel comfortable there. Nervousness is a physically unpleasant state, in which someone feels tense or shaky, and experiences trembling, rapid heartbeat and/or sweating. Anxiety usually has a number of components ranging from physical through to mental or cognitive (thought) and a physical and behavioural component that often leads to avoidance behaviour. When the anxiety becomes severe and/or prolonged, the affected person may be classed as suffering from an anxiety disorder.

There are a number of specific anxiety disorders and people with panic disorder for example, experience recurrent, unexpected panic attacks. These attacks are characterized by the abrupt onset of extreme fear, accompanied by such symptoms as rapid heart-beat, shortness of breath, trembling, shaking, the fear that one is about to die or lose emotional control, and a strong urge to flee. In people suffering from panic disorder, such panic attacks seem to come out of the blue, causing extreme fear of having another attack and great concern about one's health. Another complication of panic disorder is agoraphobia, in which people are afraid to travel far from home or go into confined places (trains, elevators, planes) for fear of having a panic attack and being unable to flee quickly or get help.

People with generalized anxiety disorder (GAD) do not experience a panic attack as their primary symptom. Rather, they chronically worry too much about a variety of things and experience symptoms such as restlessness, agitation, muscle tension, fatigue, irritability, and trouble with concentration and inevitably with sleep.

Social anxiety disorder is characterized by extreme fear and avoidance of social and/or performance situations. Some people have extreme discomfort when giving a speech, interviewing for a job, or performing in public, but are otherwise comfortable socially. When trying to perform, they get racing of the heart, sweating, trembling, blushing and a degree of mental confusion. These people are said to have non-generalized social anxiety disorder. In contrast, individuals with generalized social anxiety disorder experience extreme discomfort in many social as well as performance situations. Those with generalized social anxiety disorder are uncomfortable dating, talking to bosses or colleagues, going to parties and even chatting informally with co-workers. This is in addition to their fear and avoidance of performance-type situations.

Anyone who saw Jack Nicholson's movie "As Good As It Gets" will be familiar with obsessive-compulsive disorder (OCD). Throughout the film Nicholson presented as a man consumed with his OCD with particular fears associated with dirt, germs and contamination in general. Certain behaviours or thoughts may calm the fears temporarily but the anxiety followed by the ritualistic behaviour continues to dominate. A more extensive review of OCD is discussed later.

One of the most common clinical phenomena that has received a lot of attention over the past 2-3 decades is that of post-traumatic stress disorder (PTSD). Depending on the severity, this is potentially a very troubling condition that may follow unpleasant and severe emotional trauma. The trauma may be a single event such as a mugging or rape, a road traffic accident or a traumatic event experienced as a result of military combat, or childhood sexual or physical abuse. Affected individuals are left with a myriad of problems as they continue to psychologically re-experience the trauma. They lose interest in former pursuits and experience an emotional numbing. Many with PTSD become exceedingly jumpy, nervous and hyper-vigilant.

The revisions of the *Diagnostic and Statistical Manual of Mental Disorders (DSM)* that took place after 1980 brought major changes in the classification of the anxiety disorders. Prior to 1980, psychiatrists classified patients on the basis of a theory of causality that defined anxiety as the outcome of unconscious conflicts in the patient's mind. *DSM-III* (1980), *DSM-III-R* (1987), and *DSM-IV-R* (1994) introduced and refined a new classification that took into consideration recent discoveries about the biochemical and post-traumatic origins of some types of anxiety. The present definitions are therefore based on the external and reported symptom patterns of the disorders rather than on theories about their origins.

Anxiety disorders are the most common form of mental disturbance in the U K and anxiety difficulties remain a serious problem for individuals their families and society in general as a result of their interference with clients' work, schooling, and family life. Anxiety difficulties are an additional problem for health professionals because the physical symptoms of anxiety frequently bring people to primary care doctors and even accident and emergency rooms where individuals suffering with a severe anxiety attack are actually convinced that they are experiencing a heart attack. The formal definitions of anxiety are outlined below and this should provide a good baseline of information for therapists although most practitioners are more likely to be faced with individuals suffering with a milder form of each difficulty.

DSM-IV-R and Anxiety Disorders

DSM-IV-R defines twelve types of anxiety disorders in the adult population and these can be grouped under the following seven headings:

1 - Panic disorders with or without agoraphobia.

The chief characteristic of <u>panic disorder</u> is the occurrence of panic attacks coupled with fear of their recurrence. In clinical settings, agoraphobia is usually not a disorder by itself, but is typically associated with some form of panic disorder. Patients with agoraphobia are afraid of places or situations in which they might have a panic attack and be unable to leave or to find help. About

25% of patients with panic disorder develop <u>obsessive-compulsive disorder</u> (OCD).

2 - Phobias.

These include specific phobias and social phobia. A phobia is an intense irrational fear of a specific object or situation that compels the patient to avoid it. Some phobias concern activities or objects that involve some risk (for example, flying or driving) but many are focused on harmless animals or other objects. Social phobia involves a fear of being humiliated, judged, or scrutinized. It manifests itself as a fear of performing certain functions in the presence of others, such as public speaking.

3 - Obsessive-compulsive disorder (OCD).

This disorder is marked by unwanted, intrusive, persistent thoughts or repetitive behaviours that reflect the patient's anxiety or attempts to control it. It affects between 2-3% of the population and is much more common than was previously thought.

4 - Stress disorders.

These include post-traumatic stress disorder (PTSD) and acute stress disorder. Stress disorders are symptomatic reactions to traumatic events in the patient's life.

5 - Generalized anxiety disorder (GAD).

GAD is the most commonly diagnosed anxiety disorder and occurs most frequently in young adults.

6 - Anxiety disorders due to known physical causes.

These include general medical conditions or substance abuse.

7 - Anxiety disorder not otherwise specified.

This last category is not a separate type of disorder, but is included to cover symptoms that do not meet the specific DSM-IV-R criteria for other anxiety disorders.

All DSM-IV-R anxiety diagnoses include a criterion of severity and the anxiety must be severe enough to interfere significantly with the patient's occupational or educational functioning, social activities or close relationships, and other customary activities to be formally classed as a disorder. The anxiety disorders vary widely in their frequency of occurrence in the general population, age of onset, family patterns, and gender distribution. It is useful to note that the stress disorders and anxiety disorders caused by medical conditions or substance abuse are less age and gender-specific. Whereas OCD affects males and females equally, GAD, panic disorder, and specific phobias all affect women more frequently than men. GAD and panic disorders are more likely to develop in young adults, while phobias and OCD can begin in childhood. A number of the more common anxiety problems such as OCD and PTSD briefly outlined above will be discussed in more detail in the following chapter.

Anxiety disorders in children and adolescents

DSM-IV-R defines one anxiety disorder as specific to children, namely, separation anxiety disorder. This disorder is defined as anxiety regarding separation from home or family that is excessive or inappropriate for the child's age. In some children, separation anxiety takes the form of school avoidance. Probably the most common separation anxiety faced by children today occurs when parents separate and the child/children are inevitably going to live without one parent. Again there are numerous factors involved in the onset and development of this type of problem, although one of the most common causes can arise from an overbearing or "smothering" type of child-rearing from the primary care giver who themselves may be overly anxious.

What are the complications of an anxiety disorder?

Anxiety disorders have a number of complications. The first is suffering and reduced functioning. In the extreme, this can lead to complete disability in which an affected person can no longer go to school or hold a job. Depression is also a frequent complication, making the situation worse and heightening the risk for suicide. Substance abuse is also a frequent complication, particularly attempts at self-medication with sedatives or alcohol, and this may require primary or parallel treatment by a substance-abuse counsellor or treatment centre.

3 – Why do people suffer with anxiety?

There are of course numerous variables involved in the onset and maintenance of anxiety, however in general a combination of personality factors and life experiences will largely determine whether an individual will experience or indeed develop an anxiety disorder. In general psychologists tend to look at the differences within anxiety itself and the terms "stait" and "trait" anxiety have been used to differentiate between differing variables concerned with anxiety. In general, stait anxiety is concerned more with a particular situation and the associated anxiety that this may produce, hence it is a situational variable. Trait anxiety on the other hand is more related to an established personality factor that is far more endogenous. These components and their assessment will be discussed in more detail below. However, whether it is as a result of stait or trait anxiety everyone is capable of developing an anxiety disorder and I have witnessed numerous clients/patients who have gone on to say that they thought this type of thing would never happen to them. Naturally, whilst some individuals may appear to have a resilient emotional and psychological threshold, there are others who are perhaps a little more sensitive and anxious in nature and these individuals may be more prone to experiencing some kind of anxiety (more likely to be trait). With those generalisations acknowledged there are occasions when even the most emotionally robust individual may develop an anxiety difficulty, particularly if faced with extreme situations of danger and/or trauma and these issues and differentiations will be discussed in the following chapter when we look more closely at specific anxiety difficulties.

The odds of developing panic disorder, generalised anxiety disorder or obsessive- compulsive disorder however all seem to be greater if one of your parents or siblings has the condition. Naturally, this would suggest that some vulnerability is passed on in the genes, although it could also be modelled or taught in some way by affected parents and/or siblings. Therefore, to this extent it may be a form of learned behaviour. Even Post Traumatic Stress problems appear to require some vulnerability in most cases, since not everyone who experiences a particular trauma will go on to develop PTSD. This implies that there are personality factors or traits that will play some part in whether an individual will suffer with post-traumatic stress and/or to the degree and intensity they will suffer. We often refer to these factors as "individual differences" (self-explanatory really).

With regard to anxiety we are also aware that there is something about environmental *"triggers"* that can play a significant role in the onset of anxiety. Panic disorder for example often begins in a context of separation from loved ones and going off to college, for example, is a common precipitant. Hormonal instability may also be a trigger, and abnormal thyroid function is found in many newly diagnosed cases of panic disorder. Environmental stress may also be a trigger for *generalised anxiety disorder*. For example, loss of a job and trouble finding another or chronic health concerns about oneself or a close family member or friend etc. *Social anxiety disorder*, especially the generalized type, seems to be associated with a shy, anxious temperament as a child, but also with parental over-protectiveness, so that socially timid individuals either never learn to cope or have extreme difficulty learning to cope in the general sense. *Obsessive-compulsive disorder* may sometimes be triggered by strep infections, similar to what is found for rheumatic fever. Certain brain infections or injuries can also bring on the disorder. However, OCD is most common among individuals who appear to have anxious personalities, although individuals can develop OCD from a particular anxious episode in their lives. For Post-traumatic stress disorder to develop however, a severe trauma is required. Interestingly, a previous trauma, another anxiety disorder, or even having a family member with an anxiety disorder can significantly affect the severity of PTSD if one is unfortunate enough to experience a traumatic event.

There are numerous people who have problems with anxiety who appear to have a heightened sensitivity to the environment and react more strongly to the stimuli around them. In some people, there may exist what's called a "deficit in their stimulus barrier," in other words, noises, action, movement, smells and sights in their surroundings may be more difficult for them to "shut out" than it is for most people.

The overall causes of anxiety include a variety of individual and general social factors, and may produce physical, cognitive, emotional, and/or behavioural symptoms. The patient's ethnic or cultural background may also influence his or her vulnerability to certain forms of anxiety. Genetic factors that lead to biochemical abnormalities may also play a role. Social anxiety disorder and GAD appear most gradually, and affected adults often show milder symptoms in childhood and adolescence. It may be that as social or general responsibilities increase with age, the disorders become more manifest. OCD can begin in childhood, especially in boys, or adolescence, more often in girls. Panic disorder usually comes later; late teens or early to mid 20s is a common age of onset. In PTSD, the age of onset is understandably the most variable, since it is dependent on when a trauma is experienced.

Certain changes in brain chemistry and activity are associated with each anxiety disorder, although our knowledge about this is far from complete. Panic disorder for example appears to be associated with a lowered threshold for certain "alarm systems" in the brain. Again this is akin to a burglar alarm going off when the wind blows strongly and no one is actually breaking into the house. Often during clinical discussions with patients I will describe the *fight or flight* response as our "built in" alarm system that warns us or alerts us to danger. The problem for these clients/patients is that their "alarm system" has now become overly sensitive and now goes off when there is no real or actual danger. This is the exact parallel for many common anxiety and panic difficulties where the *fight or flight* response is triggered and it is a case of all systems go, whilst there is no actual emergency. The physiological response is automatic of course and it charges into action - this then sets up an anxiety provoking chain of events that become all encompassing and extremely distressing for the individual in question.

Interestingly, certain other conditions may produce symptoms that actually look like an anxiety state. For example, depression may be associated with nervousness, sleeplessness and social avoidance. Medical conditions like hyperthyroidism can produce nervousness, trembling, sweating and a rapid heart-beat. Excessive use of caffeine or other stimulants, or withdrawal from tranquillisers or alcohol, can produce symptoms that mimic an anxiety disorder. This is why experienced clinicians will check for these other conditions before diagnosing an anxiety problem.

4 – The CBT Model of Anxiety

The basic premise for the cognitive explanation of fear and anxiety is that people have erroneous beliefs or cognitions that lead to anxiety. For example, individuals who suffer from claustrophobia have an irrational fear of small or enclosed spaces. All of the anxiety states described earlier are actually based on erroneous beliefs, or a belief system that is not consistent with reality. Once the anxiety is set in motion however, each variable becomes inextricably linked to the next and they serve to reinforce each other thus helping to maintain and heighten the anxiety.

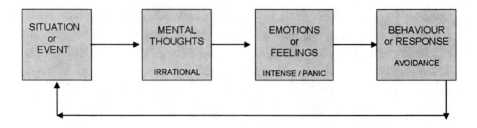

All factors remain inextricably linked often "feeding" each other and helping to maintain the overall state of anxiety

The two major questions that the cognitive explanation attempts to answer are firstly, how are these erroneous or "irrational" beliefs developed, and secondly, how are they maintained in the face of consistent contradictory evidence? Cognitive theorists currently believe that the erroneous beliefs that result in fear and anxiety states are produced as a result of an individual's earlier life experiences. These may be the result of one's actual experiences, the observation of other's life experiences, or even just hearing about a fearful event. Cognitive scientists also believe that once established, erroneous beliefs are maintained because the presence of that belief has a direct influence on a person's current and future cognitive functioning. In other words, our erroneous beliefs allow for a distorted interpretation of the events that occur around us, and it is this distorted view of things that maintains our erroneous belief system. As an example, an individual suffering from generalized anxiety disorder might see the world as a really scary and dangerous place, where trouble can occur at any moment. Whereas a person who suffers from panic disorder might be walking down the street at a fast pace (e.g., to be on time for an appointment) and start to think that the shortness of breath he or she is experiencing is a prelude to a massive heart attack which will lead to "certain" death. People who suffer from fear and anxiety could be said, according to the cognitive perspective, to have a problem with selective attention, in that they focus excessive amounts of attention on perceived threats in the environment, and thus are more aware of these threats than are other individuals. In addition, these individuals could also have a problem with selective recall, in that they are more likely to recall threatening and scary experiences than are individuals who are not anxious. Recalling these experiences will inevitably lead to the maintenance of fear and anxiety states. Furthermore, the cognitive explanation suggests that fearful and anxious individuals have a problem with misinterpretation in that they are more likely to misinterpret neutral or ambiguous situations as threatening, thus contributing to the maintenance of fear and anxiety. Therefore, problems with selective attention, selective recall, and misinterpretation could lead to the erroneous beliefs or cognitions that can contribute significantly and have a causal effect on an individual's fear and anxiety states. Given this description it is perhaps not surprising that some individuals live in a world that appears to be riddled with anxiety provoking stimuli.

5 – The Assessment & Treatment of Anxiety – Panic Attacks

Although anxiety problems sometimes go undiagnosed or unnoticed for a variety of reasons it remains imperative that once there is evidence of anxiety then some form of treatment should be considered, however minor the problem might appear. Indeed, anxiety doesn't always go away by itself; it can often progress and develop into panic attacks, phobias, and episodes of depression. Untreated anxiety problems will at the very least interfere with the patient's everyday functioning and/or their ability to perform simple tasks including holding down a job. Furthermore, many anxious patients can develop mild addictions to drugs or alcohol as they inadvertently try to "self-medicate" their symptoms. I have witnessed many relatively insightful and well-meant individuals who have resorted to small amounts of alcohol in their desperation to help alleviate their anxiety. Naturally, this is not the best way of coping even if it is understandable for many individuals.

As should be the basic premise for any therapeutic intervention, effective management of anxiety begins with a thorough and comprehensive assessment that should lead to a more accurate diagnosis or description of the problem. This remains an essential part of the clinical process when assessing someone with anxiety as the "normal" anxieties, and uncertainties associated with a chronic illness or cancer for example are often intense in themselves. Thus, there is not often a clear distinction between these "normal" fears, and fears of a specific nature that are solely anxiety related. Although there is no single test that can provide definite diagnoses of anxiety, there are several short-answer interviews or symptom inventories that therapists can use to evaluate the intensity of a patient's anxiety and some of its associated features. These measures include the Hamilton Anxiety Scale and The Hospital Anxiety and Depression Scale (HADS) that has been discussed earlier. However, whilst these instruments may help to quantify the level of anxiety it is the clinical interview where the potentially "rich" qualitative information will emanate and this is the first step in the therapeutic process.

The clinical interview

Where anxiety is concerned it is useful to be relatively relaxed in order to conduct the interview in a relatively calm and professional manner. Vulnerable clients will often "mirror" or "model" the therapist and therefore trying to maintain a calm and reassuring demeanour is probably helpful at this initial juncture. This can also create an atmosphere of having plenty of time to listen to the client and will help to elicit more information than if we appeared a little hesitant or hasty. The question of taking notes remains a necessary evil most of the time and if one explains this then it can minimize any potential difficulties. Naturally, if a client or patient is overly distressed then it is more important to fall back on the clinical and interpersonal skill discussed earlier. When the time is right (and it will be), we can then pick up and start again with the notes. Once you have the basic family or significant others noted it is best to begin with more open questions such as *"can you tell me what difficulties you are experiencing"* these can be followed later with more closed questions such as, *"how are you sleeping/ eating at the moment"*, in order to clarify the presenting complaints. There are therapists and clinicians alike who erroneously believe that there is no need to hone in on specific areas of dysfunction or difficulty and that an unstructured approach is best. This in my opinion is very much mistaken and there is much evidence to suggest that clarification of any symptoms is an important factor in determining accuracy of the presenting problems. Clinical interviewing skills that help to encourage the patient include paraphrasing or summarizing what the person has said and making good eye contact. As discussed earlier maintaining a healthy congruence with regard to the patient can be useful.

The following is a clinical interview example with some of the clients responses outlined in italics:

"How do you feel when you are asked to go to a social event or when you experience anxiety?" – *"I feel tense, anxious, nervous and worried."* – "go on" – *"I feel frightened as if something dreadful is going to happen and I keep imagining the worst, my heart starts pounding and my chest starts to feel tight and I become dizzy and light headed"*, - "What happens then?" – *"After a while I start to calm down but I always refuse to go and I just make an excuse up or I make myself so ill that I can't go anyway".*

This is a typical example of someone presenting with anxiety and it will be familiar to most therapists/clinicians. What the client is describing here is a classic *panic attack* scenario. The fact that the client has come along is generally a good sign that they want to deal with their anxiety and this needs to be checked out so that people haven't been "sent" by their partners or their doctors. It is often beneficial to ask the person what they would like to gain from their appointments and therefore it is useful to have a quantifying measure with which to review any improvement. What has been described above of course is the typical *fight or flight* response that we have discussed and somewhere along the line during a future session this aspect needs to be explained explicitly and in lay terms where possible. There is plenty of good literature available for clients and they can read this information on the "mechanics" of anxiety between sessions and any clarification or uncertainties can be discussed and reviewed at each subsequent appointment. The example above illustrates the cognitive aspect of the anxiety with the clients' thoughts being clearly governed by their anxiety resulting in emotional and irrational thinking.

In general therefore, what we are ultimately looking at when assessing the client during the clinical interview are factors relating to the onset of the anxiety, factors that may have served to maintain the anxiety, the intensity of the anxiety and what strategies has the individual attempted in order to cope with the anxiety. During this information gathering process the therapist will also seek out opportunities to establish a good therapeutic alliance. The classic panic attack features are further outlined below.

DSM IV-R Criteria for a Panic Attack

A discrete period of intense fear or discomfort, in which four (or more) of the following symptoms developed abruptly and reached a peak within 10 minutes:

1. Palpitations, pounding heart, or accelerated heart rate
2. Sweating
3. Trembling or shaking
4. Sensations of shortness of breath or smothering
5. Feeling of choking
6. Chest pain or discomfort
7. Nausea or abdominal distress
8. Feeling dizzy, unsteady, light-headed, or faint
9. De-realization (feelings of unreality) or de-personalization (being detached from oneself)
10. Fear of losing control or going crazy
11. Fear of dying
12. Paresthesias (numbness or tingling sensations)
13. Chills or hot flushes

Formal Assessment

The Hospital Anxiety and Depression Scale or HADS had already been mentioned in previous chapters and it remains an excellent instrument for measuring and quantifying anxiety. The HADS only takes a minute or two to complete and the form itself can be filled in prior to the assessment interview. The HADS is an excellent tool for separating out Depression from Anxiety with the main clinical and symptomatic difference between depression and anxiety being the general level of *autonomic arousal*. Whereby autonomic arousal remains an integral part of anxiety, this component is more or less absent when someone is suffering with depression. For example, the physiological "system" of the body *speeds* up during anxiety and more often than not *slows* down during depression. As we are now aware, autonomic responses characterised by increased autonomic arousal include sweaty hands, dry mouth, cold feet, tense muscles and accelerated heart rate. All these factors need to be taken into consideration during the assessment phase.

As briefly mentioned earlier, some therapists may want to differentiate between stait and trait anxiety and this is best achieved by using the State-Trait Anxiety Inventory for Adults. The State-Trait Anxiety Inventory (STAI) was developed by Charles Spielberger (1983) and is another excellent instrument for assessing anxiety in adults. The STAI differentiates between the temporary condition of "state anxiety" and the more general and long-standing quality of "trait anxiety." The essential qualities evaluated by the STAI-Anxiety scale are feelings of apprehension, tension, nervousness, and worry. Scores on the STAI-Anxiety scale increase in response to physical danger and psychological stress, and decrease as a result of appropriate therapeutic intervention such as cognitive therapy and relaxation training. The instruments simplicity also makes it ideal for evaluating a broad cross-section of individuals with varying social and educational backgrounds. The STAI has forty questions with a range of four possible responses to each.

Components of the State-Trait Anxiety Inventory (STAI)

- Determines anxiety in a specific situation and as a general trait
- Provides norms for different clinical patients
- Relatively easy to score and can be completed in about ten minutes

Clinical skills and techniques for working with anxiety/panic attacks

Therapeutic intervention should naturally follow information gathered from the clinical interview and the formal assessment. One of the reasons anxiety is so treatable is that there are so many potentially effective ways to intervene. Though everyone is different as to which methods or combination of methods are most effective, it is recommended that all the aforementioned skills are practiced. Unlike skills for managing depression, some of the techniques designed to help reduce anxiety necessarily cause an <u>increase</u> in anxiety prior to a lasting reduction. It is therefore important for therapists to encourage clients to continue with the techniques despite the temporary increase, as it is a necessary part of the recovery from anxiety. In general we are referring to what happens when people <u>avoid</u> situations and/or events or people over a long period of time. Whilst this phobic avoidance serves to minimize any anxiety, the individual never learns to cope and subsequently overcome the problem. Therefore, by just slowly beginning to address the difficulty of avoidance with some therapeutic skills the anxiety is naturally going to increase in the short-term.

The therapist and client should focus on the cognitive, behavioural and emotional factors related to the anxiety. Whether the anxiety is more stait (situational) or trait (personality) needs to be considered and the process of psycho-education that has hopefully been a theme during the assessment process starts to come into its own as the therapist discusses some of the reasons why we think, feel and behave when we are anxious.

Initial management of anxiety includes providing adequate information and support to the client/patient. The most useful clinical approach should include a trusting therapeutic alliance and a combination of cognitive and behavioural therapeutic techniques coupled with increasing the individuals' insight into the problem itself.

It is useful to break the treatment down into four components and these are outlined below:

1. Providing insight into the clients' anxiety / Psycho-education.
2. Reducing physical symptoms - Relaxation.
3. Altering thoughts related to anxiety – Cognitive Restructuring.
4. Changing behaviours related to anxiety – Overcoming Avoidance

<u>Understanding the clients' anxiety – Psycho-education.</u>

There will be both cognitive and behavioural insights gained from these areas. During this period and in collaboration with the therapist the client will gain insight into the development of their anxiety and into how it affects the way they think, feel and behave. The behavioural avoidance will be discussed and some small achievable goals might be considered. Therapist and client will look at specific areas where the anxiety occurs and discuss management strategies for dealing with these difficult situations. Both external situational factors will be looked at as well as the internal thinking patterns and physiology. Outside of the sessions the client will make notes of any problematic areas and these difficulties will be brought back for further discussion.

Reducing physical symptoms

This will purely focus on the physiology of anxiety as discussed earlier in the chapter. During this period the "mechanics" of anxiety will be reviewed and elaborated on helping to demystify or take away any unknown fears associated purely with the physiology of the anxiety. For example, over-breathing is very common when someone becomes anxious. The client often begins to gulp air, thinking that they are going to suffocate, or they may begin to breathe really quickly (rapid breathing). This means they end up with an inappropriate amount of carbon dioxide. This has the effect of making them feel dizzy and therefore more anxious. Clients are therefore encouraged to recognise this and are helped to slow their breathing down. Getting into a regular slow rhythm of in two-three-four and out two-three-four will soon return breathing to normal and thus reduce many of the anxious symptoms. I try to encourage clients/patients to practice this when they are not feeling anxious so that they can become familiar with what is required.

Altering thoughts related to anxiety and panic – Cognitive Restructuring.

Cognitive skills for managing anxiety involve components such as *distraction* and *de-catastrophizing*. Distraction is a very powerful means of reducing intense anxiety and panic. When one is consumed with a high level of anxiety, it is very hard to recognize and challenge distorted thoughts. However, if panic-stricken people can get away from their ruminating for a few minutes by focusing intensely and exclusively on some outside stimulus (while at the same time using the suggested breathing method) anxiety will diminish, often to a level where individuals can reason with themselves. De-catastrophizing is a disputation technique aimed at balancing anxious and irrational automatic thoughts. Many of these have been discussed in previous chapters on cognitive therapy and will not therefore be repeated. In essence, we are working with the client to help them identify long established emotional and irrational patterns of thinking related to the anxiety. Having identified these patterns there is a collaborative approach toward looking at more balanced rational responses leading to a restructuring of the way they think about the situation and themselves.

Changing anxiety/panic related behaviours – Overcoming Avoidance

When anxious, one's automatic thoughts and mental images tend to be catastrophic and there is an exaggeration of the dangerousness of the situation and a simultaneous underestimation of one's control over that danger. As we have discussed earlier the rapid activation of anxiety symptoms has one behavioural purpose – *"fight or flight"* that in general leads to continuous phobic avoidance. Countering avoidance is without doubt the most powerful means of reducing anxiety problems. Avoidance reduces anxiety in the short term, but it actually makes for more anxiety in the long term, as avoidance breeds more avoidance it creates a vicious cycle where it becomes increasingly more anxiety provoking to counter avoidance. Most clients presenting will describe situations where avoidance has been paramount when the anxiety has become extreme. Avoidance will understandably decrease anxiety, however it will then make it even more difficult to return to that situation because not only will they have an increased anxiety just considering it, but they will have a strong emotional drive to postpone again, given that the previous postponement resulted in a decrease in anxiety. *Exposure* involves placing oneself in the avoided situation, despite the anxiety, and staying there until the anxiety ebbs completely. With most forms of anxiety, a hierarchy of exposure can be established so that the client can make gradual steps, they must however reach certain levels of anxiety before they learn to habituate and manage the situations far better.

The client who gradually exposes themselves to what has been avoided, starting with a level that evokes a minimum of anxiety, and increasing the level of exposure as each level is successfully extinguished, while simultaneously utilizing cognitive and relaxation exercises will eventually overcome their fears or at the very least learn to manage them far more constructively (that's a long sentence so you may want to read over it again).

Conclusion

Anxiety problems and particularly panic attacks can be self-perpetuating, mostly by virtue of cognitive distortions and the overuse of *fight or flight* avoidance strategies. While the techniques outlined above can help reduce anxiety it is vitally important to realise that anxiety is not harmful or dangerous and this needs to be fed back continuously to clients and patients. Even if we did not use these techniques, nothing awful would happen as anxiety cannot harm us and it will eventually "burn" itself out. However, it can be extremely uncomfortable and frightening and this also needs to be acknowledged. Whilst some clients may be able to completely overcome their anxiety others will be able to make inroads that will help them manage the anxiety better and increase their overall well-being and quality of life. Educating clients to understand the "mechanics" of anxiety can be a significant stress-reducer in itself and often many clients eventually become their own therapists so to speak as they have gained a more complete understanding of the problem and are now in a position to control or manage it in the future.

Part 5: Specific Problems Associated with Anxiety

Having looked at anxiety in general we shall now turn our attention to more *specific* problems associated with anxiety. Many of these problems will be relatively common to the reader and whilst there will be a degree of overlap following on from the anxiety chapter, the following problems will be reviewed with regard to their specificity. This should draw the reader to some of the more unique components of each of the following problems. Therefore, whilst anxiety and the associated symptoms outlined earlier are very much a part of the following difficulties there are unique features within each problem that require a more specific assessment and therapeutic approach. As with the chapter on depression we shall also look at some of the personality factors associated with anxiety difficulties. The specific anxiety related problems are outlined below:

1 – Phobias

2 – Obsessive-Compulsive Problems

3 – Post-traumatic stress

4 – Personality factors and Anxiety

1 – Phobias - What are phobias?

Most of us are familiar with the word phobia and often we associate it with a situation that arouses some kind of fear reaction within us. This association is actually not far from the truth as the actual word "phobia" comes from the Greek language and literally means 'fear' or 'dread'. Suffering from a phobia has been described as having immense fear of a situation or an object that is not in proportion to the actual danger itself. Therefore it is largely an irrational fear. The fear itself however, can often lead to a strong desire or need to completely escape the situation or avoid the object altogether (phobic avoidance). Put simply a person suffering with a specific phobia can be seen as having an intense fear of something that actually poses little or no actual danger. There are of course literally 1000s of phobias and new ones are developing all the time as technology and lifestyles change. One of the most common specific phobias is centred on closed-in places and as most of us are aware this is referred to as, *agoraphobia*. About 5% of people develop agoraphobia at some time during their lives, and of these about 3% suffer with agoraphobia during any 6 month period. It is therefore a relatively common condition which, once developed, tends to persist. Interestingly, agoraphobia is three times more common among women than men. Other phobias include a fear of heights which is termed, *acrophobia* and a fear of spiders which is of course *arachnophobia*. A common phobia in the health care setting is a fear of needles, in lay-terms this might be called simply *needle-phobia*, however its formal definition would be *belonephobia* and it can be defined as a fear of sharp objects such as pins or needles. This can be severe enough in some cases to warrant people being sedated due to the fear and anxiety that the thought and/or sight of a needle may arouse There are complexities here for the *beloneophobic* as many general medical procedures of course require the insertion of a needle for taking blood etc and I have witnessed many suffering with this condition become distraught at the thought of what is a relatively simple and harmless procedure, albeit a little painful if you do not like pin pricks. This difficulty becomes particularly problematic for women intending to have children for example as there are numerous blood tests involved. Many women in this situation have had to resort to psychological intervention to help them overcome their problem so that they can eventually go on to have children. Therefore, the overall value attached to overcoming certain phobias can be extremely significant on occasion and even potentially life threatening as the example below will highlight.

The exact cause of most specific phobias such as agoraphobia is not known, but most appear to be associated with a traumatic experience or a learned reaction. For example, a person who has a frightening or threatening experience with an animal, such as an attack or being bitten, can develop a specific phobia. Witnessing a traumatic event in which others experience harm or extreme fear can also cause a specific phobia, as is receiving information or repeated warnings about potentially dangerous situations or animals. Fear can also be learned from others. For example, a child whose parents react with fear and anxiety to certain objects or situations may well respond to those objects with fear.

Phobias such as those highlighted above are not just extreme fear; they are an irrational fear of a particular object or situation For example, a person may be able to climb the highest mountain with ease yet be unable to go above the 5th floor of an office building. While adults with phobias realize that these fears are irrational, they often find that facing, or even thinking about facing the feared object or situation brings on an acute and severe panic attack. Perhaps understandably, if the object of the fear is easy to avoid, people with specific phobias may not feel the need to seek treatment. Sometimes, they may even make important career or personal decisions in order to avoid a phobic situation, and if this avoidance is carried to extreme lengths, it can be extremely disabling and restricting. People with agoraphobia for example may be so frightened of public places that they may never actually leave their homes. Others whose phobias may interfere with their employment may force themselves to look elsewhere away from their desired interests.

DSM-IV Criteria for Specific Phobia

The following outlines the formal classification for a specific phobia.

A) Marked and persistent fear that is excessive or unreasonable, cued by the presence or anticipation of a specific object or situation (for example, flying, heights, animals, receiving an injection, seeing blood)

B) Exposure to the phobic stimulus almost invariably provokes an immediate anxiety response, which may take the form of a situationally bound or situationally predisposed panic attack. In children, the anxiety may be expressed by crying, tantrums, freezing, or clinging.

C) The person recognizes that the fear is excessive or unreasonable. **Note:** In children, this feature may be absent.

D) The phobic situation(s) is avoided or else is endured with intense anxiety or distress.

E) The avoidance, anxious anticipation, or distress in the feared situation(s) interferes significantly with the person's normal routine, occupational (or academic) functioning, or social activities or relationships, or there is marked distress about having the phobia.

F) In individuals under age 18 years, the duration is at least six months.

G) The anxiety, panic attacks, or phobic avoidance associated with the specific object or situation are not better accounted for by another mental disorder, such as Obsessive-Compulsive Disorder (for example, fear of dirt in someone with an obsession about contamination), Posttraumatic Stress Disorder (for example, avoidance of stimuli associated with a severe stressor), Separation Anxiety Disorder (for example, avoidance of school), Social Phobia (for example, avoidance of social situations because of fear of embarrassment).

The Assessment of Phobias

Of all the psychological conditions that present for therapy people suffering with specific phobias are likely to be the most anxious and fearful clients. They are innately and painfully aware of their phobia and the extreme anxiety it may cause (often just by talking about it), yet they pluck up enough courage to look at how they can learn to manage and/or overcome their problems. As a consequence of this fear I often acknowledge early on that they have done extremely well just to be sitting in the room discussing their problem (I appreciate this may sound a little patronising, however if fed back genuinely and appropriately it is of considerable value). Often many feel "silly" because when they describe the problem in the "open" it can appear rather simple and this goes for a fear of needles, spiders and many other phobias. Therefore, it is important at the earliest juncture to try to engage the client in the therapeutic process. Sometimes, clients will unwittingly or unconsciously feel silly about their problems to such an extent that they may minimise its actual effect on them and possibly rationalise out that they probably don't need treatment and can manage without it. Behind this of course is the fear of having to work through the problem itself. Therefore, therapists and clinicians need to be acutely aware of these variables at this initial juncture. Early on it may be useful to mention that although the anxiety is extreme and frightening, no actual harm is going to occur. We may then want to inform them that we will discuss the anxiety itself in more detail later on in the session and in future sessions in order for them to become more at ease with it.

In general, because specific phobias are exactly that in that they are specific the information gathered will generally concern material surrounding the phobia itself. However, it still remains important that the assessment is comprehensive in nature and therefore it must concern all the general details described in the earlier chapters. Therefore, the assessment will again include information related to the immediate family and the clients' personal and social history. We must be aware of any particular life stressors at present and any general problems. Indeed, even unrelated problems are likely to impact on the phobia as they will add to a general level of anxiety, therefore we should check out all potential stressors.

When we have gathered the necessary information we can then look closer at the phobia itself and all the variables involved including when the client/patient first became aware of the problem, when the symptoms started, what have they tried to minimize the impact of the phobia (usually avoidance) and how the symptoms interfere with their overall well-being and lifestyle (they are often more restrictive that the client will let on). As previously mentioned, occasionally, there is a reason why someone has developed a phobia, for example after a particular incident or event. Often there is no obvious cause, however this should not get in the way of a successful therapeutic outcome if the situation is assessed and treated appropriately.

Factors to consider during the assessment:

1 – Relevant historical factors – Often there won't be anything specific but this shouldn't be a handicap to a successful outcome. Alternatively, there may be experiences in childhood that have contributed to the general level of anxiety and this needs to be reviewed and its overall significance evaluated.

2 – The specific phobia itself – what is it and where and when it occurs? Look at all of the key variables surrounding the specific phobia.

3 – The intensity of the phobia – scale of anxiety/fear. It is useful to get some measure of the intensity of the phobia and there are some useful rating scales outlined below.

4 – Establish the minimum baseline level – for example with someone with a needle phobia this may be, (i) can they see the needle on a computer screen without becoming anxious? (ii) Can they sit next to a needle, (iii) Can they hold a needle or (iv) does the mere mention of the word ****** set them off in an uncontrollable panic. Start at the minimum amount of the anxiety. We need to remember that the client will be nervous as a result of the session itself and therefore we should be careful not to confuse this relatively "normal" anxiety with the anxiety associated with the specific phobia.

Just to illustrate the impact of a phobia, when working with needle phobias I may write in bold felt pen the word **"NEEDLE"**. I will ask the client permission if I can show it to them first and this is usually granted. Clients are often surprised how anxious they are just by seeing the word written on a sheet of A4 paper. This also serves later on to illustrate how much the anxiety has subsided when they look at the same word on the paper at the end of a session. At the very least this should help to engage the client and serve as a parallel to illustrate how anxiety does actually dissipate when we address or confront the anxiety provoking material.

Quantifying the baseline anxiety

To gauge the scale or intensity of the phobia we may want to use a simple rating scale similar to those examples outlined below. This will again provide a useful baseline from which to assess any progress or otherwise. These are often called Visual Analogue Rating Scales (VAS Scale) and are subjective measures used to assess and provide useful feedback to the client and therapist.

A Visual Analogue Scale for measuring the level of anxiety for a specific phobia

Very little anxiety								Extreme anxiety		
0	1	2	3	4	5	6	7	8	9	10

The VAS can be used to monitor the level of anxiety to each feared situation thus providing on-going feedback throughout the therapeutic period. To some extent it may act as a positive reinforcer as the client gradually achieves their desired goals.

Clinical Skills & Techniques for Working with Phobias

Initially some clinical reassurance is required as clients are likely to be extremely anxious. Therefore, early on in the therapeutic process I will assure clients that they will have control over each step of the therapeutic process and to this extent, they will not be asked to do anything that they feel is too anxiety provoking for them. I will then reassure them again (and continuously throughout therapy) that despite the desperate feelings associated with anxiety, no actual harm is going to occur (If we calmly repeat this often enough, the message usually gets through). Naturally, early on in the therapeutic proceedings the *fight or flight* response is explained to help demystify any uncomfortable and irrational thoughts associated with the anxiety itself. Whilst giving clients a certain amount of control over the therapeutic process it is useful to inform them that as a therapist I am likely to directly encourage (where appropriate) them so that they can overcome their fears. Again this process tends to be more successful if we have established a respectful and reassuring clinical relationship. Indeed, therapeutic trust may be even more significant for this type of problem.

Psychological Treatment for Phobias

Having carried out our own assessment we then need to look at some of the more successful methods of treating this type of problem. In general there are combinations of psychological strategies for treating specific phobias. Most of these strategies however evolve around a therapeutic process referred to as, **Systematic Desensitisation**. Systematic Desensitisation is generally used with a combination of cognitive and behavioural procedures including relaxation, distraction techniques and *in vivo exposure*. In addition to these important features, much of the therapeutic success will depend on other more interpersonal factors that are an essential part of the overall therapy and in particular they include the nature and quality of the clinical relationship, the skill in teaching certain relaxation and breathing skills and the general application of the psychological procedures themselves.

Systematic Desensitisation

Systematic desensitisation has consistently been illustrated to be effective in the treatment of anxiety associated with specific phobias and when combined with basic cognitive strategies this procedure becomes the treatment of choice for many therapists and indeed, informed clients alike. This method of exposing anxious individuals gradually was originally developed by Wolpe in 1958. Wolpe had considerable success with this method when working with a range of specific phobias. Over the past 50 years, the original concept has been elaborated on and refined to become an increasingly successful therapeutic procedure.

One of the first steps in systematic desensitisation involves the development of an anxiety hierarchy in relation to the specific phobia. An anxiety hierarchy in essence is a list of fear-provoking situations arranged in order of how much fear they provoke in the client. For a man afraid of spiders, for example, holding a spider may rank at the top of his anxiety hierarchy, whereas seeing a small picture of a spider may rank at the bottom. In the second step, the therapist helps the client relax using one of the relaxation techniques described in earlier chapters. Following this the therapist asks the client to imagine each situation on the anxiety hierarchy, beginning with the least-feared situation and moving upward. For example, the man may first imagine seeing a picture of a spider, then imagine seeing a real spider from far away, then from a short distance, and so forth. If the client feels anxiety at any stage, he or she is instructed to stop thinking about the situation and to return to a state of deep relaxation and mental distraction. The relaxation and the imagined scene are paired until the client feels less anxious. The theory suggests that in time the client will be able to remain free of anxiety while imagining the most-feared situation.

In addition to asking the client to imagine a fear provoking situation a therapist is also likely to want to transfer these skills into real life situations. The technique involved when asking a client to actually encounter the feared situation is called *in vivo exposure*. It is arguable that this it is actually fundamental and necessary to have clients "testing" themselves in real life situations as it is only here where we will see the actual evidence of any therapeutic success. Indeed, if imagination is the equivalent of the client *"talking the talk"* then during *in vivo exposure* it is understandably time to *"walk the walk"*. In clinical terms this would add a degree of what we call **ecological validity** to the therapeutic process as the client is performing the behaviour in their natural anxiety-provoking environment. Indeed, many in-patient programmes for phobias and OCD problems often fail because they lack ecological validity that cannot or does not (for varying reasons) transfer or generalise outside in the natural environment.

With regard to *in vivo exposure* and the spider phobia, a therapist for example, might arrange a visit to a park or zoo where visitors can actually touch large spiders. The therapist would possibly model for the client how to approach a spider and how to handle it. This *modelling* of course could also be done by a trusted and valued friend or family member. The therapist or "modeller" may also encourage the client to walk gradually closer to the spider, reinforcing their progress with praise and reassurance. The goal for the therapist and patient would be for the client to eventually pick up the spider without experiencing any anxiety.

Systematic desensitisation for example using *in vivo exposure* for a young teacher who has experienced a trauma resulting in a work related phobia might have as an initial step, (i) driving to the school on a Sunday and just walking around the actual environment, followed by (ii) talking to a colleague on the phone, and (iii) visiting work prior to returning, starting part-time and eventually back to full time employment. Whilst this may seem a rather arbitrary procedure this is very typical of some of the phobic reactions that can occur when people have experienced anxiety in certain situations. Indeed, I have witnessed many rational and committed teachers and nurses who have developed specific phobias, often due to unpleasant work experiences and practices. These employees become consumed with fear and dread if they have to drive near or past their place of work. Indeed, many will drive miles just to avoid driving past the feared environment on a weekend. Hopefully this just illustrates how everyday people can be devastated by these conditions.

The overall therapeutic procedure involves a combination of techniques and strategies and the most successful ones are outlined below and are often used side by side in a complimentary fashion:

i)   Systematic desensitisation - establishing an anxiety hierarchy of the stimuli involved

ii) In vivo exposure

iii) Cognitive-behavioural (thoughts-emotions-behaviour)

iv) Counter-conditioning relaxation as a response to each feared stimulus beginning first with the least anxiety-provoking stimulus and moving then to the next least anxiety-provoking stimulus until all of the items listed in the anxiety hierarchy have been dealt with successfully.

v)   Modelling - Systematic desensitisation can be paired with *modelling*. During modelling, the client/patient observes others (the "models", often the therapist) in the presence of the phobic stimulus and encouraged to respond with calmness via relaxation and breathing rather than fear. In this way, the client/patient is encouraged to imitate the model and thereby gradually extinguish their phobia.

Brief clinical example

Just to briefly illustrate how some of the above principles work in practice I will briefly outline a case referred to me some 2-3 years ago. The woman in question was in her early 40s and the actual referral was in relation to an anxiety attack she had experienced prior to a kidney transplant. In essence the woman who was in desperate need of a kidney transplant had been rushed to a major hospital as they had found a "match" for her. Unfortunately, when at the hospital the woman had suffered an extreme and acute anxiety attack and was unable to go through with the potentially lifesaving operation. I will scan through the most salient and pertinent elements. The referral itself had little more to mention other than what had been outlined above. My assessment revealed however, that there were significant historical factors involved with this woman in relation to her immediate family, friends and general hospital procedures. In essence, since she was a child she had witnessed significant members of her family go into hospital and not come out alive. This included her grandmother, whom she was close to, her aunty and her mother who was in her 30s at the time. There were good physical reasons for all of the above however the assessment revealed that this woman was suffering with a classic hospital/medical phobia. The technical term for this type of phobia is, *Nosocomephobia*. The problem often significantly impacts on the persons' quality of life and it can produce panic attacks with classic symptoms that typically include shortness of breath, rapid breathing, irregular heartbeat, sweating, nausea, and overall feelings of dread. Given the nature of the woman outlined above it was all the more essential that she overcame her problem. She regularly attended her dialysis of course, albeit with some anxiety but could not overcome the anxiety in relation to the transplant.

Following the initial assessment we looked at specifics in relation to the phobia and everything appeared to come down to the anaesthetic procedure and a fear of "not knowing" and being out of control. With this in mind a combination of techniques outlined above was carefully applied including systematic desensitisation and *in vivo exposure*. At the beginning of therapy the woman could hardly mention the word <u>anaesthetic</u> or anything in relation to this. After 6 sessions she had arranged to visit an anaesthetic theatre and talked through the procedures involved in a transplant. All of this produced significant anxiety, however due to her new insight with regards to anxiety itself and the cognitive restructuring that had occurred as a result of this she was able to face her difficulties and did not resort to her previous phobic avoidance that had occurred for many years until it was revealed. There were a number of breathing exercises that were utilised to help manage the anxiety itself and possibly one of the most significant factors was the therapeutic alliance that had been carefully developed over a longer than average period of time (6 months). To illustrate the irrational nature of anxiety in general, during the initial stages when this woman was frightened out of her wits at the thought of going to the hospital I asked her, purely out of interest of course (and to illustrate a point), what would you do if it was your daughter who needed the transplant, to which she responded, *"I would carry her up there myself and force her to have it"*. Not surprising perhaps but it does illustrate the irrational nature of the phobia and the intense anxiety that accompanies it. The woman eventually went on to have a parathyroidectomy (surgery to remove parathyroid glands or parathyroid tumours.) and a subsequent transplant and she is now doing very well. The case does however illustrate the importance of managing and overcoming fears and phobias.

Summary

The overall goal of systematic desensitisation and *in vivo exposure* is to reduce the ability of certain situations to cause anxiety. This is accomplished best by helping the client confront each item, often using an anxiety hierarchy. A combination of the assessment and therapeutic procedures outlined above can have a significant impact on helping clients cope with their anxiety and in particular their often debilitating phobias. There is another procedure known as *"Flooding"*, which may be useful for some clients who are extremely motivated and courageous. In essence *"flooding"* involves a prolonged and intense exposure to the fear itself. During *"flooding"*, the client is exposed all at once to highly threatening events for a lengthy period of time until the anxiety has subsided. Prior to this of course a full and thorough explanation of anxiety etc. is illustrated. I only briefly mention this strategy as I believe that it is potentially harmful for some clients as the anxiety can be extreme and therefore I feel that clinically a more gentle desensitised approach is more ethical, less threatening and therefore more user-friendly. There are occasions however where *flooding* has been shown to be both effective and appropriate in the hands of the skilled clinician.

2 – Obsessions & Compulsions

What is obsessive-compulsive disorder?

Obsessive compulsive disorder, or OCD, involves anxious thoughts or rituals you feel you can't control. If you have OCD, you may be plagued by persistent, unwelcome thoughts or images, or by the urgent need to engage in certain rituals. You may be obsessed with germs or dirt, so you wash your hands over and over. You may be filled with doubt and feel the need to check things repeatedly. You may have frequent thoughts of violence, and fear that you will harm people close to you. You may spend long periods touching things or counting; you may be pre-occupied by order or symmetry; you may have persistent thoughts of performing sexual acts that are repugnant to you; or you may be troubled by thoughts that are against your religious beliefs. The disturbing thoughts or images are called obsessions, and the rituals that are performed to try to prevent or get rid of them are called compulsions. There is no actual pleasure in carrying out the rituals you are drawn to, only temporary relief from the anxiety that grows when you don't perform them. A lot of healthy people can identify with some of the symptoms of OCD, such as checking the oven several times before leaving the house. But for people with moderate to severe OCD, such activities consume at least an hour or more a day, are very distressing, and significantly interfere with daily life. Most adults with this condition recognize that what they're doing is senseless, but they can't stop it.

OCD is quite understandably an anxiety disorder and the presence of <u>obsessions</u> is just one of the essential features of OCD, the other component as briefly mentioned is the <u>compulsions</u>.

Obsessional thoughts have the following characteristics:

- The thoughts must be recognised by the sufferer as their own,
- They often can't be resisted, even though the subject feels compelled to try and push them out of their mind
- The thoughts are usually unpleasant and often abhorrent
- The thoughts are repetitive.

Common thoughts include:

Contamination - e.g., "my hands or my clothes are dirty".

Pathologic doubt - e.g., "did I close the front door"?

Need for symmetry - e.g., "I must put that curtain back before I can sit down and relax"

I am sure that some readers will identify a little bit of themselves in amongst these examples and indeed we all have some minor foible that is a little irrational and is probably some learned response. For example, straightening the cushions before we can "relax" and watch TV or having to have the digital volume in the car on an even number (my foible) etc. etc. However, most people suffering with OCD experience a mixture of such thoughts and people can sometimes become totally preoccupied by images rather than thoughts and these images can sometimes be of a violent and/or aggressive nature.

 DSM-IV Criteria for Obsessive-Compulsive Disorder:

Either obsessions or compulsions:

Obsessions as defined by (1), (2), (3), and (4):

(1) Recurrent and persistent thoughts, impulses, or images that are experienced, at some time during the disturbance, as intrusive and inappropriate and that cause marked anxiety or distress.

(2) The thoughts, impulses, or images are not simply excessive worries about real-life problems.

(3) The person attempts to ignore or suppress such thoughts, impulses, or images, or to neutralize them with some other thought or action.

(4) The person recognizes that the obsessional thoughts, impulses, or images are a product of his or her own mind (not imposed from without as in thought insertion).

Compulsions as defined by (1) and (2):

(1) Repetitive behaviours (e.g., hand washing, ordering, checking) or mental acts (e.g., praying, counting, repeating words silently) that the person feels driven to perform in response to an obsession, or according to rules that must be applied rigidly

(2) The behaviours or mental acts are aimed at preventing or reducing distress or preventing some dreaded event or situation; however, these behaviours or mental acts either are not connected in a realistic way with what they are designed to neutralize or prevent or are clearly excessive

At some point during the course of the disorder, the person has recognized that the obsessions or compulsions are excessive or unreasonable. (Note: This does not apply to children.)

The obsessions or compulsions cause marked distress, are time consuming (take more than 1 hour a day), or significantly interfere with the person's normal routine, occupational (or academic) functioning, or usual social activities or relationships. If the individual has an additional disorder, the content of the obsessions or compulsions is not restricted to it.

The disturbance is not due to the direct physiological effects of a substance (e.g., a drug of abuse, a medication) or a general medical condition.

Who suffers from Obsessive Compulsive Disorder?

Studies suggest lifetime prevalence is 2-3%. Peak age for onset in women is between 24-35 years of age and later in men although OCD strikes men and women in approximately equal numbers and usually first appears in childhood, adolescence, or early adulthood. One-third of adults with OCD report having experienced their first symptoms as children. The course of the disease is variable and the severity and intensity of symptoms may come and go, they may ease over time, or they can grow progressively worse. Research also suggests that OCD might run in families, again whether this is as a result of genetics or a learned or modelled behaviour is difficult to ascertain.

The Assessment of OCD

As with most recommended therapeutic approaches there will be a qualitative and a quantitative component to the assessment of OCD. To this extent, we again will ask the standard historical questions related to the clients interpersonal, social and family history and we will build a "picture" of their immediate situation and the key sources of both stress and support. With regard to the specific thoughts, compulsions and behaviours the therapist needs to gather as much explicit information as is necessary including historical influences, how the problem affects the clients quality of life and when and where these components of OCD occur.

From a quantitative perspective it is probably useful to use something like the Hospital Anxiety and Depression Scale (HADS) outlined earlier to gauge the overall level of anxiety and depression and to get an impression of the intensity of each. With regard to the OCD itself there are a number of useful instruments for assessing and quantifying OCD and probably one of the most useful ones is the, "The Maudsley Obsessional-Compulsive Inventory" outlined below. The Maudsley OCI is easy and quick to administer and it reveals the four main sub scores that are useful for specifying the particular problem. These include, (i) checking, (ii) washing/cleaning, (iii) slowness/repetitiveness, and (iv) doubting/conscientiousness.

The Maudsley OCI is also useful for monitoring change as treatment progresses.

The Maudsley Obsessional-Compulsive Inventory.

Please answer each question by putting an "x" in the appropriate column under TRUE or FALSE. There are no right or wrong answers, and there are no trick questions. Work quickly and do not think too long about the exact meaning of the question.

	TRUE	FALSE
I avoid using public telephones because of possible contamination.	x	
I frequently get nasty thoughts and have difficulty in getting rid of them.	x	
I am more concerned than most people about honesty.	x	
I am often late because I can't seem to get through everything on time.	x	
I don't worry unduly about contamination if I touch an animal.		x
I frequently have to check things (e.g., gas or water taps, doors, etc.) several times.	x	
I have a very strict conscience.	x	
I find that almost every day I am upset by unpleasant thoughts that come into my mind against my will.	x	
I do not worry unduly if I accidentally bump into somebody.		x

	TRUE	FALSE
I usually have serious doubts about the simple everyday things I do.	x	
Neither of my parents was very strict during my childhood.		x
I tend to get behind in my work because I repeat things over and over again.	x	
I use only an average amount of soap.		x
Some numbers are extremely unlucky.	x	
I do not check letters over and over again before posting them.		x
I do not take a long time to dress in the morning.		x
I am not excessively concerned about cleanliness.		x
One of my major problems is that I pay too much attention to detail.	x	
I can use well-kept toilets without any hesitation.		x
My major problem is repeated checking.	x	
I am not unduly concerned about germs and disease.		x
I do not tend to check things more than once.		x
I do not stick to a very strict routine when doing ordinary things.		x
My hands do not feel dirty after touching money.		x
I do not usually count when doing a routine task.		x
I take a rather long time to complete my washing in the morning.	x	

	TRUE	FALSE
I do not use a great deal of antiseptics.		x
I spend a lot of time every day checking things over and over again.	x	
Hanging and folding my clothes at night does not take up a lot of time.		x
Even when I do something very carefully I often feel that it is not quite right.	x	

Clinical Skills & Techniques for Working with OCD

For many years, OCD was thought to be an exceptionally problematic disorder to treat, and was often misdiagnosed. Traditional psychotherapy consistently had little impact on the disorder, and other reflective therapeutic procedures were equally unsuccessful. However, over the past fifteen years, developments within cognitive-therapy have resulted in a treatment protocol that has been found to be particularly beneficial for working with individuals with OCD. In fact, numerous clinical studies conducted over the past fifteen years have conclusively found that cognitive-therapy, either with or without medication, is dramatically superior to all other forms of treatment for OCD.

Compared to traditional psychotherapy, in which sessions are often spent merely discussing the client's problems, cognitive-therapy as we are well aware, is far more collaborative and proactive. Working together, both the client and the therapist take active roles in assessing the problem, and in devising carefully planned and structured psychological steps towards alleviating the symptoms. Using The Maudsley Obsessional-Compulsive Inventory and numerous other assessment tools, the therapist helps the client create a detailed list of his or her obsessions, compulsions and overall symptoms. This symptom list can then be used as an important adjunct to a particular form of cognitive-therapy known as *"Exposure and Response Prevention"* (ERP). Using the symptom list as a guide to the specific OCD problems the client discusses the difficulties in explicit detail. With this explicit information the therapist can often conduct micro "experiments" during therapy sessions which concern the gradual exposure to the clients' obsession with particular attention given to the thoughts, compulsions and behaviours. This is encouraged with the client resisting the urge to carry out the maladaptive behaviours.

Exposing clients to the things (or thoughts) that cause anxiety and contribute to the overall OCD is continuous until the client feels a marked relief of the anxiety. There are understandable similarities here with overcoming phobias and indeed each of these approaches has as its main goal a desire to help the client face their "demons" in a safe and far more informed way so that the irrationally based anxiety is psychologically and emotionally "re-learned" in a manner that is less threatening and eventually not threatening at all. With regard to OCD for example, it would be therapeutically useful for a client with contamination fears to make some continuous exposure with dirty and/or unclean objects. This may just be having the client sit in the kitchen with unwashed plates for a few hours or to have food on the floor etc, although the specifics should naturally be related to the obsessive-compulsive difficulty itself, and these difficulties should be relatively explicit following the assessment. Sitting close to these dirty dishes or food on the floor will understandably cause symptoms of anxiety and severe distress for clients. However, having discussed the problem in detail and with the therapist explaining the irrational cognitive and emotional components, the client will be able to become increasingly aware that no actual catastrophic event will follow this exposure and that after a period of about 10-20 minutes a decrease of anxiety symptoms occurs. Of course this procedure and others related to the obsessions and compulsions have to be repeated continuously until the client is able to adapt far more comfortably when resisting the compulsion.

Without this therapeutic approach a client is likely to be unable to resist the urge or compulsion and they will resort to washing their hands or checking things over and over with numerous repetitions depending on their particular problem. What this achieves of course is that it tends to reinforce the OCD itself. Response prevention will help the client to control and prevent these behaviours far better. Once again the client will experience anxiety and severe discomfort, however, these negative feelings will decrease and no severe negative consequences will follow. Many clients believe they might go crazy if they are not allowed to perform their obsessive-compulsive rituals. No doubt, they might feel extremely anxious and nervous; however this is actually to be expected. This type of approach can enable clients and patients to face more situations that may have previously prompted obsessive-compulsive behaviours and have subsequently been avoided. When assessed and treated appropriately techniques involving ERP and cognitive-therapy are particularly effective and there can be a marked reduction of symptoms in about 50-80 % of the clients after 8-12 sessions, naturally this will vary depending on the specific circumstances and whether the problem is mild, moderate or severe and whether there are any additional complexities. Many clients may continue to have milder obsessive-compulsive symptoms, but these symptoms do not interfere with normal everyday living.

Summary

Numerous research studies completed over the past fifteen years have concluded that cognitive therapy is the most effective treatment for OCD. In fact, in 1997, the Journal of Clinical Psychiatry surveyed over sixty OCD researchers and treatment specialists from across the world in order to determine the best treatment for OCD. The resulting publication, entitled Expert Consensus Treatment for Obsessive-Compulsive Disorder, described CBT as "the psychotherapeutic treatment of choice for children, adolescents and adults with OCD" and noted that it is "the key element of treatment". For difficult OCD problems cognitive therapy may be used in conjunction with medications. Whilst this may, on occasion be necessary, if it can be avoided then it really should be. Indeed, research suggests that those who complete a course of cognitive therapy usually have a far lower rate of relapse. With this treatment for example, the techniques learned by the client/patient are always with them and provide a set of "tools" that can immediately be utilized if and when symptoms return. Additionally, any symptomatic improvement to a vulnerable client is often misinterpreted and put down to the medication itself despite any obvious clinical improvement. That is not to say however, that medication will be needed on occasion, it is just to reinforce that if it can be avoided early on and there is access to a therapist with the respected skills then this should really be the first line approach for reasons outlined above.

3 – Post-traumatic stress disorder (PTSD)

What is Post traumatic stress disorder?

The past 20 years have seen a proliferation of research into the psychological illness that has come to be known as post-traumatic stress or post-traumatic stress disorder (PTSD). The increasing awareness of PTSD from within both the healthcare setting and the media in general has lead to PTSD becoming a relatively household term. High profile disasters such as the sinking of *The Herald of Free Enterprise*, the *Hillsborough* football tragedy and the *Gulf War* have fuelled the interest in PTSD and this in turn has lead to a greater understanding of the clinical features of the illness. Despite this popularity few healthcare professionals outside the field of mental health (and some within) are fully aware of the precise nature of post-traumatic stress and how it is clinically defined. The following therefore will outline some of the main clinical features of PTSD and highlight how best to assess and treat the problem.

Who suffers from post-traumatic stress?

Post traumatic stress disorder affects about 5.2 million adult Americans alone. It is not clear how many people in the UK have this disorder but it is believed to be of equivalent proportions. Women are more likely than men to develop PTSD and it can occur at any age, including childhood, and there is some evidence that susceptibility to PTSD may actually run in families. The disorder is often accompanied by depression, substance abuse, or one or more other anxiety disorders. In severe cases, the person is likely to experience significant difficulties when working or socialising. In general, the symptoms seem to be worse if the event that triggered them was deliberately initiated by a person-such as a rape or kidnapping.

Whatever the source of the problem, some people with PTSD repeatedly relive the trauma in the form of nightmares and disturbing recollections during the day. They may also experience other sleep problems, feel detached or numb, or be easily startled. They may lose interest in things they used to enjoy and have trouble feeling affectionate. They may feel irritable, more aggressive than before, or even violent. Things that remind them of the trauma may be very distressing, which could lead them to avoid certain places or situations that bring back those memories. Anniversaries of the traumatic event are often very difficult and ordinary events can serve as reminders of the trauma and trigger flashbacks or intrusive images. A person having a flashback, which can come in the form of images, sounds, smells, or feelings, may lose touch with reality and believe that the traumatic event is happening all over again.

Not every traumatised person gets full-blown PTSD, or experiences Post-traumatic stress disorder at all. Post traumatic stress disorder is diagnosed only if the symptoms last more than a month and are of a particular type and intensity. In those who develop Post traumatic stress disorder, symptoms usually begin within 3 months of the trauma, and the course of the illness varies. Some people recover within 6 months and others have symptoms that last much longer. In some cases, the condition may be chronic and occasionally, the illness doesn't show up until years after the traumatic event.

There is nothing new however, in the notion that traumatic events can lead to psychological distress and history is full of such examples. In the 17th Century, Samuel Pepys described his own psychological reaction to the Great Fire of London:

"It is strange to think that how to this very day I cannot sleep a night without great terrors of fire: and this very night [I] could not sleep till almost two in the morning through thoughts of fire.

("Post-Traumatic Stress Disorders – Concepts and Therapy")

This process described by Pepys is a significant clinical feature of PTSD where the trauma is relived in thoughts and intrusive memories of the traumatic event itself. There have been many theoretical attempts to explain this phenomenon and possibly the most useful is that of Yule (1999). Yule describes how all human beings are dynamic and complex organisms who constantly strive to adapt to the demands placed upon them by their physical and social environments. This is a relatively unconscious process that each individual is involved with on a daily basis as he or she learns to adapt to new situations. Most of the time these demands are relatively straightforward and whilst we tend to experience initial anxiety at a situation such as public speaking or starting a new job we eventually adapt as we repeat and get used to the situation so that little or no anxiety is experienced. However there are situations when demands can be excessive and this may place intense strain on our ability to cope. When we are threatened we react with distress and fear and experience intense psychological and physiological emotions characteristic of extreme anxiety. It is during these extreme situations of threat that we find the antecedents of post-traumatic stress. In order to develop PTSD an individual must have experienced or witnessed a major traumatic event such as a serious road traffic accident or a serious assault. As currently defined, although similar symptoms may feature in other conditions, PTSD cannot occur without this substantial trauma. The DSM-IV defines PTSD as resulting from *"an event of significant magnitude, associated with intense fear, helplessness and/or horror"*. Whilst the traumatic event is an essential component necessary for the development of PTSD there are other crucial factors that have to be taken into account and these are outlined below

Key factors involved in the development of PTSD.

- **Stressor** – nature of the stressor and the amount of traumatic exposure.

- **Personality** – coping styles, emotional hardiness, beliefs about the self, world and others, attributional style.

- **Environment** – social and material environment of the client themselves.

(Hamilton 2004)

As the key factors suggest the level of post-traumatic stress experienced by an individual is dependent on a complex interaction between the stressor itself, the individuals' personality and the social and material environment of the individual in question. All these factors are inextricably linked and help to explain why some individuals may develop quite intense post-traumatic reactions from events that may seem relatively moderate and why some individuals develop very little post-traumatic stress from quite horrific events. The primary reason for this is the individuals' pre-morbid personality. Pre-morbid personality in essence is the individuals' personality prior to the event itself and takes into account their previous ways of coping. Each individual has a different threshold for coping with stress and therefore, it is essential that the clinician allows room for these individual differences during the assessment and treatment of PTSD.

DSM-IV criteria for PTSD

A – The person has been exposed to a traumatic event in which both of the following were present:

- **the person experienced, witnessed, or was confronted with an event or events that involved actual or threatened death or serious injury, or a threat to the physical integrity of self or others**

B – The traumatic event is persistently re-experienced in one (or more) of the following ways:

- **recurrent and intrusive recollections of the event, including images, thoughts, or perceptions.**
- **recurrent distressing dreams of the event.**
- **acting or feeling as if the traumatic event was recurring e.g. illusions, hallucinations and flashbacks of the event.**
- **intense psychological distress at exposure to internal or external cues that symbolise or resemble an aspect of the traumatic event.**
- **physiological reactivity on exposure to internal and external cues that symbolise or resemble an aspect of the traumatic event.**

C – Persistent avoidance of stimuli associated with the trauma and numbing of general responsiveness (not present before trauma), as indicated by three or more of the following:

- **efforts to avoid thoughts, feelings or conversations associated with the trauma**
- **efforts to avoid activities, places, or people that arouse recollections of the trauma**
- **inability to recall an important aspect of the trauma**
- **markedly diminished interest or participation in significant activities**
- **feeling of detachment or estrangement from others**
- **restricted range of affect (e.g. unable to have loving feelings)**
- **sense of a foreshortened future**

D – **Persistent symptoms of increased arousal (not present before the trauma), as indicated by two (or more) of the following:**

- **difficulty falling or staying asleep**
- **irritability or outbursts of anger**
- **difficulty concentrating**
- **hypervigilance**

E – Duration of the disturbance (symptoms in criteria B, C and D) is more than one month.

F – The disturbance causes clinically significant distress or impairment in social, occupational or other important areas of functioning.

specify if:
- **Acute: if durations is less than 3 months**
- **Chronic: if duration of symptoms is 3 months or more**

specify if:
- **With delayed onset: if onset of symptoms is at least 6 months after the stressor**

The Assessment of PTSD

The assessment of PTSD can be guided to some degree by the DSM IV criteria itself. For example, has the individual been exposed to an event to such an extent that it would fulfil the criteria set out in criterion **A** above. In the primary care setting the most likely events would include road traffic accidents, serious assaults and military personnel, although this list is by no means exhaustive and there will be many other situations where the criteria may be met. Criterion **B** includes intrusive thoughts and dreams of the event itself and flashbacks which remain one of the key characteristics of PTSD. Indeed, ever since PTSD was officially recognised as a psychiatric disorder, intrusive thinking and imagery have been regarded as major features in its phenomenology. Even prior to the official acceptance of PTSD accounts of traumatic stress reactions often included, vivid descriptions of intrusive thoughts and images (e.g. Kardiner, 1941). The intrusive thoughts and images are often accompanied with a degree of avoidance behaviour as described in **C** above. The avoidance behaviour, whilst providing initial relief only serves to further illustrate the debilitating and restrictive effect of PTSD. The avoidance behaviour can range from mild-moderate whereby someone may be afraid to travel near a scene of an accident to severe, where the person refuses to travel in a car again and the very thought of this produces extreme anxiety.

An extremely useful clinical tool for assessing the intrusive thoughts and images and the accompanying avoidance behaviour is the *"Impact of Events Scale – IES"; (Horowitz et al, 1979)*. The scale is the most widely used self-report measure of specific responses to trauma and provides clinical guidance during the assessment process. The *IES* has two subscales, which look separately at intrusion and avoidance. Whilst the *IES* in itself cannot be used to diagnose

PTSD it nonetheless provides the clinician with a measure of symptom severity and/or symptom change.

The symptoms described in Criterion **D,** of the DSM IV are similar to generic problems associated with affective disorders and chronic anxiety and these can be adequately assessed using measures such as the *"General Health Questionnaire – GHQ-28", (Goldberg & Hillier, 1979) or* the *"Hospital Anxiety and Depression Scale – HADS", (Zigmond & Snaith, 1994).* Both scales provide useful measures of anxiety and the associated symptoms. The HADS in particular is relatively easy to administer and provides an indication of whether the individual is experiencing a mild, moderate or severe level of anxiety. Hamilton et al, (1999) have illustrated the applicability of the HADS in the primary care setting and describe how it can contribute to both the assessment and treatment process.

The assessment tools outlined above help to quantify the assessment process and give guidance to the clinician, however there is no substitute for the clinical interview. The clinical assessment interview is where the clinician will glean some of the essential information that will serve to help validate the scores on the assessments described above. The clinical assessment will also give an indication of how the individual is affected by factors associated with criterion **F,** of the DSM IV. For example, those with severe PTSD find their lives constricted to an enormous degree. The condition impacts on work, social and sexual relationships and potentially on all aspects of "normal" life.

During the clinical interview it essential to look at the individuals' pre-morbid personality and medical history in general. One must also monitor carefully their reactions when describing the events of the traumatic event itself. In their review of personality and stress disorders Clark et al, (1994) point out that personality can affect PTSD in various ways and these may not be mutually exclusive. Clark and his colleagues suggest that personality can affect the individual's vulnerability to develop PTSD and the course or expression of PTSD.

A great deal of clinical skill and care are required at the assessment stage as patients are likely to have repressed many of the thoughts surrounding the events and they will need a certain amount of reassuring when describing the events and their subsequent difficulties since. The clinical assessment can be an extremely distressing time for the patient and the clinician needs to be fully appreciative of the factors that accompany post-traumatic stress. Whilst acute reactions need to be considered one must be aware that PTSD can lay dormant for some considerable time and an initial assessment many months and sometimes years after a distressing event can give rise to an acute eruption of traumatic symptoms.

Clinical Skills & Techniques for Working with PTSD

When someone has experienced a traumatic event the individual in question is likely to be in shock for a period of time ranging from hours to days and even longer where there is evidence of disassociation. During this period there is a limited role for a clinical intervention apart from helping to "contain" the person and possibly helping to explain what they are experiencing and why. Inexperienced clinicians can inadvertently cause problems for their patients at this stage if they raise their levels of distress and do not allow the fear or anxiety to habituate. With regard to psychological treatment the empirical evidence to date focuses on the cognitive and behavioural psychological interventions. Affect is seen as a combination of 3 linked principles, *autonomic, behavioural and cognitive.* Cognitive and behavioural treatments attempt to modify the responsivity of these systems. The core of successful treatment involves confronting the feared situation and the generalised anxiety that may have developed. Most treatment packages include a selection of anxiety management techniques in conjunction with direct and/or imagined exposure. Additional techniques include breathing retraining and cognitive restructuring. Most anxiety disorders now respond very well to psychological treatments based on these behavioural and cognitive principles. Where the level of anxiety is severe an SSRI is likely to help in the treatment and management of PTSD. This can help the individual address the phobic avoidance although care should be taken when withdrawing from the SSRI, as one needs to be aware of a potential relapse. Again some vulnerable patients may also attribute all the clinical gain to the medication and not to themselves and this should be addressed early on when considering medication.

Cognitive and affective processing of post-traumatic stress

Assuming that the client either has sufficient insight and motivation, the treatment of the most extreme trauma symptoms should be achievable. There are at least three major steps in the therapeutic process, although they may recur in different orders and at various points in treatment: (i) identification of traumatic related events, (ii) gradual re-exposure to the affect and stimuli associated with a memory of the event, and (iii) cognitive/affective processing. In order for traumatic material to be processed in treatment, it must be identified as such. Although this seems an obvious step, it is more difficult to implement in some cases than might be expected. The survivor's avoidance of trauma-related material may lead either to conscious reluctance to think about or speak of upsetting incidents, or to less conscious dissociation of such events. Since such responses are avoidance defences, they should not be punished or unduly confronted, nor should the survivor be "pushed" to access more painful material than he or she can tolerate. Careful therapeutic skill is required to differentiate what the person can and cannot cope with at each stage and my advice to therapists is to go carefully at this stage and gauge where the client is as far as the traumatic material is concerned.

If there is sufficient trauma material available to the treatment process, the next step in the treatment is that of careful, graduated exposure to various aspects of the trauma memory. In this regard, the survivor is asked to recall non-overwhelming, but painful trauma-specific experiences in the context of a safe therapeutic environment. Exposure is graduated according to the intensity of the recalled events, with less upsetting memories being recalled, verbalized, and desensitised before more upsetting ones are considered. In contrast to more strictly behavioural interventions, however, this approach does not adhere to a strict, pre-planned series of exposure activities. This is because the survivor's self capacities may be unduly compromised and his or her tolerance for exposure may vary considerably from session to session as a function of outside life stressors, level of support from friends, relatives, and others, and shifting cognitions as treatment progresses.

Effective therapy also capitalizes on the effects of therapeutic safety and emotional catharsis during the desensitisation process. The positive feelings associated with emotional release (e.g., crying or raging), for example, may counter-condition the distress initially associated with the trauma, just as traditional systematic desensitisation pairs a formerly distressing stimulus to a relaxed (anxiety-incompatible) state.

At the same time that the client is encouraged to remember and to feel, he or she is also asked to think. For example, the client might explore the circumstances of the trauma and the basis for his or her reactions. This process is likely to alter the survivor's internal schema so that the trauma experience can be cognitively integrated in a more adaptive fashion.

Summary

There is great interest in rapid interventions for acutely traumatized individuals, especially with respect to civilian disasters and emergency personnel such as police and fire fighters. To this extent, there have been a number of interesting developments with regard to treating post-traumatic stress and one of these is known as *Eye Movement Desensitisation and Reprocessing* – EMDR (Shapiro, 1991, 1995). The premise of this approach is that many traumatic events are not properly "processed" by the memory network of the brain, and that the eye movements of EMDR help a person "reprocess" the traumatic memory through "rapid learning" so that it no longer has negative psychological effects. Advocates of EMDR often claim that a single 50-minute session of EMDR can be 100% successful in abolishing distress from a traumatic event. Other advocates claim that a number of sessions are required for treating post-traumatic injuries. It would appear that the potential and usefulness of this approach has yet to be realised (if indeed it can be) and it is worth watching and waiting to see what more empirical evidence is provided to assess the actual effectiveness of the EMDR approach. In the meantime it is worth acknowledging what we already know about how to treat traumatic stress and as Rachman (1997) so eloquently points out,

> *"Post-traumatic stress disorders are the simplest and also the most complex of the anxiety disorders: simplest because the initiating cause of the disorder and the resulting stress is generally all too evident, complex because of the often-puzzling unpredictability of the symptoms and the mixture of psychological processes involved".*

Rachman (1997)

In the primary care setting where most patients with post-traumatic stress will present it is both essential and wise to have an awareness of the nature of the illness and how best to assess and treat the problem. The DSM-IV-R criteria, assessment tools and treatment protocols outlined above are evidence that post-traumatic stress is now far better understood. An adherence to the empirical evidence associated with PTSD should greatly help clinicians in their work with patients' suffering with symptoms of post-traumatic stress. There are new and exciting developments on the horizon with regard to treating post-traumatic stress and only the future will reveal the true worth of these developments

4 – Personality factors and Anxiety

As with depression, there remains great controversy and debate surrounding the very term "personality disorders" and the labelling of such difficulties. Again, however I feel it is essential for all practicing therapists and clinicians alike to have some concept of what is meant by personality factors in relation to anxiety and at the very least to be aware of how these factors play a part in the anxiety process. I would like to remind readers that in general we are referring to working with personality difficulties that are on the mild end of the spectrum and not the severe end, therefore this needs to be borne in mind when reading and evaluating the following information.

What do we mean by personality and anxiety?

The word 'personality' refers to the pattern of thoughts, feelings and behaviour that makes each of us individual. We tend to behave in fairly predictable ways, yet our personalities also develop and change as our circumstances change. Usually, people are flexible enough to be able to learn from past experiences and to change their behaviour to cope with life more effectively, indeed this is a natural and adaptive process for most people. However, someone who has a personality disorder or difficulty is likely to be quite inflexible and therefore they appear resistant or incapable when faced with the need to be adaptive in certain situations or roles. To this extent, their range of attitudes and behaviours is limited, and likely to be very different from what others might expect from their background and culture. As a result of this inflexibility, their attitudes and ways of behaving often cause distress both to them and to others.

Personality disorders usually become noticeable in adolescence or early adulthood, but occasionally start in childhood. They make it difficult for someone to develop friendships, maintain a stable relationship and to work cooperatively with others because their experience, responses and coping strategies are so limited. Not surprisingly, they can feel alienated and alone and unfortunately, the risk of suicide is about three times higher than average.

Personality disorders will disrupt people's lives, and those around them, to different degrees, and the extent to which they are treatable also varies. Often, someone will have other problems going on at the same time, such as depression or a specific anxiety disorder. For instance, someone with avoidant personality disorder may also suffer from agoraphobia. Even if the phobia is treated, stressful events can still trigger problems linked with the personality disorder, such as avoidance and dependency.

When we are referring to anxiety as a personality problem we are generally referring to what is termed "Anxious (Avoidant) Personality Disorder (APD)". Like other personality disorders, 'Anxious (Avoidant) Personality Disorder' is a controversial diagnosis and at present there is no overall consensus as to its cause. The disorder itself is characterised by a pervasive pattern of social inhibition, feelings of inadequacy, and hypersensitivity to negative evaluation, beginning by early adulthood and present in a variety of contexts. Often there are, persistent and pervasive feelings of shyness, insecurity, apprehension and tension leading to restrictions in lifestyle. The individual often believes that they are un-likeable, undeserving, socially inept, and less important than other people. This often leads to reluctance to get involved in relationships unless certain of being liked and approved. The anxious personality is over-sensitive and over-concerned with the fear of being criticised or rejected in social or work situations. This often leads to an avoidance of any activity that involves having to inter-relate with other people. The complexities should be apparent from the description above and whilst these difficulties may vary in their intensity and presentation we must again be realistic with what we can achieve when working with this type of problem.

DSM IV-R Criteria "Anxious Personality Disorder" (APD)

The DSM-IV describes "APD" as a pervasive pattern of social inhibition, feelings of inadequacy & hypersensitivity to negative evaluation, beginning by early adulthood & present in a variety of contexts, as indicated by 4 (or more) of the following:

1. avoids occupational activities that involve significant interpersonal contact because of fears of criticism, disapproval or rejection

2. is unwilling to get involved with people unless certain of being liked

3. shows restraint within intimate relationships because of the fear of being shamed or ridiculed

4. is preoccupied with being criticized or rejected in social situations

5. is inhibited in new interpersonal situations because of feelings of inadequacy

6. views self as socially inept, personally unappealing or inferior to others

7. is unusually reluctant to take personal risks or to engage in any new activities because they may prove embarrassing

Assessment issues – Personality and Anxiety

A personality problem is generally a disturbance in the character, constitution and behavioural tendencies of the individual, usually involving several areas of the personality, and nearly always associated with considerable personal and social disruption. Personality disorder tends to appear in late childhood or adolescence and continues to manifest into adulthood. It is therefore unlikely that the diagnosis of personality disorder will be appropriate before the age of 16 or 17 years even if there is clear evidence of personality problems. Most of the revealing factors should appear early on in the qualitative part of the assessment process. In general we may assume that the personality has been affected in some way early on in the development of the individual and there may be pertinent historical factors that may have contributed to these difficulties. These factors could include inappropriate or inadequate parenting resulting in attachment problems, difficult early interpersonal and social experiences and possibly critical traumas that may have hindered development in some way. Since the behaviours are generally haphazard and unpredictable a quantitative assessment may only be useful in relation to some specific difficulty. For example, if the individual in question has difficulty mixing with people and becomes extremely anxious then we can do some specific work around this. With the anxious personality being so self-critical we may also want to quantify the irrational thinking and use this as a barometer of change during the therapeutic process.

It is painfully evident that individuals who suffer from this type of personality problem typically have poor self-esteem and issues surrounding any type of social interactions. They often see only the negative in life and have difficulty in looking at situations and interactions in an objective manner. This can also interfere with their self-report when they present for an initial assessment. It is therefore necessary to take a detailed assessment and evaluation and to conduct this in a relatively unobtrusive fashion. The clinician should be sensitive to nonverbal cues of the client during this session and to evaluate when information is being withheld. As with other personality difficulties, the individual is not likely to present him or herself to therapy unless something has gone wrong in their life with which their dysfunctional personality style cannot adequately cope.

Clinical Skills & Techniques for working with Anxious Personality

All personality disorders are difficult to treat, because they involve deeply rooted patterns of thoughts, feelings and ways of relating. However, many people with mild to moderate difficulties are able to change their thinking and behaviour and eventually lead more fulfilling lives if they receive appropriate treatment. The milder forms, such as avoidant and dependent personality disorders, usually have the best chances although some people with severe personality disorders may be able to modify and change their outlook, however, this is more likely to take far longer and we are not talking weeks or a few months for severe problems.

There is good evidence that psychological treatments can be helpful, especially for the milder personality difficulties. However, clients and patients who continue to lay all the blame on others and on outside circumstances (rigid cognitions) are unlikely to benefit. If the self-talk for example, of individuals with APD has become savage in its self-deprecatory intent, little progress in treatment can be achieved if this pattern is not altered. Self-statements must therefore be clearly identified and clients should be asked specifically what they call themselves or how they refer to themselves when feeling inept, inadequate, or unacceptable. The words can be quite startling in their intensity and viciousness and these must be countered in the treatment process with constructive, realistic, and self-accepting statements of encouragement and affirmations directed toward self-efficacy.

Treatment for clients with these difficult and pervasive problems is more likely to be successful if the clients themselves are:

- Motivated
- Introspective (able to examine their own thoughts)
- Honest
- Willing to acknowledge imperfections
- Able to accept responsibility for their problems.

People have to be well motivated, able to talk about their problems and be open to change. Generally, it is important to emphasise the positive aspects of someone's personality, and to encourage each individual to make the most of their strengths and abilities. Some practical changes can be brought about quite quickly but for many, progress through therapy may be slow and difficult. The avoidant personality will usually find assertiveness training useful. However, the therapist should remain cautious when giving assignments to exercise new social skills outside of therapy as failure may reinforce the patient's already poor self-esteem.

Group therapy should be considered if this is at all available as it offers individuals a chance to practise doing things differently and it can be particularly helpful for people who avoid social situations for example, or who usually depend too much on one person. Someone with borderline personality disorder tends to form intense 'special' one-to-one relationships, so a group gives them the chance to widen their range. More one-to-one therapy is useful when it takes a problem-solving approach, focusing on practical issues and analysing current relationship difficulties. Social skills training and assertiveness training for example, offer opportunities for trying out new behaviour.

Specific cognitive therapy can help someone examine their usual pattern of thoughts and attitudes, and to challenge and modify any mistaken or irrationally based thoughts and ideas very much in the same way as we have described in the cognitive therapy and depression chapter. When someone is too dependent for example therapy might focus on challenging their fixed belief that they are so helpless and incompetent that they need someone else to rely on. Situations then need to be engineered carefully so that the client is able to experience a more independent situation that challenges their "fixed" ideas of thought. Naturally this may produce anxieties however all of this would have been explained and the whole scenario, if managed carefully can be set up as quite a positive challenge for the client in question who needs to know that they are safe in the knowledge that this process is designed to help them become more secure and independent. The therapeutic relationship, as one can imagine is an important vehicle for change in this context.

Individual therapy however, should be conducted with some caution as it can make some undesirable behaviour worse; at least to begin with. A potentially intense one-to-one relationship may encourage people to become even more dependent, at least in the interim. Additionally, being judgemental and using blanket terms, such as 'immature' or 'inadequate' is unlikely to help. Indeed, we may all behave immaturely or inadequately in particular situations. It's important to identify situations that bring out the best or worst in people. For example, someone who is fearful of intimacy and ill at ease with people may lose their inhibitions when discussing a subject that really interests them, so joining a particular society or similar interest group may be a useful "vehicle" for helping people to learn to enjoy the company of others without feeling threatened. Again, this illustrates the potential benefits that can be gained from group therapy itself. Careful clinical communication however, is essential as being told for example that you are 'narcissistic' or 'dependent' without an explanation of what this means is extremely unhelpful and that probably goes for all therapeutic approaches.

Summary

For individuals with APD, the goal of treatment is to increase self-esteem and confidence in interpersonal relationships, and to de-sensitise their reaction to criticism. Treatment should be directed toward reinforcing a self-concept of competency and self-worth. These clients can be encouraged through therapy to balance caution with action and to develop a tolerance for failure. One must also be aware however, of being overprotective of the patient that can delay or hold up progress. This inevitably, sustains the poor view of the self that the client/patient has come to treatment to remedy. Conversely, we must be aware not to "force" a client unduly to face new situations prematurely, without proper preparation. The therapeutic challenge therefore, when working with this vulnerable client population is extremely evident and the ultimate aim of therapeutic intervention is to counter the tendency for individuals with APD to perpetuate a pattern of social withdrawal and perceptual hyper-vigilance that is self-defeating and self-deprecating.

Part 6: When therapy doesn't work – Factors to consider

Possibly the most difficult thing for any clinician whether they are working in mental health and/or general physical health is accepting that maybe on occasion we have exhausted all avenues and there is unlikely to be any further clinical or therapeutic gain to be had. Indeed, it is probably not in the nature of most therapists to perhaps even contemplate this prospect. However, I will maintain that it is the most professional of therapists who is able to acknowledge the limitations of therapy itself in certain situations and to accept that all therapeutic avenues have been explored. Again I will maintain that those not able to adopt this rational and professional stance risk generating an element of *"false hope"* for many clients and patients alike. Therapy therefore may not be successful for a number of reasons. One of these may actually come from the therapist where for example an inappropriate assessment has been conducted and hence both therapist and client have ventured off in the wrong direction. Of course, this is one factor that can actually be corrected and the pros and cons of this will be outlined below along with some of the more pertinent factors that are likely to be more outside of the control of the therapist.

1– "Forced or Coerced" Clients/Patients:

The reasons for someone seeking psychological help can vary significantly and naturally this can have a significant impact on the therapeutic process itself and the success or failure of that process. When I use the terms "forced" or "coerced" I am generally referring to clients and patients who have not come along out of their own volition with a desire to change or work on their problems. To this extent one of the key variables of psychological change, which is of course *motivation*, may not be present. In these instances a therapist, where possible needs to be aware of the crucial variables and reasons behind the referral itself that are likely to greatly impact on the therapeutic outcome. In particular these referrals may include, from the "forced" area, clients referred for criminal and/or legal reasons. There may be very genuine clinical issues relating to anger or impulse control, alcohol problems and general emotional and behavioural difficulties. Some referrals of course will not be as genuine and the main motivation may be to overcome or actually achieve a lesser sentence or punishment as a result of completing a course of therapy. Therefore, it is essential to try to get "behind" the reasons for the referral and to assess the motivation from the clients' perspective. This is essential otherwise we may be wasting precious clinical time. I can appreciate how much of a controversial and

215

politically sensitive issue this is, however I have assessed many young, and not so young referrals from the probation service who have had no interest whatsoever in looking at their difficulties and being able to engender psychological change through a therapeutic alliance. In essence, the motivation and investment for coming along is lacking or inappropriate and any potential therapeutic gain is likely to be sabotaged. Some of these clients are often surprised when after one assessment a letter is sent back to their probation officer.

"Coerced" referrals are a little more different although there may be parallels or similarities with the "forced" referrals. Coerced referrals are generally those that have been encouraged or "pushed" to come along by close family members and/or friends. Again, the motivation is not ideal, although a good therapist may be able to encourage someone back if the initial appointment is not too threatening. However, in general if the main motivation to come along and seek psychological treatment is to satisfy other family members or friends then of course there is unlikely to be any therapeutic gain. Indeed, I remember a sketch from a TV drama whereby the husband was seeking therapeutic intervention after his wife had threatened to leave because of his behaviour. The client in this instance was quite honest and kept saying to the therapist through each session that, *"when I'm having therapy, she (his wife) feels much better so I might as well carry on for a while just to keep the peace"* (remember this was a TV drama). Hopefully this just illustrates a point that there can be numerous reasons why someone seeks out therapy, some of these however, may be grossly inappropriate.

Whether "forced" or "coerced" the necessary and appropriate motivation may not be present and this will inevitably sabotage any real therapeutic gain. The overall situation here is probably best summed up in that old statement that asks, *"how many therapists does it take to change a light bulb – answer – one – however, the light bulb must want to change"*.

2 – Inappropriate/inadequate assessment:

One of the key areas covered throughout the book has been related to the assessment process itself and the essential variables that contribute to a thorough and comprehensive understanding of the presenting problem. Indeed, if there is just one thing I would want the reader to get from reading the book then it is how to formally assess a client or patient. Assessment as we are now aware is twofold and generally involves a thorough qualitative assessment looking at historical, interpersonal and social material among other areas. The quantitative component will look more closely at symptoms and behaviours that are occurring as a result of the difficulties themselves. The assessment therefore can be seen as the "door" to therapy. In essence if we open the wrong "door" then we are in the wrong "room" and therefore, therapeutic intervention is unlikely to produce the desired outcomes. This can be more complex than it may initially appear. If we take ourselves back to the earlier chapters of the book we would have come across the young woman who was referred because she was suffering with "post natal depression". Indeed, her GP and mid-wife knew this lady well and she was an extremely capable professional who had become depressed following the birth of her first child. The woman however, had failed to respond to some relatively straight-forward depression management advice and anti-depressants had had no affect on her mood. In retrospect, of course this was a case of the GP and mid-wife putting two and two together and getting 5 as a thorough assessment (qualitative aspect in this instance) revealed that the woman was actually grieving for her mother who had died some 13 years earlier. When we think about it on reflection, when is a young woman going to need her mother most? – Yes, when she is having a child and this had been the "trigger" for the loss of confidence and anxiety. Therefore, it is important to go back over the assessment on occasion just in case we may have missed something. Alternatively, if a referral is passed on by others who have attempted to intervene from a psychological perspective, <u>always</u> start afresh even if this means going over the same material for the client. Indeed, if we are armed with a comprehensive awareness of the finer details of the assessment then we should be in a very good position to ascertain all the salient features involved in the depression and/or anxiety.

3 – Dynamics/Transference Issues:

There are occasions when there is more or less an "unknown" or unaccountable variable involved in the therapeutic process that cannot be predicted or envisaged. In this context, I am referring to factors involved in the dynamics of the unique therapeutic process itself. The one-to-one nature of psychological therapy is embroiled in dynamism with potentially numerous unconscious dynamic variables that can impact on the therapeutic process itself. These may be variables that we are initially unaware of, yet for some reason they can have a significant impact on both therapist and client and can sabotage the therapeutic process. An example of these unaccountable variables occurs when we meet someone for the first time and for some reason, there is either an instant dislike or an unsure feeling. This of course may happen for the therapist and the client. It may be an historical feature where the person represents an unconscious reminder of a stressful or difficult experience. Indeed, it may be something as simple as their physical appearance, accent, or general demeanour. Whatever the reason these dynamics can affect the therapeutic process. If possible it may be useful to acknowledge them and use them as part of the therapeutic process itself. However if this is not possible then it may become a barrier and the client may best be served by a different therapist. This is a rare occurrence but it is one that needs to be borne in mind.

Transference issues are closely related to what we have briefly described above. However, transference and counter-transference are dynamic factors that often occur during the therapeutic process, particularly where there is an emphasis on the therapeutic relationship as a vehicle of change. Transference issues, however if managed well can actually be helpful. However, there are occasions when particular transferences can be complicating factors that can potentially sabotage the therapeutic process if one is not aware and these are the issues we need to concern ourselves with.

Transference is most generally described as the "passing on" or "transferring" of an emotion or affective attitude from one person to another person, often the therapist of course. Transference is often termed either positive or negative depending upon whether a person develops either pleasant or hostile attitudes toward the therapist. Indeed, we could write a whole chapter or book just on the issues surrounding the nature and complications involving transference. However for our own purposes a brief description of how it can sabotage the therapeutic process should suffice and at least inform the reader of what to expect on occasion.

Transference can be ambivalent as it comprises of positive (affectionate) as well as negative (hostile) attitudes towards the therapist, who as a rule is put in the place of an important "other" who is or was a significant psychological and emotional part of the clients' life. This is often illustrated when working with grief and loss. To illustrate the point I will recall a case many years ago when I was referred a woman well into her 60s who had lost her husband and was struggling to cope some 2 years later. There was a mild-moderate depression that was greatly affecting her overall well-being. At this stage I was in my early 30s and more or less at the beginning of my therapeutic career. Without my realising it, the woman had built up quite a powerful transference toward me to such an extent that it actually sabotaged the therapeutic process, just at a time when I thought she was progressing so well. The ending of therapy was so difficult that the woman made a complaint to her GP. The GP and I discussed the transference issue and acknowledged the complaint and referred her on to a female therapist. In essence, through the transference process, I had naively replaced her husband in a symbolic way and of course the end of therapy was an absolute rejection of this. Writing this now I find it hard to contemplate that I could have been so naïve and unaware, however, transference issues probably catch us out when we are least expecting it therefore, remain as self-aware as is possible and take any potential transference issues to supervision. It may also be useful to read a little more on the potentially positive and negative factors that influence the transference process in general.

Whilst transference is one part of the story, from the therapist perspective comes the term, counter-transference. Counter-transference is actually the therapists' emotional involvement in the therapeutic interaction and occurs when the therapist, during the course of therapy, develops positive or negative feelings toward the client or patient. This may be quite normal to some extent; however one must not act on such feelings and it is again essential to apply a professional level of governance and take any complicating or potentially complicating issues to supervision.

Issues relating to transference and counter-transference can occur innocently and more often than not for well-meant intentions, however, if they are not handled carefully they can greatly affect the therapeutic process and create difficulties for both therapists and clients and patients alike.

4 – Investment in illness:

Despite therapy, medication, and good support from friends and loved ones, the major reason some people remain depressed or anxious is that they don't know how else to be. I appreciate that this again may appear a controversial statement, however it is certainly not meant to say or imply that they choose to be anxious or depressed as this is a distressing state in itself. It is however, the "devil they know" and over years and in a futile effort to save them from pain, they may have learned habits that on one level feel "normal" and "natural", like part of their very "self". Of course, these emotional habits backfire and instead of reducing pain, they just perpetuate the anxiety and/or depression. Again, I would like to reinforce at this juncture that these individuals do not choose to suffer; it is just that the psychological gains involved in overcoming their problem are greatly outweighed by the problem that has become their way of life and their way of living. To illustrate this potentially controversial point (and again it is difficult to do justice to the actual situation by writing about it) I will outline a case I worked with a number of years ago. The client in question was in their mid-30s and living at home with their mother. The client was referred because of "panic attacks" and "agoraphobia". The client actually worked in a local shop 3 days a week and appeared to function reasonably well. The client presented very well, conversed well and their general appearance was immaculate with no obvious evidence of anxiety or depression. The person in question had received "therapy" on and off for 16 years. The initial assessment revealed that the client and her mother and been together from aged one with no father being involved in the care-taking and in essence they had developed a unique relationship where the client was actually still being "mothered" to a large extent. The client appeared to have insight and understanding to the anxiety and the agoraphobia, yet was unprepared to go out alone in small stages in order to begin to manage the anxiety. Yet, the client worked 3 days a week at a local shop. There was a detailed history that was conducted and the reasons for her anxiety and agoraphobia appeared relatively straightforward. However, the client was totally unwilling and unable to take part in any of the active therapeutic process, yet would have been happy to continue "therapy" for an unlimited period. I appreciate that this case example may conjure up some emotive responses for some readers, however the fact remains that on occasion we are going to be referred clients and patients who will not be able to move forward and it is the informed and professional therapist who is able to make this judgement call. In essence, what this client unconsciously wanted was a surrogate or substitute mother. Even if this was on offer it would not have impacted on the anxiety itself and would have only served the purpose of colluding with the client in question.

5 – Endings:

The success and smoothness for want of a better word of "endings" in therapy are largely related to the "beginnings" themselves and the shared and agreed goals that should naturally follow a good assessment of the problem. If this process is conducted comprehensively and collaboratively and in a rational and sensitive manner then this will go some way to ensuring that the ending of therapy is relatively smooth whether the client has moved on significantly or with minimal progress. The assessment process should, depending on the given situation create and engender room for optimism whilst guarding against engendering any potential "false hope" for the client. This may be a fine line and will largely depend on the experience and interpersonal skill of the therapist. When these situations occur, the therapist may want to go over some issues related to the initial assessment itself and together with the client look at anything that may have been missed. Courage and honesty may be required from the therapist if for some reason the client has been unable to address and overcome any of the anxiety difficulties. It is important during this difficult period to reinforce that successful treatment does require the client to be actively involved and motivated to change. The motivation may well be there, however the physical and emotional strength required to change may not be present at this particular time. Remember, the ending or agreed outcomes and how they need to be arrived at are discussed explicitly very early on in the assessment and initial therapeutic intervention. The actual ending of treatment therefore is carefully planned early on so that both therapist and client are aware of what is required to achieve a desired outcome. If there are irresolvable difficulties then it may be useful to provide clients with information and access to local resources at times of crises or acute need etc.

For some clients who have improved significantly there can still be difficulties surrounding "endings". Many clients express a fear about ending the sessions and it may be useful at this stage to suggest that we have 2-3 sessions to 'formally' close the therapy and perhaps a 3-4 month follow-up after which we may want to leave an "open door" policy should we feel that this is appropriate. The "open door" policy provides a degree of security but must be guarded against, as there is obviously a risk of unwittingly nurturing a degree of dependency here. However, the "open door" potentially gives the client 'space' to fully accept and integrate the fact that therapy has come to an end and the last session can generally reinforce what has gone before so that the client has something to work on for the occasional setback. Remember, they now have new skills to deal with their problems and hence they are in a completely different position than when they first arrived for that initial assessment. Indeed, one of the main advantages of the cognitive therapies is that each client in essence becomes their own therapist and this should help with regard to the maintenance of therapeutic gain that has occurred throughout the clinical relationship.

Whatever issues the clients bring to therapy, they must one day be sufficiently empowered to cope with the issues themselves. A therapist who accepts a client as a long term client - a client who will remain in therapy for years or even the rest of their life - may not be acting in the best interests of the client and indeed such therapy may be detrimental to the client's development. The client who assumes that therapy is a life-long commitment must also face the reality of the situation; that therapy really only prepares the client for the time when therapy is no longer needed. These issues were explicitly illustrated early on in the book when we looked at the dominant values of the long-term and short-term therapist and it is well worth revisiting these values as they clearly illustrate what good therapy is about and what it aims to achieve. There is little doubt that "endings" are a crucial part of the therapeutic process and as previously stated, they are very much linked to the "beginnings" themselves and how the therapist conducts the therapeutic dialogue in general. How a client or patient is able to cope and adjust with the ending of the therapeutic relationship will give a clear indication of the client's new-found skill at dealing with their difficulties and their overall empowerment.

Conclusion & Brief Overview

As I have repeated on numerous occasions throughout the book, it is difficult to do justice to the rich and dynamic context of the therapeutic relationship and the application of the "tools" of therapy. With regard to the cognitive therapies, it is all too easy on occasion to see them as rather "dry" and "rigid" and almost "common-sense" like in their description and evaluation of dynamic difficulties involving depression and anxiety. However, to just view them in this context is to miss the very richness and dynamism that is cognitive psychotherapy. I would therefore urge each and every therapist to at least attempt to think about some of the techniques of cognitive psychotherapy or CBT as it is most often referred to and how they may help to enhance the therapeutic process. It is often the case that many therapists are both practicing and speaking in different "languages" yet they are expressing and conveying the same or a similar message. As therapists and clinicians we must look to continuously evolve and there are elements from cognitive therapy that fit well into many other clinical orientations. Therefore, at the very least a cognitive therapeutic element can be seen as being complimentary and not contradictory for most presenting problems.

We have seen that throughout the therapeutic process cognitive therapists and their clients' work together on the presenting problems. They will develop a shared understanding of the presenting problem and identify how these issues or factors conspire to impact on the client's thoughts, behaviours, emotions and daily functioning. Based on an understanding of each client's individual problems the therapist and client work together to identify areas of difficulty and to agree on possible future outcomes and strategies. Together both client and therapist develop a shared therapeutic plan that has a clear rationale that helps the client make sense of the problem. The focus of therapy is to enable the client to generate solutions to their problems that are more helpful than their present ways of coping. This often involves the client using the time between therapy sessions to try to "test" alternative ways of thinking and behaving that hopefully will change the way they will begin to feel about themselves and the difficult situations they have come to fear. In terms of the symptoms associated with emotional distress, negative thinking is often the most powerful in terms of perpetuating anxiety and depression. When depressed people become proficient at identifying and countering cognitive distortions, depression and anxiety can begin to lose its strength and subsequent grip on the individual in question.

As pointed out at the very beginning of the book problems associated with anxiety and depression appear to be on the increase and whilst we can all gesticulate as to some of the causal social, psychological and perhaps political variables, gesticulation is not going to help resolve the immediate distress of these difficulties. Therefore, we are left with nothing more than looking at the most effective therapeutic option for working with the misery that is so much a part of anxiety and depression. When writing the book I set out with a number of aims in mind and hopefully the reader has been able to overcome some of their own prejudices and resistances and will be able to assimilate into their therapeutic practice at least some of the material that has been covered. Indeed, the easiest job in the world in my opinion is that of the critic and as I read over and over the manuscript that has gone before I can see many areas that will perhaps not be understood in the manner that I would so desire. Therefore, what I would want for the reader most of all is to just get the "gist" of what I have been trying to achieve in writing this book. This gist is that there are some great insights and benefits to be had by adopting more cognitive psychotherapeutic strategies into ones clinical practice. Furthermore, if this can be done whilst being able to conduct a thorough and appropriate assessment from both a qualitative and quantitative perspective then we are in an excellent position to be able to go about our therapeutic business. These are some of the main components of what I am referring to as the "gist". In addition to these factors I would encourage all therapists to remain as objective as they can whilst exhibiting an appropriate amount of *"rational compassion"*. Added to this, I would want therapists to be as creative as they possibly can whilst working within a therapeutic framework. If one can instil these key components into ones clinical practice then I believe that it will considerably enhance the therapy itself and the overall skill of the therapist.

A list of CBT resources

Below are some links to some up to date CBT resources and a brief description of what to expect. Logging on to these sites will give the reader a comprehensive array of cognitive material. In particular I would encourage each reader to log on to some of the computerised CBT sites such as the MoodGym training program at *www.moodgym.anu.edu.au/*. This will give readers a good idea of the principles of CBT in practice and can be a fun way to learn more about CBT.

1)　　The BABCP Guide to understanding CBT at
www.babcp.org.uk/babcp/what_is_CBT.htm

This provides a very useful outline of the core concepts of CBT and provides some useful reference points to guide the reader.

2)　　The MoodGym at *www.moodgym.anu.edu.au/*

MoodGym is an internet-based therapy program designed to prevent depression. It consists of five modules, a workbook and some interactive extras, including an interactive game. It includes assessments of anxiety and depression, 'irrational' thinking, life-event stress, parental relationships, and pleasant event scheduling. Although it is mainly intended for young people, people who are older may find it helpful. This site is definitely worth a perusal.

3)　　The Royal College of Psychiatrists at:
www.rcpsych.ac.uk/mentalhealthinformation/therapies/cognitivebehaviouralth erapy.aspx

This site has a comprehensive outline of CBT and how it applies to numerous problems. It outlines some excellent information from the Royal College of Psychiatrists and some great examples in practice and should provide the reader with a good understanding of CBT in practice.

4)　　Praxis CBT at *http://www.praxiscbt.com/cbtcdrom.html*

The Praxis CD-ROM offers training in the basics of CBT with accompanying support for local supervision for those starting out in the CBT field. The CD-ROM demonstrates CBT in a straightforward yet stimulating way, using a step-by-step approach. Emphasis is placed on the CBT model and the role of formulation. Key cognitive and behavioural strategies are demonstrated using illustrative case studies. Although CBT is a rapidly developing field, the Praxis CD-ROM provides the grounding, so there should be no difficulty in adapting what has been learned to other psychological problems for which CBT may be appropriate. This is an excellent resource for any mental health practitioner or teacher.

5)   What is Cognitive-Behavioral Therapy? At:
www.nacbt.org/whatiscbt.htm

Provides an excellent outline of 10 key features related to CBT in practice and provides some excellent links to more CBT related material.

Printed in the United Kingdom
by Lightning Source UK Ltd.
134125UK00001BA/10/P